D1156410

EVERYDAY
CHAOS

EVERYDAY
CHAOS

Technology, Complexity,
and How We're Thriving
in a New World
of Possibility

DAVID WEINBERGER

HARVARD BUSINESS REVIEW PRESS

Boston, Massachusetts

Library of Congress Cataloging-in-Publication Data

Names: Weinberger, David, 1950– author.
Title: Everyday chaos : technology, complexity, and how we're thriving in a new world of possibility / David Weinberger.
Description: Boston, Massachusetts : Harvard Business Review Press, [2019] | Includes bibliographical references and index.
Identifiers: LCCN 2018049644 | ISBN 9781633693951 (hardcover)
Subjects: LCSH: Chaotic behavior in systems—Industrial applications. | Prediction theory—Technological innovations. | Economic forecasting. | Technological innovations.
Classification: LCC Q172.5.C45 W44 2019 | DDC 006.3/101—dc23 LC record available at https://lccn.loc.gov/2018049644

CONTENTS

EVERYDAY
CHAOS

Everything All at Once

Deep Patient doesn't know that being knocked on the head can make us humans dizzy or that diabetics shouldn't eat five-pound Toblerone bars in one sitting. It doesn't even know that the arm bone is connected to the wrist bone. All it knows is what researchers at Mount Sinai Hospital in New York fed it in 2015: the medical records of seven hundred thousand patients as discombobulated data, with no skeleton of understanding to hang it all on. Yet after analyzing the relationships among these blind bits, not only was Deep Patient able to diagnose the likelihood of individual patients developing particular diseases, it was in some instances more accurate than human physicians, including about some diseases that until now have utterly defied predictability.[1]

If you ask your physician why Deep Patient thinks it might be wise for you to start taking statins or undergo preventive surgery, your doctor might not be able to tell you, but not because she's not sufficiently smart or technical. Deep Patient is a type of artificial intelligence called deep learning (itself a type of machine learning) that finds relationships among pieces of data, knowing nothing about what that data represents. From this it assembles a network of information points, each with a weighting that determines how likely the points it's connected to will "fire," which in turn affects the points they're connected to, the way firing a neuron in a brain would. To understand why Deep Patient thinks, say, that there's a

72 percent chance that a particular patient will develop schizophrenia, a doctor would have to internalize those millions of points and each of their connections and weightings. But there are just too many, and they are in relationships that are too complex. You as a patient are, of course, free to reject Deep Patient's probabilistic conclusions, but you do so at a risk, for the reality is that we use "black-box" diagnostic systems that cannot explain their predictions because in some cases they are significantly more accurate than human doctors.

This is the future, and not just for medicine. Your phone's navigation system, type-ahead predictions, language translation, music recommendations, and much more already rely on machine learning.

As this form of computation gets more advanced, it can get more mysterious. For example, if you subtract the number of possible chess moves from the number of possible moves in the Chinese game of go, the remainder is still many times larger than the number of atoms in the universe.[2] Yet Google's AI-based AlphaGo program routinely beats the top-ranked human players, even though it knows nothing about go except what it's learned from analyzing sixty million moves in 130,000 recorded games. If you examine AlphaGo's inner states to try to discover why it made any one particular move, you are likely to see nothing but an ineffably complex set of weighted relationships among its data. AlphaGo simply may not be able to tell you in terms a human can understand why it made the moves that it did.

Yet about an AlphaGo move that left some commenters literally speechless, one go master, Fan Hui, said, "It's not a human move. I've never seen a human play this move." Then, softly, "So beautiful. Beautiful. Beautiful. Beautiful."[3]

Deep learning's algorithms work because they capture better than any human can the complexity, fluidity, and even beauty of a universe in which everything affects everything else, all at once.

As we will see, machine learning is just one of many tools and strategies that have been increasingly bringing us face to face with the incomprehensible intricacy of our everyday world. But this benefit comes at a price: we need to give up our insistence on always understanding our world and how things happen in it.

We humans have long been under the impression that if we can just understand the immutable laws of how things happen, we'll be able to perfectly predict, plan for, and manage the future. If we know how weather happens, weather reports can tell us whether to take an umbrella to work. If we know what makes people click on one thing and not another in their Facebook feeds, we can design the perfect ad campaign. If we know how epidemics happen, we can prevent them from spreading. We have therefore made it our business to know how things happen by discovering the laws and models that govern our world.

Given how imperfect our knowledge has always been, this assumption has rested on a deeper one. Our unstated contract with the universe has been that if we work hard enough and think clearly enough, the universe will yield its secrets, for the universe is knowable, and thus at least somewhat pliable to our will.

But now that our new tools, especially machine learning and the internet,[4] are bringing home to us the immensity of the data and information around us, we're beginning to accept that the true complexity of the world far outstrips the laws and models we devise to explain it. Our newly capacious machines can get closer to understanding it than we can, and they, as machines, don't really understand anything at all.

This, in turn, challenges another assumption we hold one level further down: the universe is knowable to us because we humans (we've assumed) are uniquely able to understand how the universe works. At least since the ancient Hebrews, we have thought ourselves to be the creatures uniquely made by God with the capacity to receive His revelation of the truth. Since the ancient Greeks, we've defined ourselves as the rational animals who are able to see the logic and order beneath the apparent chaos of the world. Our most basic strategies have relied on this special relationship between us and our world.

Giving up on this traditional self-image of our species is wrenching and painful. Feeling crushed by information overload and nervously awaiting the next disruption of our business, government, or culture are just the localized pains of a deeper malady: the sense—sometimes expressed in uneasy jokes about the rise of robot overlords—that we are not as well adapted to our universe as we'd thought. Evolution has given us minds tuned for survival and only incidentally for truth. Our claims about what makes our species special—emotion, intuition, creativity—are beginning to sound overinsistent and a bit desperate.

This literal disillusionment is something for us to embrace—and not only because it's happening whether we embrace it or not. We are at the beginning of a great leap forward in our powers of understanding and managing the future: rather than always having to wrestle our world down to a size we can predict, control, and feel comfortable with, we are starting to build strategies that take our world's complexity into account.

We are taking this leap because these strategies are already enabling us to be more efficient and effective, in touch with more people and ideas, more creative, and more joyful. It is already recontextualizing many of our most basic ideas and our most deeply accustomed practices in our business and personal lives. It is reverberating through every reach of our culture.

The signs are all around us, but in many cases they're hidden in practices and ideas that already seem normal and obvious. For example, before machine learning came to prominence, the internet was already getting us used to these changes. . . .

The A/B Mystery

When Barack Obama's first presidential campaign tried out two versions of a sign-up button on its website, it found the one labeled "Learn More" drew dramatically more clicks than the same button labeled "Join Us Now" or "Sign Up Now."

Another test showed that a black-and-white photo of the Obama family unexpectedly generated far more clicks than the color image the site had been using.

Then, when they put the "Learn More" button together with the black-and-white photo, sign-ups increased 40 percent.

Overall, the campaign estimated that almost a third of the thirteen million names on its email list and about $75 million in donations were due to the improved performance provided by this sort of *A/B testing*, in which a site tries out variants of an ad or content on unknowing sets of random users and then uses the results to decide which version the rest of the users will see.[5]

It was even more surprising when the Obama team realized that a video of the candidate whipping up a crowd at a rally generated far fewer clicks than displaying a purely text-based message. What could explain this difference, given their candidate's talents as an orator? The team did not know. Nor did they need to know. The empirical data told them which content to post on the campaign site, even if it didn't tell them why. The results: more clicks, more donations, and probably more votes.

A/B testing has become a common practice. The results you get on a search page at Google are the results of A/B testing.[6] The layout of movies at Netflix results from A/B testing. Even some headlines used by the *New York Times* are the result of A/B testing.[7] Between 2014 and 2016, Bing software engineers performed 21,200 A/B tests, a third of which led to changes to the service.[8]

A/B testing works without needing, or generating, a hypothesis about *why* it works. Why does some ad at Amazon generate more sales if the image of the smiling young woman is on the left instead of the right? We can make up a theory, but we'd still be well advised to A/B test the position of the model in the next ad we create. That a black-and-white photo worked for Obama does not mean that his opponent, John McCain, should have ditched his color photos. That using a blue background instead of a green one worked for Amazon's pitch for an outdoor grill gives us no reason to think it will work for an indoor grill or for a book of barbecue recipes.

In fact, it's entirely plausible that the factors affecting people's preferences are microscopic and fleeting. Maybe men over fifty prefer the ad with the model on the left but only if they are coming from a page that had a funny headline, while women from Detroit prefer the model on the right if the sun just peeked through their windows after two overcast days. Maybe some people prefer the black-and-white photo if they were just watching a high-contrast video and others prefer the color version if the Yankees just lost a game. Maybe some generalizations will emerge. Maybe not. We don't know. The reasons may be as varied as the world itself is.

We've been brought up to believe that the truth and reality of the world are expressed by a handful of immutable laws. Learn the laws and you can make predictions. Discover new laws and you can predict more things. If someone wants to know how you came up with a prediction, you can trot out the laws and the data you've plugged into them. But with A/B testing, we often don't have a mental framework that explains why one version of an ad works better than another.

Think about throwing a beach ball. You expect the ball to arc while moving in the general direction you threw it in, for our mental model—the set of rules for how we think things interact—takes account of gravity and momentum. If the ball goes in another direction, you don't throw out the model. Rather, you assume you missed some element of the situation; maybe there was a gust of wind, or your hand slipped.

That is precisely what we don't do for A/B testing. We don't need to know why a black-and-white photo and a "Learn More" label increased donations to one particular campaign. And if the lessons we learned from a Democrat's ad turn out not to work for her Republican opposition—and they well may not—that's OK too, for it's cheap enough just to run another A/B test.

A/B testing is just one example of a technique that inconspicuously shows us that principles, laws, and generalizations aren't as important as we thought. Maybe—maybe—principles are what we use when we can't handle the fine grains of reality.

We've just looked at examples of two computer-based technologies that are quite different: a programming technique (machine learn-

ing) and a global place (the internet) where we encounter ot
and their expressions of meaning and creativity. Of course, thes
technologies are often enmeshed: machine learning uses the internet to gather information at the scale it needs, and ever more
internet-based services both use and feed machine learning.

These two technologies also have at least three things in common
that have been teaching us about how the world works: Both are
huge. Both are connected. Both are complex.

Their *hugeness*—their scale—is not of the sort we encounter when
we visit the home of the world's largest ball of twine or imagine all
the world's potatoes in a single pile. The importance of the hugeness
of both machine learning and the internet is the level of detail they
enable. Rather than having to get rid of detail by generalizing or
suppressing "marginal" information and ideas, both of these technologies thrive on details and uniqueness.

The *connectedness* of both of these technologies means that the
bits and pieces contained within them can affect one another without a backward glance at the barriers that physical distance imposes.
This connectedness is essential to both of these technologies: a network that connected one piece to another, one at a time, would be not
the internet but the old telephone system. Our new technologies'
connectedness is massive, multiway, distanceless, and essential.

The scale and connectedness of machine learning and the internet result in their *complexity*. The connections among the huge number of pieces can sometimes lead to chains of events that end up
wildly far from where they started. Tiny differences can cause these
systems to take unexpectedly sharp turns.

We don't use these technologies because they are huge, connected,
and complex. We use them because they work. Our success with
these technologies—rather than the technologies themselves—is
showing us the world as more complex and chaotic than we thought,
which, in turn, is encouraging us to explore new approaches and
strategies, challenging our assumptions about the nature and importance of understanding and explanations, and ultimately leading us to a new sense of how things happen.

ɔw We Think Things Happen

we've had plenty of ideas about how things hap-
ancient Greek idea that things naturally strive
ᴗ ᴗ.ossom into what they are, or our more modern idea of cause and
effect operating with the cold ruthlessness of a machine, we have,
throughout our culture's history, generally accepted four assumptions about how the next emerges from the now—assumptions that
are now being challenged.

1. Things happen according to laws

There are few worse nightmares a company can imagine than having airlines add a line to their safety spiel that instructs people to
turn off its product before it explodes.

In 2016, passengers heard that warning about the Galaxy Note 7.

After 35 of the phones had caught fire—a number that eventually
reached about 400—Samsung recalled all 2.5 million of the devices,
losing perhaps $5 billion in revenues and reducing the company's
market capitalization by $14 billion.

The issue turned out to be with the lithium-ion batteries, a defect
Samsung says affected only 0.01 percent of the handsets sold.[9]

So why didn't the other 99.99 percent catch fire? We only have a
few different sorts of answers available. First, maybe the combus-
tible ones were manufactured in some faulty way: the materials
were substandard, or the assembly process was imprecise. Or maybe
there was something unusual about the circumstances that caused
the phones to explode: perhaps they were stressed by being sat on
by users. Or perhaps we need to combine the two explanations:
some people subjected a handful of poorly manufactured units to
unusual circumstances.

No matter which sort of explanation we choose, we're holding to
an unexpressed basic tenet: if the same operation is done on the
same sort of object, if it doesn't have the same effect, then either it

wasn't really the same object (the exploding phone was different from the 99.99 percent) or the causes weren't the same (the exploding phone was squashed in a bouncy environment). Things happen in law-like ways.

But . . .

Now it's becoming increasingly clear that these laws may not always be the most useful tools for us to grapple with the world's complexity. A/B tests may be so sensitive to the minute particularities of each case that applying the laws would be as difficult as determining exactly which piece of gravel is going to strike your windshield exactly right to leave you looking through a glass spider web. We know this because if we could use laws to determine the outcome of A/B tests, we'd skip doing the testing and just apply the laws; we'd skip building Deep Patient and just let physicians predict diagnoses; we'd know which phones to leave out of our baggage; and we'd cease to murmur in wonder at how beautifully a machine is playing a complex game.

2. We can understand how things happen

The ancient Egyptians knew that if they ate some willow bark, their aches and pains would be reduced. They didn't have anything that we would recognize as a scientific theory of why it worked—their medical practices were advanced for their time, but were based on ideas about gods, spirits, and blockages in bodily channels—but the willow bark worked. The British reverend Edward Stone likewise did not have a scientific theory when he rediscovered the power of willow bark in the 1760s. Neither did the Bayer company in 1899 when it began producing what we now know as aspirin, based on the chemicals in willow bark. The theory did not arrive until the late 1970s, resulting in the 1982 Nobel Prize for its discoverers.[10].

But there is a difference between the Egyptians' lack of a theory and Bayer's: unlike the Egyptians, Bayer's chemists believed that there *is* a theory—a causal connection explained by law-governed chemical interactions—and that we would eventually discover it.

We hold firmly to the tenet that not only are changes caused by laws that apply equally to all similar cases, but we humans can know those laws. That makes us special in the universe.

But . . .

Important predictions like the ones made by Deep Patient are being made more accurately than ever before by machine learning systems that we may never be able to understand. We are losing our naive confidence that we can understand how things happen.

3. We can make things happen by pulling the right levers

Based on her examination of the BuzzFeed site, home of viral posts, Josefina Casas advises that if you want your post to go viral, give it a title with a number in it. Appropriately, the title of her post is "5 Tricks for Writing Great Headlines on Twitter and Facebook as Awesome and Clickable as BuzzFeed's."[11]

Her post repeats one of the most basic promises our theory of change makes to us: because what happens follows knowable laws, you just have to find the right levers to pull when you want to make something specific happen.

But . . .

A stunt video much like a million others is posted on the internet, and for reasons we may never understand, it inspires seventeen million people around the world to dump a bucket of ice water on their heads, raising $100 million for a good cause.[12] A thousand other charities are inspired to try some variation on that campaign. None work. Our feeds are filled with the results of all sorts of nonreproducible lever pulls, as unpredictable as which A/B is going to get more clicks.

If a lever behaves differently every time you pull it, is it a lever at all?

4. Change is proportional to effect

If you want to lift a hundred-pound bag of potatoes, it's going to take twice as much effort as lifting a fifty-pound bag. When it comes to simple physics, that's just the way it is.

But . . .

A tiny pebble that hits your windshield can shatter it. A snowball can unleash an avalanche. An amateur video can go viral, bringing millions of people out into the streets. In each of these cases, it still takes a lot of energy to make a big change, but that energy can come from tiny changes distributed throughout the system, if the system is large, complex, and densely connected enough.

Now most of us spend a good portion of our day in just such a system: the internet. And a configuration of thousands of tiny variables in a deep learning system may foretell life-threatening cardiac problems for the complex system we call the human body.

As we inch away from each of these four assumptions, perhaps our everyday understanding of how things happen is finally catching up with the way the world actually works, and how scientists have been thinking about it for a while now.

Normal Chaos

You get in your car. You drive to the mall. Along the way, you pull over to let an ambulance go by. It's a totally normal trip.

Braden R. Allenby and Daniel Sarewitz in *The Techno-Human Condition* want us to understand just how complex that normal trip actually is. Your car is what they call a Level I complex system because you can open up the hood and figure out how it works. The mall owes its existence to Level II complexity: malls weren't feasible before there were cars, yet you could not predict their rise just by examining a car. The ambulance is explicable only as part of a Level III system that exists because of the intersection of multiple systems: cars, roads, traffic laws, a health care system that relies on centralized facilities, and more. If all you knew was what you saw under the hood of your car, you could never, ever predict ambulances.[13] Allenby and Sarewitz lay this out to dissuade us from continuing to apply Level I solutions to Level III problems such as

climate change, but another consequence of their analysis is the recognition that simple things around us can only seem simple because
we ignore the complex systems that make them possible.

Yet we didn't have a theory that directly addressed complexity
until about sixty years ago. If we're willing to ironically oversim-
plify its history, we can mark Chaos Theory's rise to public awareness from a 1972 talk by Edward Lorenz, one of the parents of this
new science: "Predictability: Does the Flap of a Butterfly's Wing in
Brazil Set Off a Tornado in Texas?"[14] That arrestingly implausible
idea made it easy for the media to present the new discipline to the
public as just another one of science's crazy theories, in the "What
will they think of next?" category.

But of course Chaos Theory isn't crazy at all. In fact, before machine learning let us put data to use without always requiring us to
understand how it fits together, and before the internet let us directly experience just how unpredictable a complex system can be,
Chaos Theory prepared the ground for the disruption of our settled
ideas about how change happens.

Chaos Theory isn't crazy, but it can seem that way because it describes *nonlinear* systems—systems that work differently as they
scale up. For example, if you want to add people to your dinner party
for four, at a certain point you won't be able to just add more chairs
and increase the ingredients in your recipes; that would be a linear
system. At some precise point you're going to throw up your arms
with the realization that you have to hire a hall, find a caterer, make
arrangements with the local police to manage the traffic, and give
up on having everyone stand up and introduce themselves. It's going
to be a very different sort of party.

Weather is a more typical nonlinear system because, for example,
a tiny rise in temperature can affect the air pressure and wind speed
enough to change the pattern of evaporation and condensation, resulting in a hurricane. When a small effect produces a large change
in how a system works, you've got a nonlinear system.

Chaos Theory gave us mathematical tools for modeling highly
complex, nonlinear systems, making it possible to rigorously analyze everything from the flow of water around a boulder, to climate

change, to the direction a bead of water takes when flowing down Laura Dern's hand.[15] Of course, this new science's explanations are usually beyond the comprehension of those of us who, like me, lack advanced math degrees.

Not long after Chaos Theory started taking shape, a related type of phenomenon became an object of study: complex adaptive systems. Some of the ground for the public's appreciation of this phenomenon was prepared by Rachel Carson's 1962 best seller, *Silent Spring*, that brought to public awareness the delicacy of intertwined ecosystems—a term only coined in 1935.[16] Altering one element can have surprising and dramatic effects on entire enmeshed systems, the way a butterfly can theoretically cause a hurricane, or the way the actual reintroduction of wolves into Yellowstone National Park kicked off a set of changes that ultimately altered the course of local rivers.[17] Such complex systems can have *emergent* effects that can't be understood just by looking at their constituent parts: no matter how finely you dissect a brain, you won't find an idea, a pain, or a person.

Over the past few decades, lots of developments outside the scientific realms of Chaos Theory and complex adaptive systems theory have conspired to make the world seem not nearly as neatly understandable as we'd thought for hundreds of years. Many of these developments occurred on a global scale: World War II shook up our faith in the reasonableness of Western cultures. Philosophical existentialism taught a generation that meanings are just our inventions. Feminism has challenged the exaltation of purely analytical thinking as often a male power move. What's called postmodern philosophy has denied that there is a single reality grounding our differing interpretations of it. Behavioral economics has pointed out just how irrational we are in our behavior; for instance, hearing a lie debunked turns out to set that lie more firmly in our minds.

All of those influences and more have brought us to question whether our understanding of how things happen is too simple, too constrained by historic drives for power and mastery, too naive about the brain's reliability as an instrument that aims at truth. Instead, we are beginning to see that the factors that determine what happens are so complex, so difficult, and so dependent on the finest-grained particularities of situations that to understand them we have had to turn them into stories far simpler than the phenomena themselves.

Our vision has been clarified because at last we have tools that extract value from vast and chaotic details. We have tools that let us get everyday value out of the theory. The internet has plunged us into a world that does not hide its wildness but rather revels in it. AI in the form of machine learning, and especially deep learning, is letting us benefit from data we used to exclude as too vast, messy, and trivial.

So now, at last, we are moving from Chaos Theory to chaos practice—putting the heady ideas of that theory to everyday use.

Complexity beyond Prediction

We're going to spend the rest of this book thinking about the strategies we're adopting as we face up to and embrace the overwhelming complexity of our world, but here are some quick examples of practices that leverage our growing recognition of the chaos beneath the apparent order:

In **business**, we take *on-demand* manufacturing for granted because it helps us avoid under- or overestimating demand in essentially unpredictable markets. We talk admiringly about companies that can *pivot* or that *disrupt themselves*. Some leading companies are launching *minimum viable products* that have as few features as customers are willing to pay for so that the company can see what the users actually want. Companies often rely on *agile development techniques* that are more responsive to new ideas and developmental interdependencies than traditional task management processes are. Many companies are preparing for *black swans* that could at any moment smash a business's foundations.[18]

Governments, nonprofits, and other public institutions, as well as some for-profit companies, have been adopting *open platforms* that provide data and services without trying to anticipate what users might do with them. Using them, independent developers can create apps and services that the original institution never anticipated. By adopting *open standards*, users can *mash up* data from multiple organizations, thus creating new findings and resources not foreseen by the original publishers of the data.

In **science**, advanced statistical analysis tools can outrun hypotheses and theories. *Machine learning* and *deep learning* are opening up new domains for prediction based on more factors than humans can count and more delicately balanced interrelationships than we can comprehend.

Video games—the revenues of which dwarf the movie industry—routinely enable users to create their own *mods* and *total conversions* that transform games in ways beyond the intentions and imagination of the games' creators.

In our **personal lives**, from the *free agent nation*[19] to the *gig economy*, we've been getting used to the idea that the current generation is not going to have careers that carry them through their futures the way that Boomers did.

If all you knew were these italicized buzzwords, you might think that we've spent the past twenty years or so coming up with ways to avoid having to anticipate what's going to happen next.

You'd be right. That's exactly what we've been doing.

How This Book Works

The *aim* of this book is to reveal a shift that explains many of the changes around us in business, our personal lives, and our institutions.

The *plan* of this book is to examine the before and after of these changes in particular domains of our lives, even though in most instances we have not yet reached the full "after." What was our old system for understanding how things happened in the world, and why? How is that changing—and with what benefits (and challenges) to us as business leaders, citizens, and humans?

The *structure* of this book skips around in time a bit. Chapters 1 and 2 look at the old way we predict and then the new AI-based ways in order to see the change in how we think things happen. But AI isn't the only technology that's transforming our ideas about how the world works. So, in chapter 3, we look at the many ways we've taken advantage of digital networks over the past twenty years in order to escape from our age-old patterns of dealing with the future by trying to out-guess it. Chapter 4 looks for the ground of all the changes discussed so far. Chapters 5 and 6 explore two examples of the profound effect this new ground is having: how our high-level approaches to strategies have mirrored changes in how we think about the nature of possibilities, and what progress now looks like. Chapter 7 is a reflection on what all this means beyond business and practicalities.

The *oddness* of this book is that each chapter, except this introduction and the closing chapter, ends with an essay about how these changes are affecting some of the most basic formations of our understanding—things like how we think about what it means to be moral, or the way in which we divide the course of our lives into what's normal and the accidents that befall us. I'm calling these brief essays "codas," although a musical coda closes a piece, whereas I hope that these essays will open the chapters up, giving an indication of how deep and far-reaching these changes are likely to be in our lives.

That sense of a future opening up is entirely appropriate given the themes we are about to explore.

The *author* of this book dislikes talking about himself, but a little context might help. I've been driven toward the questions this book approaches ever since I was a philosophy major in college (although technically I majored in meaning—it was the 1960s), and I continued to pursue them throughout my doctoral studies and my six years long ago as a philosophy professor. How do our tools affect our experience and understanding of the world, and vice versa? What does our everyday experience teach us that our ideas deny? And, most of all, what have we sacrificed in our attempt to make the world understandable and controllable?

My interest in these questions only intensified when I went into high tech, initially as a marketing writer but ultimately as a vice president of marketing and a strategic marketing consultant. I became fascinated by the internet in the 1980s and then by the early web precisely because they seemed to me to tear down institutions and ways of knowing that maintained control by narrowing our possibilities; that is the subtext of the four books I've written about the internet, starting with *The Cluetrain Manifesto* (as a coauthor) and most recently with *Too Big to Know*. I have been a fellow at Harvard's Berkman Klein Center for Internet & Society since 2004 and am now a senior researcher there, and I have also been a journalism fellow at Harvard's Shorenstein Center, a Franklin Fellow at the US State Department, and a writer-in-residence at Google's People+AI Research (PAIR) group.[20] Additionally, for almost five years, I codirected Harvard's Library Innovation Lab, where I got to try out in practical ways some of the central ideas in this book.

The *why* of this book is that we are living through a deep change in our understanding of ourselves and our world. We should be "leaning in" to this by rethinking our fundamental premises about how change happens. How much control do we have? Is finding the right levers to pull still the most effective way to turn events our way? What can we learn from how our technology is already enabling us to succeed and even thrive? What is the role of explanations? What constitutes success? The pursuit of these questions and more throughout this book will lead us down some unexpected paths, and at the end there won't be a chapter with a numbered list of rules for success. If only. Instead, as we will see, leaning in means embracing the complexity and chaos our tech is letting us see and put to use.

The *hope* of this book is that we can catch a glimpse of an epochal change in our understanding that makes sense of an array of phenomena that are puzzling on their own, and more so because we've so easily come to take them as normal. It is a change in how we think things happen, which means it is a change in how we think the future arises from the present, the next from the now.

And that changes everything.

Chapter One

The Evolution of Prediction

When I was a lad, you could beat the local weather forecaster's batting average simply by predicting that tomorrow was going to be like today. Or so my fifth-grade science teacher told us.

Now, in a series of photos on the NASA website, you can graphically see one reason the app on your phone predicts the weather with scary accuracy ten days out.[1] In 2005, satellite images showed the amount of water vapor—an important predictor of hurricanes—as colored blocks each representing fifty kilometers of land. In the images from 2015, the blocks are about one-tenth the size, providing far greater detail. As an article on the site puts it, "Imagine going from video game figures made of large chunky blocks to detailed human characters that visibly show beads of sweat on their forehead."[2]

You'd think with these new predictive superpowers we'd be able to predict earthquakes by now.[3] After all, these are planet-scale events caused by the collision of massive tectonic plates that move maybe a couple of inches a year. If you slowed footage of a head-on car crash down to that pace as part of a forensic investigation, you'd be desperately pressing the "Go Faster!" button on the playback device. But earthquakes can be cataclysmic because a tiny triggering event—perhaps the slowly crashing plates vaporize a stone stuck between them, or other uncountable incidents of stress finally reach the tipping point—can set off a cascade of energy that buckles the ground and tumbles towers. As our predictions in multiple fields get better by being able to include more data and by tracking more interrelationships, we're coming to realize that even systems ruled by relatively simple physical laws can be so complex that they are subject to these cascades and to other sorts of causal weirdness.

We are thus simultaneously getting better at prediction and are being brought to recognize just how profoundly unpredictable our world is. We are less patient when predicted departure times are delayed but also more on edge about cataclysms, attacks, and our collective future. That is at least seemingly a paradox. But it is no mere curiosity, for, as we will see, how we predict shows us how we think the future happens and thus how the world works.

In this chapter we'll explore the "before" of prediction. In the next chapter we'll look at the "after," or at least the "now" and the "emerging." We'll see that our enhanced predictive powers are based on our new technology's ability to grapple with a world so detailed, so densely interconnected, and so variable that its complexity overwhelms our understanding.

Prediction's Sweet Spot

Think about the times you have uttered a prediction. Very likely you didn't just state what you think will happen and then clam up. You probably hedged it to some degree. "I bet the marriage of these two celebrities won't last a year," you might have said. Or, "If this candidate makes it through the debate without saying, 'Good jobs at good wages,' I'll eat my hat." The hedge words that acknowledge a lack of complete certainty—"I bet," "If so"—help flag a statement as a prediction.

Predictions live in a sweet spot between surprise and certainty. That's why "It looks like it'll rain on Friday" is a clearer example of a prediction than "The sun will come up tomorrow": tomorrow's sunrise is too certain. On the other hand, who will be invited to your newborn's eightieth birthday party is not subject to prediction because it's too uncertain. A prediction is a statement that attempts to say what's going to happen when there's room for belief but also for serious doubt and disagreement.

Still, not every such statement is a prediction. If I ask you why you picked a particular lottery number and you say, "I just have a hunch," your pick isn't a prediction, or at least it isn't a good example of one. In the clearest cases, we expect there to be some grounds for a prediction. For a prediction of rain, those grounds might be statistical ("It usually rains a lot in April"), might be based on a model that uses scientific laws ("A mass of moist warm air is going to collide with a cold front, causing precipitation"), or might come from the far more complex data models used by machine learning that we'll discuss in the next chapter.[4]

These two characteristics of predictions—we have a degree of certainty, but not too much, and we have grounds for that certainty—makes them an essential clue to understanding our ideas about how things happen. If you predict that it might be rainy tomorrow because tonight you saw dark clouds on the horizon, you're probably speaking not only from experience but because you also think there are scientific theories that link tonight's clouds with tomorrow's rain—something about the steadiness of the movement of clouds through the atmosphere, the composition of clouds as water vapor that can condense, and so forth. If the number 66 bus doesn't arrive at 8:17 as the printed schedule says it should, you may suppose that the traffic was bad or one of the earlier buses broke down, or you might just accept the bus system as not very reliable because of the complexity of life in a city.

In fact, predictions are such a particular type of speech that simply having them in a culture's linguistic toolkit reveals much about how that culture thinks about the world: What causes change, how regular is it, and what is the human role in its occurrence?

Let's look briefly at three early cultures that understood the world in ways that kept them from making what we would today recognize as predictions.

For three thousand years, the Egyptians held to a cyclical view that year after year proved itself to be true: the seasons came and went, life in the farms and villages remained basically the same, and the idea of progress was as foreign as soft-serve ice cream. The Egyptians didn't even bother to give sequential numbers to their years: each new pharaoh reset the clock to year one and increased it by one when the taxes were levied every two years.[5] A cyclical culture that remains unchanged for millennia is not a culture of predictions.

The ancient Hebrews had a more linear view of time, but still didn't make predictions the way we think of them. They had a promise from God that someday they would be returned to the Promised Land and the world would be redeemed, but a promise is not a prediction. That promise began a grand linear narrative for them—very different from the Egyptian cyclical sense of time—but the completion of their journey was conditional upon the Hebrews' fulfilling their side of their Covenant with God. That's why the words of the prophets are generally too intended to influence behavior to count as predictions: *if* our people continue in these wrongheaded ways, then we will face deprivation and punishment, but *if* we follow the word of God, then we will be blessed and our people's story will continue.

For the ancient Greeks, the situation was different depending on whether they were looking up or down. Looking up, they saw the same wheeling stars that the Egyptians did, and believed in their regularity just as firmly. But here on Earth, there was no telling what would happen. As a culture of sailors and traders living in tumultuous times, the contrast between the predictable, orderly heavens and the randomness of life on Earth was for the Greeks a fundamental fact of life.[6] After all, one morning the playwright Aeschylus woke up not knowing that an eagle would that day drop a tortoise on his head, killing him—out of the blue, quite literally.[7]

Life for mortals was so irregular because it was controlled by so many intersecting forces. The Fates determined your life span and some of the broad-brush themes, such as whether your marriage was going to be happy. The gods could not undo the Fates' decrees, but they could change a mortal's life in just about any other way they felt like at the moment. Then there were the ancient spirits, or daimons, who intervened in individual lives in untamed ways. So it was quite a mix of superhuman forces that determined the turning points in one's life, with only limited human control and predictability.[8]

True, the Oracle at Delphi had divine access to the future—or perhaps "was a priestess in a cave who became disoriented by volcanic fumes and babbled incoherently," as an article in *Scientific American* claims—but her pronouncements were so cryptic that sometimes they couldn't be applied until it was too late.[9] Just ask King Oedipus, who knew the words the Oracle had proclaimed but still ended up saying "Mom???" to his wife before plunging a knife into his eyes.

That's why the Greeks talked about the future not as what lay ahead of them but as what was behind them, according to the late Harvard professor of Greek, Bernard Knox. The future, he explained, was for the Greeks primordially unknowable—as invisible as what is going on behind us.[10] Nor were the Greeks alone in this. Some maintain that the ancient Israelites talked about the future in the same terms for the same reason.[11] Likewise, a scholar of African religion writes of "African peoples" who consider time to be a present that "moves 'backward' rather than 'forward.'"[12]

When the future is so unknowable that we think of it as perpetually behind us, predictions are no more possible than are prayers for societies of atheists or limericks in languages that have no rhymes.[13]

The point of this mini history is not that those three early cultures were too dumb to come up with the idea of prediction as we understand it. Rather, it is to make it clear that our idea of prediction requires a delicate balance of ideas about how the world works. In turn, predicting reveals how the world works in very particular ways.

For example, let's jump ahead to the origins of modern weather forecasting. In 1900, a Norwegian scientist named Vilhelm Bjerknes thought that we could understand the dynamics of global weather using just seven variables—the three spatial dimensions and the air's pressure, temperature, density, and water content—and laws derived from the work of Isaac Newton.[14] At last we had a model that explained how weather happens, enabling us to make predictions based on the laws of physics, rather than extrapolating from observations of the weather's prior behavior.

Over time, scientists refined Bjerknes's crude model and eventually ran it on some of the very earliest computers, making weather predictions generally good enough to tell you if you should take an umbrella to work, but still distressingly unreliable, especially for forecasts more than a couple of days ahead. Still, for all of its deficiencies, Bjerknes's approach had at last fully brought the weather into the realm of modern predictability.

If you predict tomorrow's weather by choosing seven factors governed by Newton's laws, you're revealing the world as a place that is orderly, rule-based, and knowable, at least at the large scale. If you foretell the weather for the coming season by reading bird entrails, you are revealing the world as the sort of place where what happens depends on hidden connections of meaning.[15] If you can tell that a storm is coming by sticking your finger into the wind, you reveal the world as consisting of systems so tightly interwoven that a single factor can tell the story of the whole. If you predict the weather by doing a statistical analysis of years of prior data, you reveal the world as governed by laws that may be unknown or too hard to apply because of the many factors but that tend toward repetitive patterns. And, to switch examples, if you use A/B testing to decide which version of an ad will generate the most clicks, you reveal at least the online world as a place where the causes can be so minuscule and contextual that the old ways of predicting don't work and don't much matter.

The story of prediction is therefore also the story of how we have understood how what happens happens.

To see how that story is about to hit an inflection point, we have to go back to the sweet spot that allowed the emergence of what we now think of as prediction. That sweet spot has a name: Sir Isaac Newton.

Tick. Tock.

Newtonian physics gave us a universe ripe for prediction. It's governed by rules. Those rules are knowable. They are the same for all things and throughout the universe. And they apply to a universe the state of which we can know well enough to make predictions but not so well that we are omniscient gods who don't need to make predictions.

Crucially, Newton's simple, knowable laws are sufficient to explain how things happen. They don't need gods, fates, or spirits to intervene. They don't require us to stipulate that, as acorns become oaks, things change in order to achieve their essence, as the Greeks believed. Newtonian predictions reveal the universe as a self-contained clockwork that can be explained purely on its own terms.

Think of the innards of an old windup watch or grandfather clock, each gear meshing so perfectly with the others that the only noise the system makes is the tick of the mechanism that releases the clock's pent-up energy all at once, moving the second hand one notch. The mechanism follows rules: this gear turns that one, and that one turns the other one, one tooth at a time: simple rules with simple results. The clockwork is perfectly knowable: you can open up the clock and trace how it works. Its next state depends entirely on its current state and thus is predictable: if the time is 12:01, in sixty seconds the minute hand is going to point to the 2, not the 57. If you can't predict exactly where a clock's hands will be in one hour, you're looking at a clock that may not be right even twice a day. In fact, you might check that you're not staring at your clothes dryer.

Clocks thus became a standard way of understanding and expressing how things happen: perfectly regular changes that occur in small increments, following simple, knowable rules that would be entirely sufficient to explain the change . . . if we had perfect knowledge. But, of course, we don't. That's what opens the space for prediction.

In 1814 Pierre-Simon, Marquis de Laplace, drew an inevitable, and unsettling, conclusion from Newton's work. He imagined a god-like intellect—frequently referred to as "Laplace's demon"—who could know the position of every item in the universe at any one instant, all the forces at play, and the Newtonian laws governing them. (This demon will pop up more than once in this book.) "For such an intellect," Laplace wrote, "nothing would be uncertain and the future just like the past would be present before its eyes."[16] This great intellect could apply Newton's laws to any single moment in history and deduce the entire future of the universe, as well as its entire past—"postdicting" (so to speak) as well as predicting.

Laplace was sometimes called "the Newton of France" because of his work extending the use of Newton's gravitational laws, including to explain phenomena that seemed not to fit, such as minor perturbations of the orbits of Jupiter and Saturn.[17] But in the previous passage, Laplace draws the conclusion that made Newton personally uncomfortable with the clock metaphor: once the universe is set in motion, it doesn't need God's help to keep it going. The idea that God might have no post-Creation role in the universe was unthinkable for a person as deeply religious as Newton. But he thought he saw a way to save a place for Him. Newton's theory of universal gravitation—every body attracts every other—meant that the combined gravitational pull of all the objects in the universe would slowly draw the planets out of their beautifully elliptical orbits. Newton hypothesized that God might therefore have to lob the occasional comet on exactly the right path for its gravitational pull to tug the heavenly bodies back into their perfect ellipses.[18]

Laplace, on the other hand, was a forthright atheist who felt no need to make work for God, or even to defend free will, which he viewed as "the expression of our ignorance of the true causes" of our actions.[19] Because we humans can't know everything about the universe at any one moment, prediction is for us a matter of probability, as the title of Laplace's book—*A Philosophical Essay on Probabilities*—makes clear. But since everything that happens is completely and perfectly determined by prior causes, it is perfectly predictable to an all-knowing demon.

The clockwork metaphor stuck with our culture. It felt natural because clockworks were exquisitely built, serving as representations of the magnificence of God's own handiwork. And clockworks are completely understandable within themselves, like a system of logic, making them an appropriate metaphor for the newly dawning age of reason.

Over one hundred years ago, Albert Einstein dealt the death blow to the clockwork metaphor among physicists; not only isn't the universe like a steadily ticking clock, time itself isn't a simple sequence of synchronized ticks and tocks. Then digital clocks undid the metaphor for the general public. Yet in ordinary life we still assume that everything that happens—every tock that follows a tick—arises in a knowable and determinate way from the present state of the mechanism. We still make predictions using laws that let us "skip ahead" to see the future—for example, predicting how far a plane will have flown in four hours as easily as predicting the distance it will have traversed in two hours.

Beneath these predictions is a confidence that not only are the rules pretty simple, but simple rules create a predictable world. We can think of this as the first level of predictability.

But from the beginning, Newton knew that there's a second level where simple rules get complicated quickly.

A Summer of French Aristocrats

In 1676, Isaac Newton modestly wrote to his rival Robert Hooke, "If I have seen further it is by standing on the shoulders of Giants."[20] Yet in the preface to his masterpiece, the *Principia*, there is only one giant whom Newton acknowledges: "the most acute and universally learned Mr. Edmund Halley," who not only edited the book but was responsible for nagging Newton into publishing it.[21] Halley even helped to finance it after the Royal Society had blown too much of its budget on a history of fish, thereby avoiding what would have been perhaps the worst trade-off in history. Newton appreciated his friend's efforts: he sometimes referred to the *Principia* as "Halley's book."[22]

Yet when Halley asked Newton for help calculating the path of the comet that would come to bear Halley's name, Newton said no. The task was just too complicated.

For Halley to prove that the heavenly body he had observed in 1682 was the same one recorded in 1607, 1531, and multiple times earlier, he had to predict when it would again return. This would be straightforward if the interval between observations were constant, but there was about a year's difference in them. Halley thought that this might be caused by the gravitational attraction of Jupiter, Saturn, and the sun as the comet passed through the solar system. All he had to do was use Newton's equations to factor in the pull of the planets and the sun, and out would pop the comet's path and the date of its next pass through our solar system.

That sounds easy. But the combined gravitational pulls of those three bodies is different at every moment because they are in constant motion relative to one another, which means the gravitational forces they exert on each other are also constantly changing. This makes it a classic "three-body problem." Such problems were so notoriously difficult that Newton declined Halley's request because it would simply take too long to do the calculations. He had bigger thoughts to think.

Halley took a swing at it on his own. Through mathematical cleverness and some approximations, he came to expect the comet sometime around the end of 1758. He died fourteen years before he could see whether his hypothesis would be confirmed.

The predictability of the return of that particular light in the sky became a thumbs-up or thumbs-down moment for Newton's theories themselves, touted by well-known intellectuals such as Adam Smith.[23] With that much riding on it, three French aristocrats—Alexis Claude Clairaut, Joseph Jérôme Lefrançois de Lalande, and Nicole-Reine Étable de Labrière Lepaute (back when names were names!)—stepped in. They spent the summer months of 1757 filling in row after row of a table, calculating where the sun, Saturn, and Jupiter were relative to each other at one moment, how their gravitational fields would affect the course of the comet, and where their slightly altered positions would put the comet at the next moment. They did this in incremental steps of one or two degrees for each of 150 years of the comet's path, with Clairaut checking the results for errors that, if not caught, could throw off all the subsequent calculations based on them.

It was painstaking work, day after day from June through September, that Lalande later claimed left him permanently ill. On the other hand, Clairaut reported that Lepaute exhibited an "ardor" that was "surprising"—perhaps surprising to him because Lepaute was a woman; he later removed the acknowledgment of Lepaute's considerable contribution from the published text. (Much of her later work was published without attribution by other people, including her husband, France's royal clockmaker.)

Clairaut presented the trio's findings to the Académie des Sciences in November 1757, giving a two-month stretch during which they believed the comet would return. On March 13, 1758, a German astronomer spotted it, just two days outside that window. Modern scientists attribute this minor inaccuracy to the team's failure to figure in the gravitational influence of Uranus and Neptune, planets undiscovered at the time. Later scientists also found two errors in the trio's calculations that, luckily, canceled each other out.[24]

In this story we see the next level of complexity in applying Newton's laws. At the first level, those laws let us skip ahead: plug in the right data and you can tell that there will be a solar eclipse on January 30, 2921, as easily as you can predict the one on June 10, 2021. But there was no jumping ahead to predict the path of Halley's comet—not because Newton's laws don't govern its motion, but because when multiple bodies are moving relative to one another and that movement affects where they are in relation to one another, the numbers to be plugged into the equations are constantly changing. The formulas remained simple, but the computation process was complicated. That's why solving the problem took a summer of three aristocrats walking through it one step at a time.

At this level, the complexity merely requires the patient reapplication of the known laws. We still do this today, although our computers do many summers of French aristocratic work in instants.

Level-two predictions show the world as a complicated but still predictable place. Their success maintains and reinforces our traditional paradigm of how things happen: knowable rules ensure that similar causes have similar, knowable effects.

The path of a comet between massive moving bodies is a relatively simple problem involving only a tiny handful of moving parts, isolated from each other in the vastness of space. Prediction soon took the first of two turns. The first turn, toward statistics and probability, acknowledged what Newton knew: the universe is so complicated that in fact we can't always know the conditions under which the rules are operating. The second, as we'll see, found an important problem with one of Newton's—and our—assumptions about laws.

Simple but Complicated

We flip a coin to come up with a random decision because we can't predict how it will land. But we also know that Newton's laws fully explain the coin's flight, its descent, and whether it lands on its face or its tail. But we also flip coins because we know something else: the odds are fifty-fifty that it will land either particular way.

Probability theory originated several decades before the publication of Newton's major work. It's usually traced back to correspondence between Blaise Pascal and Pierre de Fermat in the mid-1600s about a question posed by a gambler: If you roll a pair of dice twenty-four times, were the chances that one of those rolls will be double sixes really fifty-fifty, as was assumed at the time? Pascal and Fermat's work led to the publication of the first book on probability, written in 1657 by the mathematician and astronomer Christian Huygens. *De Ratiociniis in Ludo Aleae—The Value of All Chances in Games of Fortune*—was about gambling, a specialized case in which we want randomness to reign, but its math applied more broadly.

The idea of probability arose far earlier but was not pursued as a science. In fact, Plato himself dismissed it as the opposite of mathematics because the point and beauty of math was its provable, knowable, absolute rightness; the perfection of the heavenly sphere was embodied in its geometric precision.[25] Here on Earth, the Greeks assumed that the gods determined the outcome of what we think of as random events.

But by the seventeenth century, science was on the rise, the gods were well in retreat, and the world seemed to be ruled by systematic, repeatable causes. The roll of dice obeyed the causal laws, although the outcome was determined by minute, unmeasurable differences in the starting positions of the dice, the strength of the toss, the bounciness of the surface they landed on, and who knows (literally) what else. We realized that in some controlled instances, such as dice throws in which there's a limited set of causes and possible outcomes, we can use the logic of mathematics to predict the probability of the various possible outcomes.

Then, beginning with a paper in 1774, Laplace inverted probability theory, giving impetus to what we today call statistics. As Leonard Mlodinow puts it in *The Drunkard's Walk*, probability "concerns predictions based on fixed probabilities": you know the likelihood of rolling double sixes without having to gather data about the history of dice rolls. But statistics "concerns the inference of those probabilities based on observed data."[26] For example, based on the data about the punctuality of the number 66 bus, what are the chances that you're going to arrive on time?

From the early nineteenth century on, statistics have had a tremendous influence on policy making. While from its start some have argued that it demeans human dignity to say not only that our behavior is predictable but that it can be read from mere columns of numbers, it's demonstrably true that clouds of facts and data can yield insights into the behavior of masses of people, markets, and crowds, as well as into systems that, like the weather, lack free will.

This has at least two profound effects on how we think about how what happens next emerges from what's happening now. First, statistical research still at times shocks us by finding regularities in what appear to us to be events subject to many influences: people walking wherever they want on errands of every sort nevertheless wear paths into the ground. Second, probability theory and statistics have gotten us to accept that Plato was wrong: a statement that is uncertain can still count as scientific knowledge if it includes an accurate assessment of that uncertainty. "There's a 50 percent chance that this coin will land heads up" is as true as "This coin just landed heads up." Without these two consequences of probability theory and statistics, we would not be able to run our modern governments, businesses, or lives.

But for all their importance, probability theory and statistics remain solidly within the Newtonian clockwork universe, usually yielding level-two predictions. They assume a causal universe that follows knowable laws. Their outcomes are probabilistic because the starting conditions are too complicated or minute to measure. These mathematical sciences not only did not contradict the clockwork paradigm about how the universe works but confirmed it by extending its reach to outcomes that once seemed to be random or accidental, due to the gods' machinations, or the result of unpredictable free will. Such events may not be completely explicable, but they are probabilistically predictable because they are fully determined by the same laws that explain and predict the comets.

From dust to stars, one set of laws shall rule them all.

Simple and Complex

When the age of computers began in the 1950s, it further cemented the Newtonian view of how things happen. A computer program was a tiny universe completely governed by knowable laws, with the important difference that humans got to decide what the laws would be. And we saw and it was good, and we called it programming. Once programmed, a computer operated like a perfect clockwork, resulting in completely reliable and predictable output no matter what data was entered—assuming the programmers had done their jobs well and the data was good.

For sure, back then computers were very limited in the amount and complexity of the data they could deal with, even though it seemed so overwhelming that in the 1960s we started hearing about "information overload" as an imminent danger.[27] That's why computers looked like instruments of conformity to much of the culture: Exactly the same set of information was tracked for every person in a human resources database, and a different but equally uniform set for every product in a computerized inventory system. Because of the limits on computer memory and processing speed, these systems tracked the minimal information required. So, while IBM's own internal personnel system tracked employees' names, social security numbers, and wage scales, it's highly unlikely that there was a field to note that that troublemaker in operations sometimes showed up to work in a sports coat instead of a conservative blue suit, or that Sasha in accounting is a serious student of flamenco dancing. Computers were a domain of perfect order enabled by a ruthless and uniform concision.

So it was when, in 1970, John Conway invented a simple little game.

Conway has held a distinguished professorship at Princeton for over twenty-five years and has authored seminal books on everything from telecommunications to particle physics. In 2015, the *Guardian* called him "the world's most charismatic mathematician" and "the world's most lovable egomaniac." Outside his scholarly fields, he is best known for "the Game of Life," a "no-player neverending" game."[28] The game may not have players or winners, but it does have a board, counters, and rules.

The board is a grid. Each square represents a space where a person (represented by a counter) might live. At each turn, four rules are applied to each square to determine whether that square will have a counter placed in it; the rules look at how many of the eight surrounding squares are occupied.[29] A turn in the game consists in the application of the rules to each of the squares. This may sound a bit like the French aristocrats calculating the path of Halley's comet, but the results are startlingly different.

When the game was first made famous by a *Scientific American* column about it by Martin Gardner, computing time was so expensive that the Game of Life was designed to be played with graph paper, a pencil, and an eraser.[30] In addition to being laborious, applying the rules by hand can mask what the computer's rapid application of them makes clear: some of the starting patterns can fly.

Most initial sets of filled-in squares either fritter away into random patterns or become uninterestingly repetitive, perhaps the same two squares blinking on and off forever. But some mutate into unexpected shapes. Some endlessly cycle between a set of quite different patterns. Some spawn "spaceships" or "gliders" that, when looked at in sequence, move across the page or shoot "bullets." To this day, enthusiasts are still discovering patterns that move particularly quickly, that complexify rapidly, or that "eat" other shapes that come near them. Even in 2016, forty-six years after the invention of the game, people were breathlessly announcing new finds.[31]

That's evidence of the depth and complexity of this four-rule game. And that's the point: Conway's puzzle shows that simple rules can generate results that range from the boring, to the random and unpredictable, to animated birds that flap their wings and fly off the page. If, in a clockwork universe, simple rules yield simple, predictable results, in this universe, simple rules yield complexity and surprises. A clockwork that generated such results would be not just broken but surreal.

The Game of Life was taken up as no mere game. The philosopher Daniel C. Dennett in the early 1990s thought the ideas behind it might explain consciousness itself.[32] The technologist Raymond Kurzweil thinks that simple rules instantiated as computer programs will give rise to machines that not only think but think better than we do.[33] The Game of Life influenced the mathematician and chaos theorist Stephen Wolfram's development of a "New Kind of Science," which explains the universe as a vast computer.[34] Wolfram uses this approach—simple rules with complex results—to explain everything from the patterns in shattered glass to the placement of branches circling a sapling's trunk.

The Game of Life might even have confounded Laplace's demon. Put yourself in the demon's position. The board is set up, and some counters are already in place. How do you take the board to its next state? Apply the rules to square 1, and record the result. Then square 2. Continue until you've gone through all the squares. But now suppose you, the Imp of All Knowing, want to know how the board will look in two moves, or ten moves, or a thousand moves. Even someone with your powers can only get those answers by going through each of the moves. There are no shortcuts, no way to leap ahead, not even for an all-knowing imp. (Wolfram calls this the principle of computational irreducibility.) Isn't it odd that we think we can leap ahead in predicting our own lives and business, but not when playing a game not much more complicated than tic-tac-toe?

The Game of Life shows that a universe with simple rules doesn't itself have to be as predictable as a clock, where each tick is followed by a tock. Instead, what follows might be a tock, or it might be the blare of a foghorn or the smell of rye toast . . . and the only way to find out is to wind it up and give it a go. When small changes can have giant effects, even when we know the rules, we may not be able to predict the future. To know it, we have to live through it.

While this third level of prediction means we have less control than we thought, it also has a certain appeal. Few of us would trade the net for a medium as predictable as the old three-network television was. Likewise, few of the generation brought up on open-world video games long to go back to the arcade days when, for a quarter, you got to move your avatar left and right while shooting at a steadily advancing line of low-resolution space aliens that inevitably overran you. And who would ban today's best, most unpredictable television shows so we can go back to the good old days of 1950s TV?

But even in the realms where the surprises that simple rules can generate are not pleasant diversions but rather global threats—biological, geopolitical, climactic—we are accepting this lack of predictability for two reasons. First, it's a fact. Second, we are—seemingly paradoxically—getting better at predicting. We can predict further ahead. We can predict with greater accuracy. We can predict in domains—including the social—that we'd thought were simply impervious to any attempts to anticipate them.

We are getting so much better at predicting in some domains because our technology—especially machine learning—does not insist on reducing complexity to a handful of simple rules but instead embraces complexity that far surpasses human understanding. When we were unable to do anything with this complexity, we ignored it and cast it aside as mere noise. Now that unfathomable complexity is enabling our machines to break the old boundaries of prediction, we're able to open our eyes to the complexity in which our lives have always been embedded.

As we'll see in the next chapter, our new engines of prediction are able to make more accurate predictions and to make predictions in domains that we used to think were impervious to them because this new technology can handle far more data, constrained by fewer human expectations about how that data fits together, with more complex rules, more complex interdependencies, and more sensitivity to starting points. Our new technology is both further enlightening us and removing the requirement that we understand the *how* of our world in order to be able to predict what happens next.

Such a radical change in the mechanics of prediction means fundamental changes in how we think the world works, and our role in what happens. In the next chapter, we'll explore these changes by asking how AI "thinks" about the world.

Coda: The Kingdom of Accidents

You're driving on a residential street in Boston. It's winter. The streets have been plowed, but there are occasional slippery patches where the scraped snow has melted and refrozen. So you're driving as if you're not from Boston: slowly and considerately.

As you glide to a stop at an intersection, working the steering wheel to compensate for the car's sideways slippage, you feel a bump on the back of your car: a canonical fender bender. You can't get too angry. The bump was more like a gentle tap, so it's likely that the car behind you was also going slowly and carefully. The roads are just impossible. What are you going to do? It was an accident.

Classifying an event as an accident puts it into a kingdom with its own special rules. "It happened by accident" is meant to imply not that there wasn't a cause but rather that we were unable to exert control over that cause. It thus wasn't our fault. While any particular accident perhaps could have been prevented, not all can be; the persistence of the Kingdom of Accidents is a given.

Accidents are the exception. They are unexpected, unasked for, and usually unwelcome, visitors to the Kingdom of the Normal. In the Normal, we make our plans and succeed at them with some well-calibrated degree of confidence. We normally get to work within ten minutes of the mandated start of our workday, but if our car gets bumped or a subway track loses power, we'll feel we've been paid an unwanted visit from that other kingdom.

These two worlds have fluid borders, unlike the line the ancient Greeks drew between the perfectly orderly heavens, where the sun rises and falls without mishap, and Earth, where chaos outlives every mortal. These days we assume we control what happens in this human world to a degree that is new in history—if we could sue tornadoes, we would—but we still need the Kingdom of Accidents to explain why things don't always go as planned.

What makes the Normal normal is not simply that it's what is usually the case. The Normal feels as if it's the *real* world, the way things are, even the way things should be. When we say about outrageous behavior, "That's not normal," we're not just making a statistical observation. The Normal is our home. Accidents are home invaders.

But if the Normal is our home, it's like the perfect suburban neighborhood, with perfectly manicured lawns and perfectly coiffed wives who take care of the kids all day and have martinis waiting when their menfolk return from work. Later in the movie, we find out it's too perfect to be real and too gendered to be desirable. The Normal is a fiction that simply ignores the galaxies of accidents that enable it.

The Normal arises from a trick of focus. The Accidental looks like the exception to the Normal because we define the Normal around our plans . . . and we make plans only about that which we can control to some degree. Even gaining that imperfect degree of control has required us to build massive, interconnected systems to do something as simple as take a long drive. We have cars with controls and instrumentation to enable us to keep them apart from other cars. We have laws governing how we drive them and penalties for those who fail. We have motels spaced out along the highways and Airbnbs filling the gaps. We have GPS systems, credit card systems, and car-resale systems all designed to keep automobile trips predictable. The rare visitors from the Kingdom of Accidents look like strangers because we've worked so hard on keeping them out.

Meanwhile, our cross-country trip runs on and through accidents beyond count: The opacity of the lane markings varies according to which cars wobbled over them and which trucks braked so hard they wore away the edge of the stripe your car just drove past. The grass untrimmed around the edge of a sign grew from seeds whose stories can't be found. Each of the cars you pass is going somewhere for some reason that arose through the billions of accidents of biology, emotion, politics, and the pure luck of living in this time and place. The asphalt was poured by workers whose boots were splashed black in patterns no one could have outlined beforehand. A worker in those boots was surprised on some Tuesday by the extra bag of chips he found in his lunch bucket.

The Normal is a poorly paved road running through the endless territory belonging to the Kingdom of Accidents. Our plans are low beams that point wherever we look and leave the rest in the dark.

Chapter Two

Inexplicable Models

Until a chick is five or six weeks old, it's surprisingly difficult to tell the pullets from cockerels—or the boys from the girls, if you're not in the trade. This is a problem if you're a commercial egg producer who sees males as nothing but a waste of chicken feed.

In the 1920s, the Japanese hit on a technique to address this. There are two ways to determine the sex of a chick: check their wingtips or their cloacae—better known as their buttholes.[1] Japanese chicken sexers settled on this second approach because it is more reliable for more breeds of chicken. (This decision explains the title of an NBC report in 2015: "Chick Sexer: The $60K a Year Job Nobody Wants.") But the odd thing is there's nothing about a male chick's cloaca that obviously differentiates it from a female's. At least there's nothing that anyone can point to or describe. So a student learns how to tell the males from the females by guessing which is which, while an expert confirms or rejects the decision. After classifying thousands of chicks this way, eventually, somehow, the student starts getting it consistently right, but still can't tell you how they know.

Training people how to sex chickens therefore is not like training soldiers to identify enemy aircraft or teaching people how to become proficient bird watchers, as Richard Horsey points out in a philosophical article about chicken sexing.[2] Planes and birds have distinguishing features you can learn to notice: a Japanese Zero has rounded wingtips; a robin has an orange chest. Chicken sexers have nothing they can point to. If you ask them how they knew a particular chick was male or female, they cannot tell you. Yet a trained chicken sexer is able to classify up to 1,200 chicks an hour—one every three seconds—with 98 percent accuracy.

Philosophers who study knowledge find this fascinating. Because the accuracy of the chicken sexers' predictions is so high—the world record is 1,682 chicks sexed in an hour with 100 percent accuracy—their decisions demonstrate they know the genders of the chicks.[3] But since the ancient Greeks, we've considered knowledge to consist not just of true beliefs but of true beliefs that are justifiable.[4] Saying, "I know it's a pullet, but I can't tell you how I know or why you should believe me," is like saying, "I fully know that the next card is going to be an ace but I have no reason for thinking so"—a textbook example of guessing versus knowing, even if you turn out to be right.[5]

But commercial egg operations don't care about the philosophical conundrum chicken sexing poses. They care about identifying the male chicks so they can grind them up alive to avoid wasting food on them. Since people are reluctant to make a career out of staring up the butts of hundreds of chicks an hour, we might figure that this is a process ripe for traditional computer-based automation.

It's not. Traditionally—before machine learning—we'd teach a computer to recognize birds by programming in a *model* of birds. A model of a thing or system lists its salient features and how they're arranged relative to one another. For example, for a computer program designed to identify birds, a model might include the sorts of things a field guide points out in its illustrations: the beak, the shape of the head, the body shape and color, the length and shape of the wings relative to the body, the length of the legs, and the shape of the feet attached to those legs. The model also specifies where each of those parts is located in relation to the others. If the computer is intended to identify still photos of perched birds, its model won't bother to include the way the bird glides or what it sounds like. The model is also likely to ignore whether a bird has sand on its claws, although that might in fact be a clue to its habitat. The model works if it enables the machine to sort birds into the right bins, using the same sort of criteria that human birders would use when arguing about whether they just saw a downy or a hairy woodpecker. "Its beak was as long as its head" is likely to be a convincing argument that it was the latter, for that's what the models of those two birds tell the quarreling birders.

That's exactly the sort of *conceptual* model that chicken sexers cannot provide for themselves—or to computer programmers trying to build a *working* model that will let technology replace the sexers. A conceptual model is the idea of a system's parts and relationships. A working model is a representation of the conceptual model, built out of atoms or bits, that you can manipulate to see how the system behaves. Your old classroom's solar system made out of small balls, representing the sun and the planets, that you can crank to see their relative positions is a working model. It crudely represents the astronomer's conceptual model that includes the mathematical relationships that express each planet's position, mass, and velocity.

Traditional computers may be stopped by the chicken sexers' lack of a conceptual model, but now there's a new type of computer program in town. With machine learning, we could in theory build a chicken-sexing computer without programming a model into it at all. We would train it the same way that chicken sexers are trained: feed it lots of examples of chicks with their sex noted and let the computer figure out for itself what the salient differences are. The result would be a working model, quite possibly without a conceptual model.[6] And, as we'll see in this chapter, that threatens to upend one of our core assumptions about our position as human beings: we are the special creatures who can understand how the world works.

Working Models, Conceptual Models

Good news: we can now stop talking about chicken butts, for handwriting recognition has become a standard example of machine learning's way of acquiring a new skill.[7]

Traditionally, in the old world of working models based on conceptual models, we would train a computer to recognize handwritten numbers by telling it what the salient characteristics of the numerals are. For example, to recognize an 8, look for a stack of two circles, with the top one the same size or smaller than the bottom one. With machine learning systems, instead of telling the computer about the geometry of 8s, we would give it thousands of examples of handwritten 8s. Many of those will violate the geometry of penmanship we were taught in grade school: the circles might lean, they will rarely be perfect circles, and many of the circles won't be fully closed because people write hastily. The machine learning algorithms would analyze those scanned-in samples as grids of various shades of gray (because our writing implements don't just lay down perfectly black lines) and come up not with a rule about circles but rather with a way to compare a new sample against the distribution of gray dots in all the samples. If the new sample is in fact an 8, the system will—if it's working—assign it a high probability that it's an 8, perhaps a lower probability that it is a 3 or a B, and probably a very low probability that it is a 1 or 7.

This is how the National Archives of the United Kingdom has been teaching its machines to read ancient documents written with quill pens in characters that are hard for us to recognize and that have changed over time. Volunteers transcribed sixty thousand words—the length of a short book—from old manuscripts to create what in machine learning language is called ground truth: because humans identified the letters the pen strokes stand for, we can be highly confident that the identifications are correct. A machine learning system called Transkribus, funded by the European Union, analyzed the scanned-in manuscripts, figured out the range of patterns for the letters, and then applied what it learned to new manuscripts. The pilot project resulted in machines getting more than 86 percent of the characters right, which means humans are still more reliable at the task, but we are far slower. Even with Transkribus's current level of accuracy, the National Archives thinks it will make its manuscript collection searchable for the first time, which will fling the doors open to researchers.[8]

Machine learning systems with varying degrees of accuracy now recognize faces and objects in photographs, translate over one hundred languages, identify teens who may be contemplating suicide, and—highly controversially—are used to identify defendants that are likely to skip out on bail.[9] They do this with varying degrees of accuracy, sometimes without having been given a conceptual model, and sometimes using models that they've built for themselves that are too complex for humans to understand.

The inexplicability of some machine learning models may not matter when a machine sexes chickens, or is used to make movie recommendations, but it does when it's diagnosing a woman's likelihood of developing breast cancer or recommending a prison term at the end of a trial. The patient may well want to know *why* the machine has concluded that she needs preemptive surgery, and the defendant may well want to know whether his race had anything to do with the sentence the system recommended. There are tremendous controversies now about whether and how we want to limit the use of this technology in such cases, and perhaps in all cases.

No matter how that political, cultural, and intellectual struggle resolves itself, it is making us ever more aware that what happens can sometimes be best predicted by models that we may not be able to understand. As we saw in the previous chapter, prediction discloses the source of the constant change that surrounds us: supernatural creatures that can be swayed by sacrificing animals to them, hidden relationships that let us read the future in a swirl of tea leaves, or immutable laws of physics than can be expressed in mathematical equations. In this chapter we'll see that the models we rely on when making predictions have assumed not only how things happen but also that our human essence is to be the knowers of the world. That's why we like it when our working models not only work but also reflect our conceptual models.

Our success with machine learning is teaching us to question those assumptions by showing us a new way to see how things happen—a way that changes our idea about where we as humans stand.

Models We Can Understand

We have not always insisted on understanding our predictions. For example, some of the Founding Fathers of the United States made daily records of the weather and the factors they thought were related to it: when plants start blooming, the first frost, and so forth. They hoped this aggregated data would reveal reliable correlations, such as the daffodils' blooming early signifying that there's a good chance it will be a wet summer. Until the early 1900s, that sort of weather forecasting worked better than not predicting at all.

As Nate Silver explains in *The Signal and the Noise*, this is statistical forecasting: we gather data and use it to make an informed guess about what will happen, based on the assumption that the data is expressing a regularity.[10] Silver says that is how hurricanes were predicted until about thirty years ago. It works pretty well, at least as long as the natural system is fairly consistent.

Statistical forecasting doesn't need a model of the sort proposed in 1900 by Vilhelm Bjerknes, which we looked at in chapter 1. Bjerknes's model explained the dynamics of global weather using seven variables and Newtonian physics: relevant factors connected by rules governing their interactions.[11] But there was a problem: even using only seven variables, the computations were so complex that in 1922 a mathematician named Lewis Fry Richardson spent six full weeks doing the work required to predict the weather on a day years earlier, based on data gathered on the days before it. He wasn't even close. After all that grueling work, Richardson's calculated air pressure was 150 times too high.[12]

These days we track hundreds of variables to forecast the weather, as well as to predict the longer-term changes in our climate. We do so with computers that chortle at the 1940s computer—the ENIAC (Electronic Numerical Integrator and Computer)—that took twenty-four hours to predict the next day's weather.[13] Nevertheless, until machine learning, we relied on the model-based technique that harks back to Pierre-Simon Laplace's demon: if we know the rules governing the behavior of the seven factors that determine the weather, and if we have the data about them for any one moment in the life of the Earth, we should be able to predict what the next moment's weather will be.

The problem is that so very many factors can affect the weather. In fact, Silver says "the entire discipline of chaos theory developed out of what were essentially frustrated attempts to make weather forecasts."[14] Literally everything on the surface of the planet affects the weather to one degree or another. It is not a coincidence that the example forever associated with Chaos Theory involves a butterfly that creates a catastrophic weather event thousands of miles away.

So if we want to make a prediction about a system like the weather—a third level of predictive complexity, in the terms discussed in the previous chapter—we seem to be left with bad choices. We can rely on statistics and hope that we've been gathering the relevant ones, and that the future will repeat the patterns of the past as surely as the Nile overflows after the Dog Star returns. Or we can figure out the laws governing change and hope that the system is as simple as the model we're using . . . and that it is not disrupted by, say, the Krakatoa volcano that erupted in 1883, spewing forth enough ash to cool the seasons for a year and to chill the oceans for a full century afterward.[15]

Bjerknes's seven-factor weather model has the advantage of providing a working model that at least crudely reflects its conceptual model. But we don't always insist on that. The following four examples show different ways successful working models may or may not coincide with our conceptual models. They'll also let us see how deeply machine learning models break with our traditional practices and age-old assumptions about how things happen . . . and our assumptions about how suited we humans are to understanding what happens.

Spreadsheets

Although computerized spreadsheets date back to the early 1960s,[16] they only became widely used after 1978 when Dan Bricklin, a student working on his MBA at Harvard Business School, was annoyed by a class assignment that required calculating the financial implications of a merger. Having to recalculate all the dependent numbers when any single variable changed was more than irksome.[17]

So, in the spring of 1978, Bricklin prototyped a spreadsheet on an Apple II personal computer, using a gaming controller in place of a mouse.[18] With the rise of PCs and with the decision by Bricklin and his partner, Bob Frankston, not to patent the software,[19] spreadsheets became a crucial way businesses understood themselves and made decisions: a company's conceptual model of itself now could be expressed in a working model that let the business see the effects of the forces affecting it and of decisions the company was contemplating.

In a remarkably prescient article in 1984, Steven Levy wrote, "It is not far-fetched to imagine that the introduction of the electronic spreadsheet will have an effect like that brought about by the development during the Renaissance of double-entry bookkeeping."[20] He was right. "The spreadsheet is a tool, and it is also a world view— reality by the numbers," Levy wrote.

A spreadsheet is what a business looks like to a traditional computer: quantitative information connected by rules. The rules— formulas—and some of the data, such as fixed costs, are relatively stable. But some of the data changes frequently or even constantly: sales, expenses, headcount, and so on. Personal computers running spreadsheets made keeping the working model up to date so easy and fast that a new decision-making process was made feasible: a spreadsheet is a temptation to fiddle, to try out new futures by plugging in different numbers or by tweaking a relationship. This makes them very different from most traditional models, which focus on representing unchanging relationships, whether they're Newtonian laws or the effect that raising taxes has on savings. Spreadsheets are models that encourage play: you "run the numbers," but then you poke at them to try out "what if this" or "what if that." This was a model meant to be played with.

A spreadsheet thus is a simple example of a working model based on a fully understandable conceptual model. It lets you plug in data or play with the rules to see what the future might or could look like.

Of course, they are inexact, they can't capture all of the relationships among all of the pieces, and the predictions made from their models may be thrown off by events that no one predicted. Because spreadsheets are tools and not perfect encapsulations of every possible eventuality, we accept some distance between the working model and the conceptual model, and between the conceptual model and the real world. We continue to use them because, as George E. P. Box said, "[a]ll models are wrong but some are useful."[21]

Armillary

In the Galileo Museum in Florence sits a beautiful set of nested geared rings, 6.5 feet tall.[22] If we today had to guess the point of this intricate mechanism just by looking at it, we might suppose that it's some type of clock. If we were contemporaries of it, we'd be far more likely to recognize that it shows the positions of the major heavenly bodies in Earth's skies for any night.

Antonio Santucci finished this object, called an armillary, in 1593, after five years of work. Although forty-six years earlier Nicolaus Copernicus had shown that the Earth revolves around the sun, Santucci still put the Earth at the center, circled by seven rings that display the positions of the seven known planets. An eighth ring has the fixed stars on it, as well as the markings of the zodiac. Adjust the rings on this wood-and-metal machine, and the planets and fixed stars will align relative to one another and to the Earth. Now gild it and paint in the four winds, the shield of your patron's Medici-related family, and an image of God Himself, and you have a beautiful room-size model of the universe.[23]

According to no less an authority than Galileo, even Santucci eventually came around to Copernicus's idea.[24] But the armillary's model of the universe is odd beyond its Earth-centric view. It simulates the movement of the heavenly bodies using only circles as components of the mechanism because, from the early Greeks on, it was commonly assumed that because the heavens were the realm of perfection, and circles were the perfect shape, the heavenly bodies must move in perfect circles. That makes the planets a problem, for they wander through Earth's sky in distinctly noncircular ways; *planet* comes from the Greek word for *wanderer*. Therefore, if the armillary were to be truthful to its conceptual model, not only did it have to get the planets in the right places relative to Earth, it also had to do it the way the universe does: by using circles. So Santucci set smaller gears turning as they revolved around larger gears that were themselves turning, adding in as many as necessary to model the paths of the planets accurately.[25]

The result is a successful working model that uses a convoluted mechanism dictated by a conceptual model that has been shown to be wildly wrong.

The error in its conceptual model also happens to make the working model quite beautiful.

Tides

"Unlike the human brain, this one cannot make a mistake."[26]

That's how a 1914 article in *Scientific American* described a tide-predicting machine made of brass and wood that made mistakes all the time. And its creators knew it.

Newton had shown that the gravitational pull of the sun and moon accounted for the rise and fall of the tides around Earth. But his formulas only worked approximately, for, as the *Scientific American* article pointed out,

> *the earth is not a perfect sphere, it isn't covered with water to a uniform depth, it has many continents and islands and sea passages of peculiar shapes and depths, the earth does not travel about the Sun in a circular path, and Earth, Sun and Moon are not always in line. The result is that two tides are rarely the same for the same place twice running, and that tides differ from each other enormously in both times and in amplitude.*[27]

In his book *Tides: The Science and Spirit of the Ocean*, Jonathan White notes, "There are hundreds of these eccentricities, each calling out to the oceans—some loudly, some faintly, some repeating every four hours and others every twenty thousand years." Newton knew he was ignoring these complications, but they were too complicated to account for. (It's quite possible that he never saw an ocean himself.)[28]

It was Laplace who again got Newton righter than Newton did, creating formulas that included the moon's eight-year cycle of distances from the Earth, its varying distance north and south of the equator, the effect of the shape and depth of the ocean's basin, the texture of the ocean floor, the water's fluctuating temperatures, and other conditions.[29]

This added nuance to Newton's model, but a vast number of additional factors also affect the tides. It took about another hundred years for Lord Kelvin, in 1867, to come up with a way of predicting tides that takes all the factors into account without having to know what all of them are.[30]

As the 1914 *Scientific American* article explains it, imagine a pencil floating up and down in an ocean, creating a curve as it draws on a piece of paper scrolling past it. Imagine lots of pencils placed at uniform distances from one another. Now imagine the ocean lying still, without any bodies exerting gravitational forces on it. Finally, imagine a series of fictitious suns and moons above Earth in exactly the right spots for their gravity to pull that pencil to create exactly those curves. Wherever you have a curve that needs explaining, add another imaginary sun or moon in the right position to get the expected result. Lord Kelvin ended up with a "very respectable number" of imaginary suns and moons circling the Earth, as the article puts it. If adding sea serpents would have helped, presumably Lord Kelvin would have added them as well.[31]

With the assistance of George Darwin—brother of Charles—Lord Kelvin computed formulas that expressed the pull of these imaginary bodies, then designed a machine that used chains and pulleys to add up all of those forces and to draw the tidal curves. By 1914, this had evolved into the beast feted in the *Scientific American* article: fifteen thousand parts that, combined, could draw a line showing the tides at any hour.

Lord Kelvin was in fact not the first to imagine a science-fiction Earth circled by multiple suns and moons that create the wrinkled swells and ebbs of tides caused by the vagaries of the Earth's geography, topology, weather, and hundreds of other factors. Laplace himself "imagined a stationary Earth with these tide components circling as satellites."[32] Lord Kelvin's machine and its iterations took this to further levels of detail, while accepting that the actual tides are subject to still more factors that simply could not be captured in the machine's model—the influx of melted snow from a particularly long winter, the effect of storms, and all the other influences Earth is heir to. The *Scientific American* article could claim the machine never makes a mistake because Kelvin's machine was as accurate as the tools and data of the time allowed, so it became the accuracy we counted as acceptable . . . all while relying on a fictitious model.

It set this level of accuracy by building a working model that is knowingly, even wildly, divorced from its conceptual model.

The River

In 1943, the US Army Corps of Engineers set Italian and German prisoners of war to work building the largest scale model in history: two hundred acres representing the 41 percent of the United States that drains into the Mississippi River. By 1949 the model was being used to run simulations to determine what would happen to cities and towns along the way if water flooded in. It's credited with preventing $65 million in damage from a flood in Omaha in 1952.[33] In fact, some claim its simulations are more accurate than the existing digital models.[34]

Water was at the heart of another type of physical model: the MONIAC (Monetary National Income Analogue Computer) economic simulator built in 1949 by the New Zealand economist Alban William Housego Phillips.[35] The MONIAC used colored water in transparent pipes to simulate the effects of Keynesian economic policies. Tanks of water represented "households, business, government, exporting and importing sectors of the economy," measuring income, spend-ing, and GDP.[36]

It worked, given its limitations. The number of variables it could include was constrained by the number of valves, tubes, and tanks that could fit in a device about the size of a refrigerator.[37] But because it only took account of a relative handful of the variables that influ-ence the state of a national economy, it was far less accurate than the Mississippi River simulator. Yet the flow of water through a river the size of the Mississippi is also affected by more variables than humans can list. So how could the Mississippi model get predictions so right?

The Mississippi had the advantage of not requiring its creators to have a complete conceptual model of how a river works. For ex-ample, if you want to predict what will happen if you place a boul-der in a rapids, you don't have to have a complete model of fluid dynamics; you can just build a working scale model that puts a small rock into a small flow. So long as scale doesn't matter, your model will give you your answer. As Stanford Gibson, a senior hydraulic engineer in the Army Corps of Engineers, said about the Mississippi basin project, "The physical model will simulate the processes on its own."[38]

So this working model can deal with more complexity *because* it doesn't have a conceptual model: it puts the actual forces to use in a controlled and adjustable way. Because the model is not merely a symbolic one—real water is rolling past a real, scaled-down boulder—the results aren't limited by what we know to factor in. That's the problem with the MONIAC: it sticks with factors that we know about. It's like reducing weather to seven known factors.

Still, the Mississippi River basin model may seem to make no as-sumptions about what affects floods, but of course it does. It assumes that what happens at full scale also happens at 1/2000 scale, which is not completely accurate for the dynamics of water; for example, the creators of a model of San Francisco Bay purposefully distorted the horizontal and vertical scales by a factor of ten in order to get the right flow over the tidal flats.[39] Likewise, the Mississippi model does not simulate the gravitational pull of the sun and the moon. Nor does it grow miniature crops in the fields. The model assumes those factors are not relevant to the predictions it was designed to enable. Using the Mississippi model to simulate the effects of climate change or the effect of paddle wheelers on algae growth probably wouldn't give reliable results, for those phenomena are affected by factors not in the model and are sensitive to scale.

The Mississippi model wasn't constructed based on an explicit conceptual model of the Mississippi River basin, and it works without yielding one. Indeed, it works because it doesn't require us to understand the Mississippi River: it lets the physics of the simulation do its job without imposing the limitations of human reason on it. The result is a model that is more accurate than one like the MONIAC that was constructed based on human theory and understanding. So the advent of machine learning is not the first time we have been presented with working models for which we have no conceptual model.

But, as we'll see, machine learning is making clear a problem with the very idea of conceptual models. Suppose our concepts and the world they model aren't nearly as alike as we've thought? After all, when it comes to the Mighty Mississippi, the most accurate working model lets physical water flow deeper than our conceptual understanding.

Despite the important differences among all these models—from spreadsheets to the Mississippi—it's the similarities that tell us the most about how we have made our way in a wildly unpredictable world.

In all these cases, models *stand in* for the real thing: the armillary is not the heavenly domain, the spreadsheet is not the business, the tubes filled with colored water are not the economy. They do so by *simplifying* the real-world version. A complete tidal model would have to include a complete weather model, which would have to include a complete model of industrial effects on the climate, until the entire world and heavens have been included. Models simplify systems until they yield acceptably accurate predictions.

Models thereby assume that we humans can identify the elements that are relevant to the thing we are modeling: the factors, rules, and principles that determine how it behaves. Even the model of the Mississippi, which does not need to understand the physics of fluid dynamics, assumes that floods are affected by the curves and depths of the river and not by whether the blue vervain growing along the sides of the river are in flower. This also implies that models assume some degree of *regularity*. The armillary assumes that the heavenly bodies will continue to move across the skies in their accustomed paths; the tidal machine assumes the gravitational mass of the sun and moon will remain constant; the spreadsheet assumes that sales are always going to be added to revenues.

Because the simplification process is *done by human beings*, models reflect our strengths and our weaknesses. The strengths include our ability to see the order beneath the apparent flux of change. But we are also inevitably prone to using unexamined assumptions, have limited memories and inherent biases, and are willing to simplify our world to the point where we can understand it.

Despite models' inescapable weaknesses due to our own flawed natures, they have been essential to how we understand and control our world. They have become the *stable frameworks that enable us to predict and explain the ever-changing and overwhelming world in process all around us.*

Beyond Explanation

We are transitioning to a new type of working model, one that does not require knowing how a system works and that does not require simplifying it, at least not to the degree we have in the past. This makes the rise of machine learning one of the most significant disruptions in our history.[40]

In the introduction, we talked about Deep Patient, a machine learning system that researchers at Mount Sinai Hospital in New York fed hundreds of pieces of medical data about seven hundred thousand patients. As a result, it was able to predict the onset of diseases that have defied human diagnostic abilities. Likewise, a Google research project analyzed the hospital health records of 216,221 adults. From the forty-six billion data points, it was able to predict the length of a patient's stay in the hospital, the probability that the patient would exit alive, and more.[41]

These systems work: they produce probabilistically accurate outcomes. But why?

Both of these examples use *deep learning*, a type of machine learning that looks for relationships among the data points without being instructed what to look for. The system connects the nodes into a web of probabilistic dependencies, and then uses that web— an "artificial neural network"—to refine the relationships again and again. The result is a network of data nodes, each with a "weight" that is used to determine whether the nodes it is connected to will activate; in this way, artificial neural networks are like the brain's very real neural network.

These networks can be insanely complicated. For example, Deep Patient looked at five hundred factors for each of the hundreds of thousands of patients whose records it analyzed, creating a final data set of two hundred million pieces of data. To check on a particular patient's health, you run her data through that network and get back probabilistic predictions about the medical risks she faces. For example, Deep Patient is unusually good at telling which patients are at risk of developing schizophrenia, a condition that is extremely hard for human doctors to predict.[42]

But the clues the system uses to make these predictions are not necessarily like the signs doctors typically use, the way tingling and numbness can be an early sign of multiple sclerosis, or sudden thirst sometimes indicates diabetes. In fact, if you asked Deep Patient how it came to classify people as likely to develop schizophrenia, there could be so many variables arranged in such a complex constellation that we humans might not be able to see the patterns in the data even if they were pointed out to us. Some factor might increase the probability of a patient becoming schizophrenic but only in conjunction with other factors, and the set of relevant factors may itself vary widely, just as your spouse dressing more formally might mean nothing alone but, in conjunction with one set of "tells," might be a sign that she is feeling more confident about herself and, with other sets, might mean that she is aiming for a promotion at work or is cheating on you. The number and complexity of contextual variables mean that Deep Patient simply cannot always explain its diagnoses as a conceptual model that its human keepers can understand.

Getting explanations from a machine learning system is much easier when humans have programmed in the features the system should be looking for. For example, the Irvine, California–based company Bitvore analyzes news feeds and public filings to provide real-time notifications to clients about developments relevant to them. To do this, its dozens of algorithms have been trained to look for over three hundred different sorts of events, including CEO resignations, bankruptcies, lawsuits, and criminal behavior, all of which might have financial impacts. Jeff Curie, Bitvore's president, says that it's like having several hundred subject experts each scouring a vast stream of data.[43] When one of these robotic experts finds something relevant to its area of expertise, it flags it, tags it, and passes it on to the rest, who add what they know and connect it to other events. This provides clients—including intelligence agencies and financial houses—not just an early warning system that sounds an alarm but also contextualized information about the alarm.

Bitvore's system is designed so that its conclusions will always be explicable to clients. The company's chief technology officer, Greg Bolcer, told me about a time when the system flagged news about cash reserves as relevant to its municipal government clients. It seemed off, so Bolcer investigated. The system reported that the event concerned not cash reserves but a vineyard's "special reserve" wines and was of no relevance to Bitvore's clients. To avoid that sort of machine-based confusion, Bitvore's system is architected so that humans can always demand an explanation.[44]

Bitvore is far from the only system that keeps its results explicable. Andrew Jennings, the senior vice president of scores and analytics at FICO, the credit-scoring company, told me, "There are a number of long standing rules and regulations around credit scoring in the

US and elsewhere as a result of legislation that require[s] people who build credit scores to manage the tradeoff between things that are predictively useful and legally permitted."[45] Machine learning algorithms might discover—to use a made-up example—that the Amish generally are good credit risks but, say, Episcopalians are not. Even if this example were true, that knowledge could not be used in computing a credit score because US law prevents discrimination on the basis of religion or other protected classes. Credit score companies are also prohibited from using data that is a surrogate for these attributes, such as an applicant's subscribing to *Amish Week* magazine or, possibly, the size of someone's monthly electricity bills.

There are additional constraints on the model that credit score companies can use to calculate credit risk. If a lender declines a loan application, the lender has to provide the reasons why the applicant's score was not higher. Those reasons have to be addressable by the consumer. For example, Jennings explained, an applicant might be told, "Your score was low because you've been late paying off your credit cards eight times in the past year," a factor that the applicant can improve in the future.

But suppose FICO's manually created models turn out to be less predictive of credit risk than a machine learning system would be? Jennings says that they have tested this and found the differences between the manual and machine learning models to be insignificant. But the promise of machine learning is that there are times when the machine's inscrutable models may be more accurately predictive than manually constructed, human-intelligible ones.

As such systems become more common, the demand for keeping their results understandable is growing. It's easy to imagine a patient wanting to know why some future version of Deep Patient has recommended that she stop eating high-fat foods, or that she preemptively get a hysterectomy. Or a job applicant might want to know whether her race had anything to do with her being ruled out of the pool of people to interview. Or a property owner might want to know why a network of autonomous automobiles sent one of its cars through her fence as part of what that network thought was the optimal response to a power line falling onto a highway. Sometimes these systems will be able to report on what factors weighed the heaviest in a decision, but sometimes the answer will consist of the weightings of thousands of factors, with no one factor being dominant. These systems are likely to become more inexplicable as the models become more complex and as the models incorporate outputs from other machine learning systems.

But it's controversial. As it stands, in most fields developers generally implement these systems aiming at predictive accuracy, free of the requirement to keep them explicable. While there is a strong contingent of computer scientists who think that we will always be able to wring explanations out of machine learning systems, what counts as an explanation, and what counts as understanding, is itself debatable.[46] For example, the *counterfactual* approach proposed by Sandra Wachter, Brent Mittelstadt, and Chris Russell at Oxford could discover whether, say, race was involved in why someone was put into the "do not insure" bin by a machine learning application: in the simplest case, resubmit the same application with only the race changed, and if the outcome changes, then you've shown race affected the outcome.[47] It does not at all take away from the usefulness of the counterfactual approach to point out that it produces a very focused and minimal sense of "explanation," and even less so of "understanding."

In any case, in many instances, we'll accept the suggestions of these systems if their performance records are good, just as we'll accept our physician's advice if she can back it up with a study we can't understand that shows that a treatment is effective in a high percentage of cases—and just as many of us already accept navigation advice from the machine learning–based apps on our phones without knowing how those apps come up with their routes. The riskier or more inconvenient the medical treatment, the higher the probability of success we'll demand, but the justification will be roughly the same: a good percentage of people who follow this advice do well. That's why we took aspirin—initially in the form of willow bark—for thousands of years before we understood why it works.

As machine learning surpasses the predictive accuracy of old-style models, and especially as we butt our heads against the wall of inexplicability, we are coming to accept a new model of models, one that reflects a new sense of how things happen.

Four New Ways of Happening

Suppose someday in the near future your physician tells you to cut down on your potassium intake; no more banana smoothies for you. When you ask why, she replies that Deep Asclepius—a deep learning system I've made up—says you fit the profile of people who are 40 percent more likely to develop Parkinson's disease at some point in their lives if they take in too much potassium (which I'm also making up).

"What's that profile?" you may ask.

Your physician explains: "Deep Asclepius looks at over one thousand pieces of data for each person, and Parkinson's is a complex disease. We just don't know why those variables combine to suggest that you are at risk."

Perhaps you'll accept your physician's advice without asking about her reasons, just as you tend to accept it when your physician cites studies you're never going to look up and couldn't understand if you did. In fact, Deep Asclepius's marketers will probably forestall the previous conversation by turning the inexplicability of its results into a positive point: "Medical treatment that's as unique as you are . . . and just as surprising!"

Casual interactions such as these will challenge the basic assumptions of our past few thousand years of creating models.

First, we used to assume that we humans made the models: in many cases (but not all, as we've seen) we came up with the simplified conceptual model first, and then we made a working model. But *deep learning's models are not created by humans*, at least not directly.[48] Humans choose the data and feed it in, humans head the system toward a goal, and humans can intercede to tune the weights and the outcomes. But humans do not necessarily tell the machine what features to look for. For example, Google fed photos that included dumbbells into a machine learning system to see if it could pick out the dumbbells from everything else in the scene. The researchers didn't give the system any characteristics of dumbbells to look for, such as two disks connected by a rod. Yet without being told, the system correctly abstracted an image of two disks connected by a bar. On the other hand, the image also included a muscular arm holding the dumbbell, reflecting the content of the photos in the training set.[49] (We'll talk in the final chapter about whether that was actually a mistake.)

Because the models deep learning may come up with are not based on the models we have constructed for ourselves, they can be opaque to us. This does not mean, however, that deep learning systems escape human biases. As has become well known, they can reflect and even amplify the biases in the data itself. If women are not getting hired for jobs in tech, a deep learning system trained on existing data is likely to "learn" that women are not good at tech. If black men in America are receiving stiffer jail sentences than white men in similar circumstances, the training based on that data is very likely to perpetuate that bias.[50]

This is not a small problem easily solved. Crucially, it is now the subject of much attention, research, and development.

The second assumption about models now being challenged comes from the fact that our conceptual models cover more than one case; that's what makes them models. We have therefore tended to construct them out of general principles or rules: Newton's laws determine the paths of comets, lowering prices tends to increase sales, and all heavenly bodies move in circles, at least according to the ancient Greeks. Principles find simpler regularities that explain more complex particulars. But *deep learning models are not generated premised on simplified principles, and there's no reason to think they are always going to produce them,* just as A/B testing may not come up with any generalizable rules for how to make ads effective.

Sometimes a principle or at least a rule of thumb does emerge from a deep learning system. For example, in a famous go match between Lee Sedol, a world-class master, and Google's AlphaGo, the computer initially played aggressively. But once AlphaGo had taken over the left side of the board, it started to play far more cautiously. This turned out to be part of a pattern: when AlphaGo is 70 percent confident it's going to win, it plays less aggressively. Perhaps this is a generalizable heuristic for human go players as well.[51] Indeed, in 2017, Google launched a program that brings together human players and AlphaGo so that the humans can learn from the machine.[52]

A later version of AlphaGo took the next step. Rather than training AlphaGo on human games of go, the programmers fed in nothing but the rules of the game and then had the machine play itself. After just three days, the system so mastered the game that it was able to beat the prior version of AlphaGo a hundred games out of a hundred.[53] When experts studied the machine-vs.-machine games that Google published, some referred to the style of play as "alien."[54]

Isn't that the literal truth?

If so, it's because of the third difference: *deep learning systems do not have to simplify the world to what humans can understand.*

When we humans build models for ourselves, we like to find the general principles that govern the domain we're modeling. Then we can plug in the specifics of some instance and read out the date and time of an eclipse or whether the patient has type 2 diabetes. Deep learning systems typically put their data through artificial neural networks to identify the factors (or "dimensions") that matter and to discern their interrelationships. They typically do this several times, sometimes making the relationships among the pieces understandable only by understanding the prior pass, which may have surpassed our understanding on its own.

The same holds for the data we input in order to get, say, a diagnosis from my hypothetical Deep Asclepius system. Deep Asclepius doesn't have to confine itself to the handful of factors a patient is typically asked to list on a three-page form while sitting in the waiting room. It can run the patient's lifetime medical record against its model, eventually even pulling in, perhaps, environmental data, travel history, and education records, noting relationships that might otherwise have been missed (and assuming privacy has been waived). Simplification is no longer required to create a useful working model.

The success of deep learning suggests to us that the world does not separate into neatly divided events that can be predicted by consulting a relative handful of eternal laws. The comet crossing paths with Jupiter, Saturn, and the sun is not a three-body or four-body problem but rather an all-body problem, for, as Newton well knew, every gravitational mass exerts some pull on every other. Calculating a comet's path by computing the gravitational effect of three massive bodies is a convenient approximation that hides the alien complexity of the truth.

As we gasp at what our machines can now do, we are also gasping at the clear proof of what we have long known but often suppressed: our old, oversimplified models were nothing more than the rough guess of a couple of pounds of brains trying to understand a realm in which everything is connected to, and influenced by, everything.

Fourth, where we used to assume that our conceptual models were stable if not immutable, everything being connected to everything means that *machine learning's model can constantly change*. Because most of our old models were based on stable principles or laws, they were slower to change. The classic paradigm for this was put forward by Thomas Kuhn in his 1962 book *The Structure of Scientific Revolutions*. Historically, Kuhn says, a science's overarching model (which he calls a paradigm) maintains itself as data piles up that doesn't fit very well.[55] At some point—it's a nonlinear system—a new paradigm emerges that fits the anomalous data, as when germ theory replaced the long-held idea that diseases such as malaria were caused by bad air. But changes in machine learning models can occur simply by retraining them on new data. Indeed, some systems learn continuously. For example, our car navigation systems base our routes on real-time information about traffic and can learn from that data that Route 128 tends to get backed up around four o'clock in the afternoon. This can create a feedback loop as the navigation system directs people away from Route 128 at that time, perhaps reducing the backups. These feedback loops let the model constantly adjust itself to changing conditions and optimize itself further.

As we'll see, this reveals a weakness in our traditional basic strategy for managing what will happen, for the elements of a machine learning model may not have the sort of one-to-one relationship that we envision when we search for the right "lever" to pull. When everything affects everything else, and when some of those relationships are complex and nonlinear—that is, tiny changes can dramatically change the course of events—butterflies can be as important as levers.

Overall, these changes mean that while models have been the stable frameworks that enable explanation, *now we often explain something by trying to figure out the model our machines have created.*

The only real continuity between our old types of models and our new ones is that both are representations of the world. But one is a representation that we have created based on our understanding, a process that works by reducing the complexity of what it encounters. The other is generated by a machine we have created, and into which we have streamed oceans of data about everything we have thought might possibly be worth noticing. The source, content, structure, and scale of these two types of representations are vastly, disconcertingly different.

Explanation Games

"JAL 123 was twelve minutes into its flight when a bang was heard on the flight deck."

On August 12, 1985, thirty-two minutes after that, the pilots lost their struggle to keep the plane aloft as its right wingtip clipped a mountain. The Boeing 747 came down with such force that three thousand trees in its path were destroyed. Of its 509 passengers, 505 were killed. It is to this day the plane crash that claimed the most victims.[56]

The task facing the investigators who arrived from multiple organizations and countries was made more difficult by the impending nightfall, which prevented immediate access, and by the mountainous terrain—inaccessible by helicopter—across which pieces of the plane were strewn. But once the one surviving flight attendant reported that she had seen the sky through the aft part of the plane after a tremendous explosion, the investigators knew where to look: the pressure bulkhead that sealed the rear of the plane.

To these skilled forensic experts, the nature of the tear marks indicated metal fatigue. They checked the aircraft's repair history and found that seven years earlier it had struck its tail while landing, necessitating a repair. This led them to a hypothesis that they confirmed by inspecting the pattern of rivets used to repair the bulkhead. Where there should have been three rows of rivets, there was only one. "Instead of replacing the whole bulkhead, Boeing had merely replaced half of it."[57] This put extra stress on the single line of rivets. Each takeoff and landing stressed it a bit more. A back-of-the-envelope calculation told the investigators that the plane was within 5 percent of the number of takeoffs and landings likely to break the seam open.

From there the sequence of events was relatively straightforward to read. The bulkhead blew, knocking out the hydraulics to the tail, catastrophically limiting the pilots' ability to control the flight.

This story has all the classic elements of what we mean by explaining something:

First, the investigators had a model of what factors count. So they knew to examine the rivets in the bulkhead, but not to bother asking the flight attendant what had been served for lunch or if she had been thinking bad thoughts. Instead, they looked for evidence based on an interrelated set of models that our aircraft flight models are embedded in: laws of physics, properties of metals, systems that record repair and flight histories of planes, and so on.

Second, the investigators fulfilled the expectations of what constitutes an explanation within that domain. An airplane crash requires forensics by a government body that delivers a highly detailed account. But if your car starts to wobble, a single phrase—"rear axle's bent"—well might suffice. Or perhaps your local mechanic will point out that if it's wobbling because of a manufacturer's fault in the axle, the warranty might cover it. In that case, a quick inspection might be enough to establish the explanation. No matter the particulars, the rules for explaining a broken axle are quite different from what constitutes a satisfactory explanation of a plane crash, the fall of the Roman Empire, or why you're not your usual sparkly self today. The philosopher Ludwig Wittgenstein would count these as different "language games" and would warn us not to think that all explanations are played the same way.

Third is a rule so obvious that we don't even think of it as a rule: we offer explanations only when there is an element of mystery. If I take milk out of the refrigerator and ask why it's cold, you won't be sure how to reply because the right explanation—"It was in the fridge"—should be no mystery to me at all. If it's cold after I have just taken it out of the oven, though, an explanation might well be called for.

Fourth, there is some reason why we want an explanation. Boeing wanted to know why JAL 123 crashed so that it could fix the problem. The relatives of the victims wanted an explanation in order to know whether they should sue. But if I'm sitting quietly next to a stranger on a bus and she taps me on the shoulder and starts telling me, unasked, about Bernoulli's principle, which explains the role the shape of wings plays in flight, she is an odd duck who does not know the basic rules of explanation or perhaps cannot tell a bus from a plane.

Finally, we look for explanations only when we think the thing to be explained *can* be explained. The question, "Why did he die so young?" hardly ever is actually looking for an explanation because, for many of us, there is no answer that differs from the answer to the question, "Why did he die?": "Because he got hit by a car." That is neither an explanation nor any comfort. Or perhaps we reply, "The Lord works in mysterious ways," which is not much of an explanation but may be a comfort.

In short, explaining is a social act that has social motives and is performed according to rules and norms that serve social purposes. What counts as an explanation depends on why we're asking, and what counts as a satisfactory explanation depends on the domain we're in: doing fundamental physics research, investigating an air crash, or trying to learn from a fallen soufflé.

We have developed the rules of these explanation games over many centuries. They are exquisitely well worked out, and we inhabit them as if they were as obvious as using a spoon to drink hot soup.

What if we wanted to use a model to explain what causes war?

What factors would we include? Economic disparities? Clashing cultural values? Freudian ideas about aggression and the death wish? The historical dominance of men? Struggles for raw power? These models lead to different predictors to look for: The assassination of a leader. Economic instability. Religious differences. Plans for world domination. In reality, any of these can start a war. Each of them has at some time done so. But each has also existed without resulting in a war.

None of these is sufficient on its own. No one particular factor is necessary. Each is a "cause" only in conjunction with many, many other factors. If we say Hitler started World War II, then we also have to ask about the conditions in Germany that let Hitler come to power, the economics and military relationships in Europe that made invading Poland seem feasible to him, the cultural attitudes toward Germany in Europe and around the world, the effect of the Treaty of Versailles that ended the prior world war, the class system that enabled the calling up of soldiers in Germany and elsewhere, the historic relationship of Germany and the Sudetenland, the effect of Neville Chamberlain's personality on the policy of appeasement, the attitude toward war shaped by the art and entertainment of the time, the history of the Jews, the history of the Poles, the history of the French, the history of everyone. . . .

In short, there may be no set of factors common to the start of all wars. Even if there were, in each case the factors may have different weights in their interrelationships with all the other factors.

This would be a tricky model for us to build using our old assumptions. But this is the sort of world that deep learning assumes.

While the old models continue to shape our decisions about what data we think is relevant enough to feed into a deep learning system, the shape of the new models doesn't much resemble the traditional models we've looked at in this chapter. A deep learning system as a working model can behave differently as well, producing more finely tuned results, and results that are more subject to cascades due to small differences, the way in the real world one stray bullet, a can of spoiled rations, or a squad mate with a contagious disease in World War I could have meant that young Lance Corporal Hitler would not have survived to lead Germany into a worldwide cataclysm.

We sometimes think about our own lives this way: the time we got out at the wrong bus stop and met the love of our life, or missed a job interview at a company that later became fabulously successful or infamously awful. But those are exceptional moments, which is why we recount them as stories. Far more commonly, we look for explanations and answers that bring a situation down to what we can manage. That's what's normal about the normal.

We know the world is complex, but we desperately want it to be simple enough for us to understand and to manage. Deep learning doesn't much suffer from this tension. Complexity wins. But the tension is very much front and center as we humans try to come to grips with deploying deep learning systems, for these systems don't play by the rules of our traditional language games for explanations. Policies such as the European Union's requirement that AI be capable of explaining its processes when its conclusions significantly affect us demand more explicability than we generally ask of nondigital systems. We don't expect to be able to explain an axle failure with anything much beyond "We must have hit a bump" or "It was a faulty axle," but we may require autonomous vehicles to be able to explain every lane change in a ballet of traffic choreographed on the fly by the ad hoc collaborative of networked vehicles on the road at that moment.

It's possible that this demand on AI for explanations has been so well and widely received because most people's expectations of this new realm of digital technology have been shaped by traditional computers, which are little controlled worlds. A traditional computer can tell us about all the data it's dealing with, and the computer does nothing to that data that a human didn't program it to do. But a deep learning program that has constructed its model out of the data we've given it can't always be interrogated about its "decisions." While there are still elements humans control—which data is put in, how that data is preprocessed, how the systems are tuned, and so forth—deep learning may not meet the first requirement of explanations: an intelligible model.

Yet many who want AI's outputs to be as explicable as plane crashes *do* understand how deep learning works. They want explicability for a truly basic reason: to prevent AI from making our biased culture and systems even worse than they were before AI. Instances of algorithmic unfairness are well documented and appalling, from racist bail risk assessment algorithms to AI that, when translating from languages without gendered pronouns, automatically refers in English to a nurse as "she" and a programmer as "he."[58]

Keeping AI from repeating, amplifying, and enforcing existing prejudices is a huge and hugely important challenge. It is a sign of hope that algorithmic unfairness has become such a well-recognized issue and has engaged many of our best minds. And if for this book the question is, "How is our engagement with our new technology changing our ideas about how things happen?" then perhaps the first thing we should learn is that the very difficulty of removing (or sometimes even mitigating) the biases in our data makes it clear—in case anyone had any doubt—that things happen unfairly.

Our insistence on explanations makes two more things clear.

First, we have thought, in an odd way, that an explanation is a readout of the state of the world. But the argument over requiring AI's explicability brings us face to face with the fact that explanations are not readouts but tools. We *use* explanations to fix our planes, to determine whether our axle is under warranty, to decide whether we should stop eating banana smoothies, or to be reassured that our race did not affect the severity of our jail sentence. There are certainly situations in which we'll want to confine our AI to drawing conclusions that we can understand, as Bitvore and FICO already do. This is clearly appealing for the use of AI by institutions such as the courts, where trust in the system is paramount. We are going to have to work out together exactly where we think the trade-offs are, and it will be a messy, difficult process.

But no matter how we work this out, differently in each domain, we should also recognize that the demand for explicable AI is only a question at all because the inexplicable "black box" AI systems we're developing *work*. If they didn't do what we intended more accurately, faster, or both, then we'd just stop using them. We are thereby teaching ourselves, over and over, that systems that surpass our ability to diagnose and predict may also surpass our understanding.

The unexpressed conclusion that we are leading ourselves to is that they're better at this because their model of the world is a more accurate, more useful, and often more true representation of how things happen ("often" because it is mathematically possible for models that yield the most accurate predictions to be based on some elements of falsehood).[59] Even so, the demand for explanations may therefore be leading us to recognize that the inexplicability of deep learning's models comes straight from the world itself.

Coda: Optimization over Explanation

During the oil crisis of the 1970s, the US federal government decided to optimize highways for better mileage by dropping the speed limit to fifty-five miles per hour,[60] trading shorter travel times for greater fuel efficiency. We could similarly decide to regulate what driverless cars (more accurately, autonomous vehicles [AVs]) are optimized for as a way of achieving the results we want, without insisting that the machine learning systems literally driving these cars always be explicable. After all, if explanations are a tool, we should be asking the questions we implicitly ask before using any tool: Will it do the job? How well? What are the trade-offs? What other tools are available? Given our overall aims—in this case, our social goals—is this the best tool for the job? What's true of dutch ovens is also true of explanations.

Let's say we decide the system of AVs should be optimized for lowering the number of US traffic fatalities from forty thousand per year. If the number of fatalities indeed drops dramatically—McKinsey and Elon Musk's Tesla blog both imagine it could be reduced by 90 percent—then the system has reached its optimization goal, and we'll rejoice, even if we cannot understand why any particular vehicle made the "decisions" it made;[61] as we've noted, the behavior of AVs may well become quite inexplicable particularly as AVs on the road are networked with one another and decide on their behavior collaboratively.

Of course, regulating AV optimizations will be more complex than just checking that there are fewer fatalities, for we're likely to say that AVs ought to be optimized also for reducing injuries, then for reducing their environmental impact, then for shortening drive time, then for comfortable rides, and so forth. The exact hierarchy of priorities is something we will have to grapple with, preferably as citizens rather than leaving it to the AV manufacturers, for these are issues that affect the public interest and ought to be decided in the public sphere of governance.

Not that this will be easy. Deciding on what we want the system of AVs optimized for is going to raise the sorts of issues that have long bedeviled us. For example, suppose it turns out that allowing trucks to go 200 miles per hour marginally increases the number of fatalities but brings an economic boom that employs more people and drives down child poverty rates? How many lives would we be willing to sacrifice? Or, as Brett Frischmann and Evan Selinger ask in *Re-engineering Humanity*, might we want to optimize traffic so that people with more urgent needs get priority? If so, do we give priority to the woman on the way to an important business meeting or to the woman on the way to her child's soccer game?[62]

Lest these examples seem too remote, consider the explanation of why in March 2018 one of Uber's experimental AVs hit and killed a pedestrian in Arizona.[63] The National Transportation Safety Board's initial report said that the AV detected the person as much as six seconds earlier but didn't stop or even slow down because its emergency braking system had been purposefully disabled. Why? Uber said it was done "to reduce the potential for erratic vehicle behavior."[64] Turning off the emergency braking system on an AV traveling on public roads seems on the face of it to be plainly irresponsible. But it may be related to a known and literally uncomfortable trade-off between safety and a smoother ride for passengers.

That trade-off seems baked into the intersection of machine learning systems and physics. AVs use lidar—light-based radar—to constantly scan the area around them. Everything the lidar reveals is evaluated by the AV's computer as a possible cause of action. These evaluations come with a degree of confidence, for that is how machine learning systems, as statistical engines, work. So, what's the degree of confidence that an object might be a pedestrian that should get the AV to put on its brakes? Fifty percent? Sure. Why not five percent? Quite possibly. So why not insist that AVs be required to brake if there is even a .01 percent possibility that an object is a pedestrian?

The answer is the same as for why we're not going to prevent AVs from ever going over fifteen miles per hour on the highway, even though that restriction would lower fatalities. As the confidence levels we require go down, the vehicle is going to be slamming on its emergency brakes more and more frequently. At some point, passengers will be treated to a ride on a bucking bronco from which they will emerge shaken, late, and determined never to ride in another AV. So if we are to deploy AVs to gain the important societal benefits they can bring, then we are going to have to face a trade-off between passenger comfort and safety.

Deciding on what we want these systems optimized for is obviously going to require some difficult decisions. But we make these sorts of decisions all the time. Police departments decide whether they're going to ticket jaywalkers to reduce traffic accidents and injuries at the cost of pedestrian convenience. Cities decide whether to create bicycle lanes even if it means slowing motorized traffic. Zoning laws are all about trade-offs, as are decisions about budgets, school curricula, and whether to shut down Main Street for the local sports team's victory parade. All decisions are trade-offs—that's what makes them decisions. AVs and other machine learning systems are going to force us to be more explicit and more precise in many of those decisions. Is that really a bad thing?

These conversations and, yes, arguments are ones we need to have. Insisting that AI systems be explicable sounds great, but it distracts us from the harder and far more important question: What exactly do we want from these systems?

In many if not most cases we should insist that AI systems make public the hierarchy of optimizations they're aimed at, even if those systems are not subject to public regulation. Is the navigation system you use optimized for fuel efficiency, for getting you where you're going in the shortest time, for balancing the traffic loads throughout the system, or for some combination? Does your social networking app aim at keeping you deeply involved with a small circle of your closest friends, reminding you of people drifting out of orbit, or introducing you to new possible friends? What's its hierarchy of goals? Maybe users might even be given a say about that.

When systems are transparent about their goals, we can then insist that they be transparent about how well they're achieving those goals. If they're not living up to goals we've socially decided on, we can hold their creators and managers accountable, just as we hold automobile manufacturers responsible if their cars fail to meet emission standards. We can employ the usual incentives, including legal action, to get what we want and need—although sometimes this will mean learning that we were unrealistic in our expectations.

Notice that none of this necessarily requires us to demand that the technology be fully explicable.

But achieving the goals for which we've optimized our machine learning systems is not enough.

Suppose we agree that we want our system of AVs to dramatically reduce traffic fatalities. And suppose when we put the system in place, fatalities drop from forty thousand to five thousand per year. But now suppose that after a month or two (or, preferably, in simulations even before the system is deployed) it becomes apparent that poor people make up a wildly disproportionate number of the victims. Or suppose an AI system that culls job applicants picks a set of people worth interviewing, but only a tiny percentage of them are people of color. Achieving optimizations is clearly not enough. We also need to constrain these systems to support our fundamental values. Systems need to be extensively tested and incrementally deployed with this in mind not as an optimization but as a baseline requirement.

Even achieving this fundamental type of fairness does not necessarily require the sort of explicability so often assumed to be essential. For example, since old biases are often inadvertently smuggled into AI systems in the data that those systems are trained on, transparency of data—not explicability of operations—often will be the best recourse: How was the data collected? Is it representative? Has it been effectively cleansed of irrelevant data about race, gender, and so forth, including hidden proxies for those attributes? Is it up to date? Does it account for local particularities? Answering these questions can be crucial for assessing and adjusting a machine learning system. Answering them does not necessarily require understanding exactly how the model created from that data works.

There are some good reasons to move to governing optimizations rather than through a blanket insistence on explicability, at least in some domains:

1. It lets us benefit from AI systems that have advanced beyond the ability of humans to understand them.

2. It focuses the discussion at the system level rather than on individual incidents, letting us evaluate AI in comparison to the processes it replaces, thus swerving around some of the moral panic AI is occasioning.

3. It treats the governance questions as social questions to be settled through our existing democratic processes, rather than leaving it up to the AI vendors.

4. It places the governance of these systems within our human, social framework, subordinating them to human needs, desires, and rights.

By treating the governance of AI as a question of optimizations, we can focus the necessary argument about them on what truly matters:

What is it that we want from a system, and what are we willing to give up to get it?

Chapter Three

Beyond Preparation

Unanticipation

We have long known that the world is too big for us to fully understand, much less control, but we have long thought that underneath the chaos there must be an order. For the past few hundred years, we thought that order consisted of simple rules governing a complicated universe. The rules were enough to make the place explicable, and when the inevitably unexpected happened, we would just put it in the "accidents" column.

Even before machine learning began to give us a different model, the old model had been shaken up by twenty years of online life. We have developed tools and processes that make perfect sense given the internet's capabilities and weaknesses, but that implicitly present us with a view of how things happen that's very different from the classical one we've continued to think we inhabit.

Our experiences on the net have not just retrained our thinking. They have proved the pragmatic benefits of adopting a new stance that undoes one of the most basic premises of our decision making and plans. Perhaps thriving in a scaled, connected world requires at least sometimes forgoing anticipating and preparing for the future.

After Henry Ford spent more than ten years selling millions of cars with no changes beyond removing an unnecessary water pump, engineers showed Ford a prototype of an updated version. Ford's response was to smash it to pieces with a sledgehammer. He then turned and walked out without saying a word. Henry Ford was the paragon of getting something right from the start—a strategy (or perhaps just a personality trait) that assumes the future is predictable in ways our new models are bringing us to question.[1]

He had gotten his car right, but it hadn't come easy. In 1906, Ford initiated a two-year design process by handpicking a small group of engineers he knew and felt comfortable with. He installed them in a fifteen-by-twelve-foot room with blackboards and metal machining tools because Ford would rather hold a part in his hand than evaluate its design specification written on paper. Day after day, Ford and his team focused on designing a car that would meet the minimum requirements of customers. It had to be easy to learn how to control because for most buyers it would be the first car they'd ever driven. It had to be high off the ground because it would be traveling rutted roads designed for horses. It had to be cheap to manufacture so they could make and sell them like four-wheeled hotcakes.

After it launched, Ford made no significant alterations to the Model T's design for nineteen years. The company by then had sold fifteen million of them, revolutionizing transportation, manufacturing, what it means to be middle class, and the open road as a symbol of freedom. The room where it was designed is now a national heritage site.[2] That's a great American success story.

But the Model T's design process is also a great Paleolithic success story, for its design methodology was essentially the same one humanity employed for tens of thousands of years. The seventy-one-thousand-year-old arrowheads that anthropologists found in a cave on the southern coast of South Africa were produced via a process as inflexible as Ford's: Find a type of stone called silcrete. Build a fire to heat it so you can begin the slow process of chipping away at it with other rocks gathered for the purpose. Gather wood or bone to make mounts so that you can attach the arrowheads to wooden shafts using resin gathered from particular plants. Let it dry. This was such a complex and extended process that some have said it's evidence that our forebears must have had language at that point.[3]

The particulars of Ford's design process are of course very different from those of our Paleolithic ancestors', except for their most fundamental element: both succeeded by *anticipating* the future and *preparing* for it.

Anticipations need not—and usually do not—rise to the level of a prediction in which one makes an explicit statement about what the future holds. An anticipation can be as implicit as the expectations that let us confidently fish our keys out of our pocket as we approach our house. Or anticipation can be as deliberate as Ford's correctly thinking that customers would want headlights on their car so they could drive it at night.

Either way, anticipation that leads to some preparatory action is the fundamental way we engage with our world. If we were to stop anticipating and preparing, we literally would not dip a spoon into a bowl of soup or look ahead at where we're walking. It's at the heart of our strategies, as well as the way we navigate the most mundane of our everyday activities.

For example, it explains why there's a bottle of cream of tartar over forty years old on my spice shelf. At some point many decades ago, some recipe—probably for lemon meringue pie—called for it; it's not the sort of item one buys on a madcap impulse. Whatever its origin story, I have dutifully moved that bottle from apartment to apartment and house to house, always thinking it makes more sense to pack it than to toss it. You never know when a recipe is going to call for a pinch of the "spice" officially known as potassium bitartrate.

This is a perfectly rational strategy. But it's also a slightly crazy one, since at this rate I'm going to be buried with the bottle without ever having used it again. Assuming that I am not a pathological hoarder, why do I still have it? Because this is how we prepare for an unknown future.

It's obviously a good strategy, since we have survived so long by employing it. But it's not without its costs. Otherwise, we would all be proud owners of the Wenger 16999 Swiss Army Knife, an eighty-seven-tool beast that makes you ready for anything. Got a divot stuck between your golf shoe cleats? One of its tools is designed precisely for that. Need to adjust your gun sight? It's got just the thing. Ream a chisel point, disgorge a fishhook, and then clip a congratulatory cigar? Yes, yes, and yes.

So why don't we all have Wenger 16999 Swiss Army Knives? For one thing, it costs about $1,200. But even if it were free, we still wouldn't be rocking one in our tool belts because, weighing in at seven pounds and with a width of about nine inches, it's only technically portable and requires two hands to use, which makes it an awkward screwdriver and renders its nail clipper useless for anything except your toes. The Wenger 16999 is a collector's item, a curiosity, a conversation piece, not a real tool, even though on paper a single Boy Scout equipped with one would be as well prepared as a troop of about thirty Scouts with their pathetic three-blade knives in their pockets.

The 16999 makes clear the risks inherent in our anticipate-and-prepare strategy. There's a price to being overprepared. Each additional blade, useful on its own, makes the knife more unwieldy. Cream of tartar lurks on our spice shelves and gathers dust. Cave people may have wasted time preparing arrows for a flock of birds that never showed up. But go too far in the other direction and we run the risk of being underprepared, as when a cave person makes five arrowheads and then runs into a flock of a hundred slow birds. Worst of all, if the cave person prepares arrows but runs into a saber-toothed tiger that requires a spear to be subdued, then she is misprepared, and probably dead.

Affluent societies routinely over-, under-, and misprepare without even recognizing them as failures, just as no one cares that a spice shelf holds an undisturbed jar of cream of tartar that will be a silent witness as we marry, we have children, and then our children have grandchildren who one day ask, "What's that dusty bottle of white powder for, Gramps?" We don't count that as a failure of the anticipate-and-prepare strategy because its cost is so low. But we also discount far more consequential failures as just the cost of doing business. Factories tend toward overpreparation when stocking materials because a single missing component can bring the entire operation to a halt. Your local artisanal ice cream shop probably tends to underprepare because it knows that if it runs out of strawberry crème brûlée, it can always plop in a bucket of burnt banana cacao instead and not lose any customers.

But the cost of the anticipate-and-prepare strategy can also be tragic. In a horrifying testament to the problem of over- and mispreparing, we Americans throw out a full 40 percent of our food and ingredients—equivalent to $165 billion each year—because we cooked too much or bought supplies that outran their use-by dates.[4] In 1995, at the height of the personal computer boom, one study showed that costs related to "mismatches between demand and supply leading to excess inventory . . . equaled the PC business's total operating margin"; excess inventory is just part of the cost of doing business—CODB.[5] Likewise, publishers so accept that they will print more books than they'll sell that they have had to establish a process to deal with the overstock without burdening the bookstores: booksellers rip the covers off of paperbacks, mail the covers to the publisher, and pulp what remains. CODB.

There's a simple reason none of this goes onto the scales when we assess our reliance on our prehistoric strategy of anticipating and preparing for a future most marked by its unpredictability: we have no scales and we do no weighing because we have had no alternative.

Now we do. We can adopt strategies of *unanticipation.*

Modes of Unanticipation

Unanticipation has shown itself in how we've been conducting business and living our lives over the past twenty years. Here are some of the more illustrative, important, and sometimes quite familiar examples.

Minimum Viable Anticipation

In 2004 the software startup IMVU was feeling some urgency to get its product into people's hands. So, says cofounder Eric Ries, they decided to do "everything wrong." In his 2011 best seller, *The Lean Startup*, Ries explains, "[I]nstead of spending years perfecting our technology, we build a minimum viable product . . . that is full of bugs. . . . Then we ship it to customers way before it's ready." He adds, "And we charge money for it."[6]

IMVU was developing an instant messaging app that would represent users with visual avatars in a simulated 3-D space of the sort familiar to video game players. The users would be able to create and sell the online items that would turn this space into an inhabited world. Ries notes that shipping product before it's ready goes against every best practice developed over the past generation for ensuring quality, but, he writes, "[t]hese discussions of quality presuppose that the company already knows what attributes of the product the customer will perceive as worthwhile."[7] These practices assume that the company can anticipate customer needs and values.

Often we only think that we can. For example, IMVU assumed that customers would want to be able to move their avatars around. But adding the programming code to enable animated walking was relatively complex since it meant not only doing the graphics work but also creating path-finding algorithms that would let avatars move from point A to point B without bumping into the objects customers had unpredictably plopped down into their world. So IMVU shipped the product without providing even this most basic animation. Instead, users could "teleport" their avatars from A to B without any transitional animation, or even any fancy sound effects.

"You can imagine our surprise when we started to get customer feedback," Ries recounts. "[W]hen asked to name the top things about IMVU they liked best, customers constantly listed avatar 'teleportation' among the top three." Many of them even specifically said that it was an advance over the slick animated travel in the game *The Sims* that IMVU had assumed had set the bar for this type of visualization.[8]

IMVU may seem to have lucked out, but the real strength of its approach was that it diminished the role of luck. If customers hated the lack of animations, then IMVU would know what feature to add next—not because it guessed correctly, but because real, paying users were bellyaching.

IMVU was following the new strategy of releasing a "minimum viable product" (MVP), a term coined by Frank Robinson, the co-founder of a product development consultancy, in 2001.[9] An MVP reverses the usual order of "design, build, sell," a process followed even by the earliest arrow-makers, except they would have replaced "sell" with "shoot." Or, in our terms, it replaces "anticipate and prepare" with "unanticipate and learn."

It is hard for even the most diligent of companies to anticipate customer needs because customers don't know what they want. That's not because we customers are dumb. It's because products are complex, and how they best fit into our complex workflows and lives can only be discovered by actually using them. And then those usages can give rise to new needs and new ideas.

That's why when Dropbox launched in September 2008, it shipped a product that did just one thing well: users could work on the same file from multiple machines without hitting any speed bumps.[10] Since then, Dropbox has incrementally added more features based on what users turn out to want: publicly shareable files, automatic backups, collaborative editing, and more. Dropbox has continued to add major features as it learns from customers what they will actually use.

There's a similar story behind Slack, a workgroup chat app modeled on an ancient internet service, IRC (Internet Relay Chat), that lets people create "channels" over which they can communicate by typing. When it launched in 2013, Slack offered minimal functionality. As it got taken up by more and larger organizations, it discovered it needed to provide better navigation tools for users who may now have dozens of channels. Slack continues to devote a great deal of its resources to learning what its users actually want. Founder Stewart Butterfield says they get about eight thousand help and enhancement requests every month, and ten thousand tweets, "and we respond to all of them." "Whenever they hear something new that seems like it's actually a really good idea—or it's a pretty good idea but it's very easy for us to implement—it gets posted to a [Slack] channel where we discuss new features. That's an ongoing, daily thing." He adds, "There have already been 50 messages posted today."[11]

Why anticipate when you can launch, learn, and iterate?

The MVP approach is now familiar to many segments of business. It was even featured in *Harvard Business Review* in 2013. But we should pause to remember just how counterintuitive the MVP process is . . . or at least was, until our success with such strategies changed our intuitions.

Business has worked on systematizing quality processes at least since W. Edwards Deming started teaching his management techniques to Americans in the 1950s. In the early 1980s, the US Navy started applying Deming's techniques and dubbed the program Total Quality Management. As taken up by companies such as Ford, Motorola, and ExxonMobil, TQM is a cultural and organizational commitment to "[d]o the right things, right the first time, every time"—very Henry Ford.[12]

It's hard to argue with that. But not impossible. The emphasis on quality has often led to efforts to systematize "best practices" on the grounds that "there's only one best way to do things," as adherents say. For repetitive processes on an assembly line, a best practices approach—mirroring Taylorism, with its clipboards and stopwatches—makes sense, except of course for its abject dehumanization of workers. But when best practices apply uniform processes to unique situations, as they do in virtually every nonmechanized environment, they can miss opportunities or create inefficiencies. They can become ritualized and outlast their utility. As Tom Peters, coauthor of *In Search of Excellence*, says, "[I]n a world with so much change . . . what is the shelf life of a best practice anyway?"[13]

Our temptation to rely on best practices is backed by the real benefits they can bring, but also by a misapplication of one of the rules of how things happen we discussed in the introduction: equal causes have equal effects, but only if the situations are truly the same. Only in the most mechanized of environments are the situations so self-similar, and even there, emergencies and opportunities arise that can turn best practices into suboptimal practices or even disastrous practices.

Certainly the companies that have released MVPs are not arguing against quality, even as they charge customers for the privilege of using underfeatured and possibly buggy products. Rather, they are against the idea that quality is best achieved the way Ford did: by knowing beforehand exactly what you want and then planning the perfect procedures that will get it right every time. Releasing an imperfect, incomplete product to users who want to help shape its future often results in a higher-quality product that is more highly valued by its users.

An Agile Approach to the Unpredictable

In 2009, Aneesh Chopra, the first US national chief technology officer, watched the HealthCare.gov site launch, crash, and burn.

"When the law was passed, the overriding assumption was that states would implement the exchanges" where people sign up for one of the available plans, he told me. The federal government's role would be to create the standards by which the state health care insurance sites could communicate with a central hub. But, motivated in part by rancorous partisanship, some states left it to the federal government to create their sites for them. With the short deadline stipulated in the Affordable Care Act, the government didn't have time to go through the usual procurement process and instead used a provision that allows them to ask for bids from the official list of prequalified providers—"exclusively beltway bandits," says Chopra.[14]

These were the old names in project development, and they behaved like it. They used traditional software development techniques and came up with a cumbersome, slow, underfeatured, and utterly unreliable site that almost sank the entire health care program.[15] "On Healthcare.gov's first day, six people successfully used it to sign up for health insurance," reported NBC News.[16]

HealthCare.gov's turnaround began when White House digital strategist Macon Phillips stumbled on a mockup of a possible health care site on Twitter, created by Edward Mullen, a designer in Jersey City, New Jersey. Phillips was so impressed with its ease of use that he invited Mullen to come to the White House to help make his design real.[17] The White House then hired a group of Silicon Valley developers in what became known as the Tech Surge. A team of young coders moved into a McMansion in Georgetown and started replacing the software produced by the original contractor with code that worked, at one-fiftieth the cost.[18] After their approach rescued HealthCare.gov, this approach was given institutional prominence in the new US Digital Service and the federal digital agency named 18F.

The project management technique that saved HealthCare.gov relied upon *agile development*. It's another way in which we're developing products while minimizing the need to anticipate.

The traditional process of software development carefully divides a project into phases, each with its own timetable and milestones. This is called the "waterfall" process because in some project diagrams, the tasks are connected by curved arrows, resembling cascading water.[19] More to the point, as with a waterfall, once you complete a phase, there's no way of getting the water to go back uphill. That one-way flow seemed acceptable because, as one history of programming explains, "it was taken as gospel . . . that the more time you spent planning, the less time you would spend writing code, and the better that code would be."[20]

That makes sense when you're putting atoms together to create a Model T, but it fails to take advantage of what bits and networks allow. Software creation can be spread across a network of developers working simultaneously and cooperatively, freed from overengineered plans that try to predict every feature and every step. But doing so requires restructuring the code, breaking it into small, functional units—modules—each of which takes in data, operates on it, and outputs the results. One module might take in a username and password, and output whether that user is registered with the system. Another might be responsible for taking in a user's age and profile and outputting an actuarial prediction. The other developers don't need to know if the developer of a module has modified its algorithms, so long as the inputs and the outputs continue to work— just as a customer in a diner doesn't have to worry if the cook is using a new fryer, so long as the input ("Onion rings, please!") results in the same delicious output.

One developer explained why 95 percent of companies are doing at least some agile development: "Waterfall assumes that one can model the process in one's mind, sufficiently enough to plan a project start to finish."[21] Agile development knows better: if someone comes up with a new idea for a feature, it can be implemented quickly and cleanly by relying on the already-existing modules. It works because it minimizes anticipating and planning.

Agile development can be traced back to the 1990s with roots that go decades further back, but as geek culture has spread far beyond the engineering cubicles, its radical lesson is now sinking in: even projects as large as a national health insurance program can succeed by routing around overly rigorous planning.

Platforms of Unanticipation

Unanticipation is showing up not only in the product development process—prerelease (agile development) and postrelease (MVP)— but also in an architecture of technology designed for use outside the bounds of expectation.

For example, Sheryl Sandberg, Facebook's original chief operating officer, in 2011 told Chopra that in 2008 she came across a job board that listed thirty thousand Facebook developers. Since at that time Facebook only employed about 2,600 people, she was puzzled.[22]

Then Sandberg realized what was going on.

Although the early versions of Facebook went the traditional route of anticipating and meeting its initial users' needs, early on,

Mark Zuckerberg had come up with a secret plan. As the app started to reach beyond the Harvard campus, Facebook launched a new photo-sharing feature that lagged far behind what the dedicated photo services were offering. Yet users were swarming to it. Zuckerberg realized it wasn't because the feature was particularly good but because the Facebook application understood its users' social networks, making it far easier for users to share their photos.

Facebook calls the integrated data about its users and their networks its "social graph," and Zuckerberg knew it was immensely valuable not just because of the uses to which Facebook would put it but also because of all the uses of it that Facebook could never imagine. No company or set of developers, no matter how smart, could. So why not let everyone try?

In fact, Zuckerberg understood that developers were likely to take advantage of its social graph whether or not Facebook let them. After all, one of his earliest projects—an app that showed students who else had signed up for a course so they could decide if they wanted to take it—used data Zuckerberg had gathered without asking Harvard for permission.[23] Then came Zuckerberg's Facemash, an unfortunate "hot or not" app that let students compare photos of Harvard women. It got Zuckerberg into deserved trouble with the school's administration not just for its crass sexism but also because the photos came from the official "facebooks" of nine of twelve of Harvard's residences, again without permission, in one case by hacking the residence's computer over the network. The *Harvard Crimson* charitably referred to this as "guerrilla computing."[24]

So while Facebook's 2007 launch of its open development platform—introduced as F8—may have surprised the world, it was consistent with Zuckerberg's vision. The platform provided an online interface that enabled software engineers anywhere in the world to use Facebook software services and social graph data to create their own apps. Facebook of course did not give untrammeled access to all of its users' private data or to all of the site's internal functionality, but it provided enough that if you had an idea for an app that needed some of what Facebook knows about its network of users—carefully but inadequately vetted, as time would show—you very likely could create it. Not only didn't you have to work for Facebook, you didn't even have to ask Facebook's permission.

The success of the Facebook platform accounted for the number of Facebook developers that had puzzled Sandberg. The vast majority of those thirty thousand developers, Sandberg realized, were not working at Facebook, even though they were deeply engaged in creating new applications based on the social graph. Within six months of the open platform launch, twenty-five thousand new applications had been created, and half of Facebook's users were using at least one of them.[25]

When Zuckerberg first surveyed what had been submitted, most of the apps seemed trivial. But he quickly realized that even an app that was just a silly game could be helping Facebook achieve its avowed (but not always followed) mission of bringing people together. And simply opening the platform to developers had created financial value too: two years after the platform's launch, the aggregate value of the companies building apps on top of Facebook was roughly equal to Facebook's own value.

Open platforms were not a new idea in 2007 when Facebook launched its own. But an open platform created by one of the most important and information-rich sites on the web was a big deal. As *Fortune*'s main tech writer put it, this brought about a "groundbreaking transformation" that "began to change how the world perceived Facebook."[26]

It also was a significant step forward in weaning our culture from tens of thousands of years of relying on anticipation, validating for companies and organizations—for-profits and nonprofits—that making a subset of one's resources openly available could generate unanticipated financial and cultural value.

The benefits of open platforms are varied and often remarkable:

Increasing presence

Like most newspapers in the mid-2000s, the *Guardian* was struggling to make the transition to the digital era. So when Matt McAlister came to the paper in 2007, he found its management ready to listen to the case he laid out: to increase its web presence, the paper ought to launch an open platform where external developers could easily find relevant content from the *Guardian* and incorporate it into their own sites, without jumping through administrative hoops. McAlister told me that he argued that "media organizations needed to extend beyond their domain to grow, and to be present in all the places that readers are."[27]

Such a platform is known technically as an application programming interface (API): software that translates a program's request for information into a language that the back-end servers understand, and vice versa. The same strategic use of an API has been crucial to making Wikipedia one of the top ten most visited sites on the web. Its API provides access to all of Wikipedia's content, as well as to the categories, links, "information boxes," and more that enrich its content. For example, a music site might use the Wikipedia API to get the first paragraph of the biography of any musician and run it on its own site without asking permission. This is one reason Wikipedia is a preferred source on more sites than it can count.

Resilience

As with many organizations that adopt open platforms, there was a second motivation for the *Guardian*'s adoption of open platforms: an organization's technology infrastructure—its software and processes—based on this approach is far more resilient. For example, when you search for content at the *Guardian*, your search request goes to the API, which puts it into a form that the *Guardian*'s back-end software understands. The API then takes the results from the database and translates them into a form that the website understands. Likewise, when you sign in to your account at the *Guardian*, the API sends your name and password to the module that authenticates users. The *Guardian* and many other sites use an API for this internal purpose because it means that if, for example, they change the processes by which the site validates logins, none of the internal services that rely on that function have to be updated. This enables the site to develop new services and support new devices far more easily.

For instance, when Apple gave National Public Radio only a few weeks to create an app for the initial launch of the iPad, the fact that NPR had an API meant its developers didn't have to write new code to handle searching the NPR content library, to authenticate users, and all the rest. The new iPad app's user interface could just ask the NPR API to perform those services.

NPR made the deadline and was featured at the launch.

Adding value to products

In 1981, the game *Castle Wolfenstein* was released for the Apple II, and then for MS-DOS, the Atari, and the Commodore 64. Its graphics were state of the art, which meant they were incredibly primitive by today's standards: you navigated your little blocky character through a top-down map of corridors and rooms, encountering little blocky Nazi soldiers who fired tiny pixel-bullets at you.

Then, in 1983, some users decided that while they enjoyed the gameplay, they weren't crazy about the Nazi theme. So they altered the game's image files on their own computers, replacing German soldiers with Smurfs. They altered the audio files so that instead of your enemies sounding German, they sounded Smurfy.[28] *Castle Smurfenstein* was *Wolfenstein* with a new coat of Smurf-blue paint.

This sort of hacking was simpler back then. In fact, even with my primitive technical skills, in the early 1990s I turned the then-current version of *Wolfenstein* into a mockup of "document management software of the future" that you could visually run through to find your files; it was a hit at our annual users conference because it was so ridiculous.

In the early 1990s, "modding," as the practice was called, flipped from hack to feature. Game companies started supporting user creation of new maps or levels for games, new functionality, and even new rules. For example, in 1996 id Software released a version of its hit game *Doom* that included levels designed by users. These days, some game companies provide access to the very same tools the in-house developers used. For customers, knowing that there would be endless mods to play made buying a game a better investment.

Enabling users to build what the company developers might never have thought of is now part of the PC gaming mainstream: *Grand Theft Auto V* has earned $2.3 billion since its launch, in part because mods keep it fresh, enhancing the game's value.[29] Beyond that, by treating their users as cocreators, game makers strengthen the emotional bond between them.

Other industries are going down the same path. For example, the open development environment provided by Pebble, one of the first smartwatch companies, resulted in users creating not only new watch faces but also apps, games, and the occasional art project. Fitbit eventually bought Pebble, in part for its open development environment.[30]

It's always been the case that play teaches us our first lessons about how the world works. A generation of gamers is learning a new set of rules about rules.

Integrating into workflows

At the Slack app store, you'll find hundreds of contributed apps in eighteen categories, including analytics, customer support, health and medical, human resources, marketing, office management, project management, sales, and travel—all free. Many of the most important apps integrate Slack into existing workflows. For example, the Tact app integrates Slack into the major sales force management systems, and Airtable integrates Slack into a database management system. These sorts of apps stitch Slack more tightly into existing business ecosystems.

This is so important to Slack that the company created an $80 million fund to help developers and small companies build apps that Slack could not anticipate. "We expect our portfolio to feature a diverse array of entrepreneurs working on solving problems for teams in every industry, function, and corner of the world," said the announcement.[31] Each problem solved will make Slack more indispensable.

Data.gov, a site established at the beginning of the Obama administration, provides open access to over two hundred thousand government data sets. Jennifer Pahlka, the founder of Code for America and a deputy federal chief technology officer in the Obama White House, told me, "Some [government] data sets that no one would have thought would be popular have been highly used, such as the location of fire hydrants, storm drains, [and] tsunami alarms."[32] For example, Code for America wrote an Adopt-a-Siren app that lets local Hawaiians sign up to make sure that the islands' hundreds of tsunami warning sirens are in good working order—a helpful service since there's a 5–10 percent failure rate each month.[33]

Tim O'Reilly, the head of a major tech media company, thinks our vision of government itself ought to be based on this open model. He sums up the idea in the phrase "government as a platform."[34] Like an API, the government should be a set of services that can be used and extended by citizens so we can create what we need without always having to petition the government to provide it for us. The aim is to let a government accomplish its mission of serving its citizens without having to anticipate and provide every service citizens may decide they need. O'Reilly's idea had a strong constituency in the Obama White House.

Moving unanticipation upstream

A manufacturer of playing cards can never know whether a customer is going to use a deck to play Go Fish or to prop up a wobbly table. The Bee Gees couldn't know if someone has bought a copy of "Staying Alive" to dance to the disco beat or to train people on the right tempo for performing CPR. Manufacturers can't anticipate all of the uses of the products they make, but they should recognize that unanticipated uses represent customers getting unanticipated value from the product. Open platforms can deliberately push that moment further upstream: sometimes users can use the pieces before they've been combined into a product, as if Henry Ford let people take parts off the assembly line and build new cars, windmills, and pasta makers out of them.

The *New York Times* did this sort of upstream unanticipation with the data behind a 2014 article.[35] After thousands of people took to the streets in Ferguson, Missouri, to protest police violence against African Americans, the *Times* posted the raw data that documented the article's claims about the transfer of equipment from the military to local police. It did this so people could analyze the data, check it, look for information about their own local police, or try to find correlations between the availability of military equipment and police abuses. Then, to the surprise of the *Times*, people started to improve the data, reporting errors and compiling it into more usable forms.[36] The *Times* now has a site—The Upshot—dedicated to hosting the data behind its reportage because you can never tell what people will find in it or do with it. The Upshot is a platform built to take advantage of upstream unanticipation.

There's more to the story, though. The Upshot is hosted by GitHub, a site used by developers around the globe to enable teams to collaborate fluidly and agilely. Because developers can post code to the site in a way that is publicly available, people can reuse or alter it without first asking permission. Furthermore, if you reuse a part of someone else's open-source code in your own project, GitHub remembers that and makes the relationship public. If the original developers incorporate a change that you've made, GitHub records that reuse as well. This not only gives credit where it's due, it creates an ecosystem for the sharing of code. GitHub thus has become an enormous upstream repository of code and code fragments that can be put to use in entirely unanticipated ways: in September 2017, GitHub had twenty-eight million users and hosted over eighty-five million projects.[37]

Arfon Smith, chief scientist at Github when I spoke with him, told me that although GitHub was originally built for software developers, "the platform turns out to be for collaboration in general."[38] According to Smith, by 2014 people were using GitHub to share and improve on knitting patterns, to gather home repair procedures, to organize weddings, and to write jointly authored papers. "People are forking cocktail recipes," Smith said with delight, referring to the process of altering someone else's code in order to create something new.

GitHub began by allowing developers not to anticipate how their code could be used. By refusing to anticipate even what type of projects might benefit from unanticipated upstream sharing, GitHub's utility has reached far beyond the world of software development.

As the success of all these techniques shows, the true price we paid for the old way of doing things became apparent once we had tools and technology that let things happen differently.

Preparing for Spontaneity

Embracing unanticipation doesn't mean that we must bid adieu to all prediction and planning.

"The event was designed with a funny combination of persnickety attention to some details, and a sanguine letting go of others," says Sara Winge, cocreator and producer of the first of Tim O'Reilly's Foo Camp "unconferences." (This is the same Tim O'Reilly behind the "government as platform" idea.) "I do think we hit on a pretty good system that takes care of enough stuff—both physical infrastructure and social norms—that the participants can get a sense of what's going on and also understand that they have a responsibility to make wonderful and/or meaningful things happen."[39]

Getting there meant the O'Reilly organization had to have many discussions about whom to invite, how many simultaneous sessions should be allowed, whether to put whiteboards in the discussion areas, whether on the first night there should be an all-attendee ice-breaking exercise, how big the grid of available rooms and times should be, and whether attendees should write directly on the scheduling whiteboard or use sticky notes instead.

Winge remembers one particular discussion vividly. She argued strongly that the name badges should not list attendees' affiliations, even though the group was eclectic and thus contained many strangers. She acknowledged that not listing affiliations would make some people "cranky," but "it reinforces the point that the event is about the people who are there," not the organizations they work for. Plus, it was a bit of social engineering: "If you want to know where somebody works, you have to ask them."

In short, Foo was an event carefully planned to enable unplanned discussions.

We have been learning that, more often than not, enabling the unanticipated requires this type of thoughtful anticipation. Simply opening up an API or publishing open-source software and hoping people will use it often doesn't work. For example, many of the news media's APIs have been underutilized, and some have been closed. So long as humans do X in order to gain Y, unanticipation is never going to replace the old anticipate-and-prepare strategy entirely. We're still going to resupply our larders. The local theater company is going to print up more than enough programs for the attendees. Businesses are still going to stock inventory and plan for the holiday rush. But there is nevertheless something new in the world: we are increasingly willing to give up control in order to enable the emergence of things of value that we didn't predict.

We are thereby learning that creating a future that's even further out of our control can be a surprisingly productive strategy.

The Platform for Platforms for Unanticipation

In their 2010 book *The Power of Pull*, John Hagel, John Seely Brown, and Lang Davison argue that open platforms are an essential part of the major shift business is undergoing from "push" to "pull." "Push operates on a key assumption—that it is possible to forecast or anticipate demand."[40] Pull, on the other hand, attracts contributors from outside the business and gives them the tools—often in the form of open platforms—that let them extend and repurpose products. The authors of *The Power of Pull* consider this to be an epochal change that transforms not just economies but also the production of knowledge and culture overall. Likewise, the technology writer Kevin Kelly considers open platforms to be one of the "12 inevitable forces that will shape our future," as he says in *The Inevitable*'s subtitle.[41]

Beneath all of these changes is one of the most profoundly unanticipatory technologies in human history.

That the internet was architected for unanticipation is apparent in one of its foundational documents: "End-to-End Arguments in System Design," published in 1984 by Jerome Saltzer, David Reed, and David Clark.[42] This technical paper makes the counterintuitive argument that the best network provides the fewest services. For example, it might have seemed obvious to the internet's early designers that its users would need a search engine. But if the network designers built one into the system, it would address only the needs that the designers could anticipate. It'd be far better to enable any user to build a search engine. That way competition can work its magic, producing far better search engines than any centralized committee of network engineers could manage. It means niche engines can arise. The same is true for security services, archiving, and the other services one can anticipate users of networks would want.

As Reed put it to me, "Optimizing for one service de-optimizes for others."[43] That's the problem with overanticipating what your product is for and building it to address that use. It is also why Reed has been a strong advocate for a policy of net neutrality that forbids internet access providers from deciding what they think the internet is "really" for—delivering the movies their parent companies own, perhaps?—and optimizing it for delivering those bits ahead of others.

Because the net was held back from anticipating its uses, it became useful for everything, from reading research papers, to making phone calls, to watching videos, to holding collaborative drawing sessions, to taking online courses, to controlling our household appliances, to whatever is the next thing someone invents.

We now have a generation that has grown up with the internet as a fact of life. They take it for granted that if they have something they want to share, they can post it. They take it for granted that if they have an idea for a service to offer over the internet, they can just build it. These are core assumptions for them. But they are assumptions that imply the power of a system that refuses to anticipate and prepare for what it might be used for.

Every time we touch the net, we relearn the same lesson: unanticipation creates possibilities. It means we no longer need to pay the heavy price of wasted resources or missed opportunities that come from over-, under-, or mispreparing. More importantly, instead of limiting the value of what we build by anticipating and preparing for the few narrowed-down possibilities that we could foresee, we are now building to meet needs that a connected world of users might invent for one another. By anticipating and preparing, we were not only gambling that our idea of a customer's first automobile was right but also making it harder—often virtually impossible—for users to add value to our products by extending them, adapting them, and customizing them for their own workflows.

We had little choice about the matter. Anticipating and preparing was the right strategy until digitization made our products more extensible, and our new global network connected users who were eager to collaborate and share what they've made.

The effect goes beyond increasing customer satisfaction and loyalty. Being able to make more of a product than we anticipated lets the world show itself to us in a new light. "This is for that" becomes a needlessly limited way of thinking. Yes, this was *intended* for that, but it could be for this, for that, or for something no one has thought of yet. And if we're learning that often there are serious benefits to holding off on locking things into their anticipated uses, then how things interact is also freer, more possible, and more complex than we'd thought.

Indeed, as we will see in the next chapter, in a world that bursts the bonds of anticipation, everything affects everything. All at once. Forever.

Coda: Libraries of Anticipation

Open Text, a developer of searching software . . . and Yahoo Corp., publisher of a comprehensive directory to the on-line universe, are now sharing their technologies.[44]

This was news in 1995, and very big news for Open Text, where I was vice president of marketing. We were a small company with a great text search engine, and Yahoo! was the queen of the internet; from the early days of the web, it was where you went to find stuff. As *PC Magazine* put it at the time, "Every day, Yahoo serves up over 6 million pages to 400,000 users."[45] That's what dominance looked like back then.

Before the incorporation of the Open Text search engine, if you wanted to find information about, say, art therapy, at Yahoo! you'd scan the fourteen categories on the home page and choose Health. Clicking on it took you to a new page with a couple dozen subcategories. Choose Mental Health, then Therapies, and then Arts Therapy, and at last you'd be looking at links leading to eight pages on the topic.[46] Each of those links had been chosen by hand by Yahoo!— originally by the site's two creators, grad students at Stanford— and individually placed into its tree of topics.

If you knew what you were interested in, browsing through a tree of topics was far better than just poking around the thousands of pages on the web at that point, but it was not nearly as efficient as searching. That's why it was a big deal when Yahoo! decided to put a search box right at the top of its home page. Now you could put in the words you were looking for and the site would find pages that talked about, say, art therapy, no matter what branch they were hanging from.

The matchup of browsing versus searching was decisively settled a few years later when two other Stanford grad students created a search engine they whimsically named Google—as whimsical as "Yahoo!"—that kicked browsing's butt. Yahoo! pivoted to become a media and entertainment site, struggling as Google bestrode the Earth like a colossus.

Anticipation is at work in both searching and browsing, just as it is for any purposive action we humans undertake, but searching's anticipations are very different from browsing's. We search when we have a narrow enough idea of what we need for our project: "Prius 2007 headlight change" or "Dallas vegetarian barbecue restaurant with jukebox." The very nature of a search box encourages us to be highly specific about what we want.

We browse when we're asking a question that has many right answers. "What would I like to read?" is very different from "What is the capital of Peru?" The right response to a search is one-dimensional: the end point of a straight line, the house at the end of the street, the light at the end of the tunnel—a right answer. Browsing requires as many dimensions as we can manage—dimensions not as physical spaces but as pathways through a set of possibilities. In a library, the physical shelves arranged by topic create one dimension, but users also have the ability to browse by author, by strong reviews from other readers, by new acquisitions, by books on sale for one dollar, by librarians' recommendations that are purposefully just different enough from our usual fare that we are surprised and then delighted.

There is an art to creating a place to browse, a game of overpreparing and unanticipating. The library has anticipated that we might enter to look for books, and the clothing store has anticipated that we're there to find something to wear. But while both searching and browsing involve anticipations and intentions, browsing is defined by its relative lack of anticipation. Browsing is to searching as the weekend is to the week.

That means libraries are in the business of being overprepared because they cannot finely predict all the works that their communities might want. Only about 3 or 4 percent of Harvard University Library's magnificent collection is checked out every year, and it's not a completely different set of works each year, so there are more than a few books that have not been checked out within living memory.[47] Imagine a restaurant that keeps an item on the menu that hasn't been ordered in over fifty years. It takes almost a thousand librarians to run Harvard's library system, with an annual budget of over \$150 million, but it's worth it to the university because it enables the faculty and students to find answers to questions that they did not know they were going to be asking, and that may literally never have been asked before.[48]

In fact, a browsing space like a library *needs* noise: choices we can consider and reject, choices we can skip over. For any individual user on any particular trip to a library, well over 99 percent of it will be noise. Done right, books in a library are going to be rejected so frequently that if they were young actors who just arrived in Los Angeles, they'd be on the next bus back to their hometowns, brokenhearted.

Being overprepared is expensive, but when it comes to the ingredients of creation, not of consumption, it is a necessary gift. Granted a free rub on a genie's lantern, most librarians would prefer to create libraries that are so overprepared that they could provide every resource to every user. Someday perhaps the law will permit what technology already enables: making all resources freely available online under reasonable copyright constraints. (The United States started with copyright lasting for fourteen years; we're now at seventy years after the death of the author, and climbing.) Until then, the extravagance of possibility libraries offer announces their commitment to resolutely not anticipating precisely what their community should be interested in.

Meanwhile we see all over the internet the growth of collections of information where the economics of anticipation have flipped: it is now usually cheaper to include digital content than to exclude it. That's why site after site lets users upload whatever they want without permission. If there are legal issues or abuse, that can be weeded out afterward. And if there's too much stuff uploaded higgledy-piggledy—which is to say, if the site succeeds—the service may need to come up with better ways to let users filter content on the way out, rather than resorting to filtering it on the way in.[49] The result is collections the value of which is vastly amplified by the fact that they were not limited by the curators' anticipation of what users will use them for. What is true of the open collections on the net is true of the net itself.

The internet has taught us many lessons, and one is that anticipation doesn't scale. Another is that anticipation constrains possibilities. Unanticipation liberates them, the way a great library does.

Chapter Four

Beyond Causality

Interoperability

We don't expect things to happen on the internet the way they happen in the real world. Not only is the pace of change exponentially faster on the internet, it also gives us a direct experience of unpredictability every day. We check to see what the latest quirks are online and off. We see tiny internet sparks ignite worldwide flames. We see ridiculousness paraded for our entertainment or scorn. We prowl to see what new thought has been thought and what new invention has been invented. Just as a vessel flying through outer space never knows what piece of space dust, drawn to some large but distant mass, might breach its hull, a web browser flying through internet space never knows if it's going to come across a video game—*Pokémon*—controlled by the simultaneous but conflicting flicks of hundreds of users, or a page with dots of dust whose path across the screen you can alter by clicking to make "gravity points" wherever you choose.[1] There seem to be no rules guiding change on the internet, and we have come to accept that, to count on it, and to like it.

In chapters 1 and 2 of this book, we also saw how machine learning is giving us a model of models so complex that we often cannot fully comprehend them. What happens, we are learning, is the result of everything that is happening, all at once. While our new technology lets us predict more accurately and makes predictable domains we formerly thought were too complex, it simultaneously reveals the immense complexity we skate over.

We are so far down the path of this new model of change that we take for granted minimum viable products, open application programming interfaces (APIs), and so much more, even though they fly in the face of tens of thousands of years of anticipating the future and preparing for it.

It turns out that all these changes in our understanding of how the future happens are rooted in a single but profound change in our most basic model: it no longer resolves to the laws of causality. Beneath causality, we are discovering something even more fundamental.

Plug-in World

If you need to buy an audio cable to plug your mobile phone into your car's stereo system, you can get one at your local dollar store and it will work in any car that has an auxiliary plug. But if you need a replacement bulb for the car's headlights, you may end up paying over a hundred dollars, and not just because headlights are more expensive to manufacture than audio plugs. The car manufacturer has you over a barrel because you need a bulb designed for that one type of car. You are, in effect, paying the noninteroperability tax.

Interoperability is the ability to use elements designed for one system in another system the designers may never have heard of, and in ways that they did not anticipate. In slide deck after slide deck, the concept of interoperability is introduced with a photo of Lego pieces. But that's misleading. The Lego Group fiercely kept other companies from producing interoperable toy brick sets for as long as its patent held out. On the other hand, Lego pieces are a great example of things that *intra*operate—they work beautifully with other pieces from the same system. A 3.5 mm audio plug is a better example of *inter*operability because it can be plugged into so many different types of devices from many, many different manufacturers.

John Palfrey and Urs Gasser give another type of example in their book *Interop*: the standardization of the vocabulary used by air traffic controllers.[2] Pilots must speak English or at least learn Aviation English: three hundred words relevant to flying a plane.[3] Likewise, standardized barcodes on commercial items enable products to interoperate with checkout systems in stores around the world. Credit cards enable people's wallets to interoperate across different national currencies. Standardized export formats for spreadsheet files, such as CSV (comma-separated values)—invented in 1972—let you load a Lotus 1-2-3 spreadsheet you created in 1995 into a modern spreadsheet app, as well as into most database software and graphic charting applications.[4]

Indeed, interoperability is at the heart of many of the examples we have looked at so far:

- Platforms with public APIs crack open a site's internal services so that applications written by others can interoperate with those services.

- Open data lets information be put to use by any app or system that needs it.

- With agile programming, developers create interoperable functional modules that can work with any other module that knows how to provide it with the expected inputs.

- A user can mod a computer game if the game accepts new objects, graphics, and rules of interaction that work with its core mechanics.

- The ability of computers to interoperate with other hardware devices enables on-demand printing, embedded insulin pumps, household thermostats, and the Internet of Things.

- Machine learning works by bringing together massive amounts of data generated by many different systems in forms that the system can ingest and analyze. Now vendors are finding ways to enable their machine learning systems to interoperate with other machine learning systems. For example, six giant technology corporations—Amazon, Google, IBM, Microsoft, Oracle, and Salesforce—have taken the Cloud Healthcare Pledge to develop open standards by which health data can be shared among their systems.[5] Judea Pearl in *The Book of Why* talks about his own work in making data "transportable"—that is, usable across machine learning systems.[6]

- The internet itself makes local networks interoperable so they can pass along information packets using standard data formats and transmission protocols.

We've gone with interoperable solutions in these cases because interoperability makes systems more efficient, flexible, sustainable, and expandable. But the effect that is most directly altering our understanding of how things happen is interoperability's math: when the resources and services designed for one system are interoperable with other systems, unexpected value can, and probably will, emerge.

The Useful Unpredictability of Standards

You can see this in an important joint effort by Google, Bing, Yahoo!, and Yandex (a Russian search site) called Schema.org, which specifies a vocabulary of terms that website owners can invisibly embed in their web pages so that information on those pages can be better understood by the search engines.

For example, imagine the word *bridges* is somewhere on a web page. To respond to user queries with relevant results, a search engine would first want to know whether the page is about architecture, travel routes, movies, or orthodontics. Schema.org provides a standard way for the page creator to embed a hidden tag that says explicitly that the page is about, say, movies. Then the search engine wants to know what sort of thing "bridges" is referring to on that page. Is it a word in a title (*The Bridges of Madison County*), the name of an actor (Jeff Bridges), or part of the marketing description ("bridges the gap between love and desire")? Schema.org provides a vocabulary to express just this sort of information, all hidden from the people visiting the page but visible to the search engines. Likewise, with Schema.org, a site about the book *Sense and Sensibility* could indicate that Jane Austen is the name of the author while Elinor Dashwood and Colonel Brandon are names of characters in that book. With information like this, when someone searches for Jane Austen's *Sense and Sensibility*, the search engines can confidently offer a list of characters in the book, as you often see in the information boxes Google provides on the right-hand side of many search results pages.

Schema.org thereby makes the search engines smarter and their users happier. But, not coincidentally, it also makes the information on web pages far more interoperable.

Schema.org does this by providing sets of tags for scores of different types of things that pages talk about, including organizations, people, events, recipes, medical conditions, news articles, and local businesses.[7] These vocabularies are created in collaboration with the relevant communities of practice in an open fashion that has more in common with how the internet was created than with how Henry Ford designed the Model T.

Once Schema.org's tags have made it clear that a page is about a book, and has tagged the book's title, the name of the author, the names of characters, the date of publication, its geographic settings, and so forth, Google can cluster that information with what it has learned from other pages. It can connect all that it has learned about Jane Austen with other works of fiction, with geographical data, with weather information, with historical information about the role of marriage, with the structure of British royalty, and with other Oscar-winning movies starring Emma Thompson. By making information on billions of web pages *intra*operable, these webs of information—"graphs," as they are known technically—have made search engines the most knowledgeable institutions in the history of the planet.

Because Schema.org's vocabulary of tags has to be public so web page creators can insert them, it also increases *inter*operability by enabling any application on the web to locate, extract, and reuse the information on web pages just the way the search engines do. Evan Sandhaus, who was executive director of technology at the *New York Times* when we spoke, said that Schema.org is "probably even a bigger deal in terms of how news organizations get their data out there than APIs." He explained that sites such as Facebook and Twitter automatically scan pages linked to by users, looking for Schema .org's hidden tags in them. This lets those sites do things like identify and format the headline appropriately for their site, display the date in a way consistent with their users' preferences, and embed topic tags so that the site can suggest related links. What Facebook and Twitter do, literally any developer with access to the web can do for her or his own purposes. "The page itself becomes kind of like an API," Sandhaus said, in that it can be queried for information about itself. "That's huge!"[8]

So what started as a simple way for website creators to identify the nature of their contents to all the major search engines has become an open-ended resource for any app that can think of a use for that information. For example, Yext began as a service that provides the search engines with trustworthy information about the locations, hours, and so forth of its clients. Then in 2018 it began a new initiative, called Yext Brain, that builds knowledge graphs for businesses—connecting a wide range of information about, and relevant to, a company. "Why should you have to be a Facebook or Google to have that resource for your company?" asks Marc Ferrentino, Yext's chief strategy officer. As a primary way to represent information in those graphs, Yext has repurposed Schema.org, with some extensions. By turning this publishing standard into an internal data standard, Yext is not only benefiting from a well-thought-out data structure, but is also making it easier to publish information developed by the Brain to the web by embedding it in Schema.org tags—a virtuous circle of interoperability.[9]

Or, as another example, Microsoft Cortana—Microsoft's Siri, as it undoubtedly hates to be described—uses hidden Schema.org tags about flight information to show users a flight's status.[10] That makes Windows a slightly more valuable product for Microsoft, but the real value of making all this data interoperable is what the next developer will do with it. Perhaps she'll mash it up with astronomical information so hobbyist plane-spotters can identify the flights overhead. Perhaps she'll start a lost luggage recovery business based on that data. Perhaps she'll look at data about the geographic clustering of illnesses to disprove the contrail conspiracy theory that planes are releasing harmful chemicals when they fly. "But that's not what it was designed for!" is not a criticism of Schema.org but a statement of its value.

The adoption of this system is driven by the economic and attentional power of search sites. But exercising that power most effectively required the search sites to give up some of their control. Rather than specifying their own standards from on high and shoving them down the throats of website owners, the search engines wisely adopted the *microformats* approach that had begun in the mid-2000s. Its early advocates were impatient with the typical methods industries had used when they wanted to make information in their documentation interoperable. For example, a standard called SGML (Standard Generalized Markup Language) was created in the 1960s to enable entire industries to make the documents they share with their supply chains interoperable by agreeing on those documents' structures and their tags for common elements. But SGML standards were complex and prone to becoming mired in years of contentious arguments about trivialities, such as whether a table in a document is a set of rows intersected by columns or a set of boxes aligned into rows and columns. Microformats, on the other hand, are developed by small groups of knowledgeable people who skip over the contentious parts so they can come to quick agreement on the 80 percent that everyone agrees on. The result is quick and dirty standards that are simpler to implement, and from which companies can quickly benefit. The more companies that adopt a particular microformat, the greater its attractive force for getting yet more companies to adopt it.

Standards, whether a niche microformat or the more encompassing Schema.org, shape the space around them and enable further interoperability. For example, currently, if you gathered up college course syllabi from around the world to see how patterns of assigned readings vary geographically, or how the same sources are used in units on different topics, you would face a difficult computing problem, for there is no standard way in which syllabi express the information they contain and no Schema.org-like way of tagging that information. So a computer program trying to identify the information in a syllabus can't easily distinguish a book title from the title of a study unit, or the topic of an article from the topic of the final paper. As a standard emerges for how the elements of syllabi are to be tagged, it will become far easier to extract, aggregate, and interrelate those elements. With interoperable syllabi, professors could learn from how their colleagues around the world are organizing courses and readings.[11] This would encourage yet more professors to make their own syllabi interoperable. Perhaps apps will be written to let the information about required books interoperate with used-book services to help drive down the cost to students. The uniformity of the data format would also make quantitative analysis far easier and machine learning more accurate, which is likely to unearth relationships that could unveil hidden currents in our educational systems and culture. Educational platforms could use that information to create new learning services and to guide students to interests they might never have otherwise discovered.

It will also . . . who knows? And that's the point. In the causal clockwork universe, we look for the dials to turn and the levers to pull. The essence of levers is that they have predictable outcomes. The essence of interoperability is not simply that the information in syllabi can be more effectively shared, or that an audio cable fits many different devices, or that search engines can show us local times for the movies we ask about or list the cast and the characters they play. Rather, the essence of interoperability is that it specifies what pieces do and how they fit together so they can be used in unpredictable ways, sometimes for projects the original creators couldn't have imagined and will never hear about.

Interoperability Is the New Causality

If you grasp a pool cue, your hand is interoperating with it. When you slide the cue forward into a ball, the stick interoperates with it. When the ball hits another ball, it interoperates with it. When that second ball hits the side of the pool table, they interoperate.

These interactions within the material world are *causal*: an action brings about a determinate effect. Newton did a superb job enabling us to predict the outcome of colliding objects, and we've obviously made advances in understanding the causal relations among everything from microbes and diseases to windshields and pebbles.

Now our new technology is leading us to think about causality as just one—obviously crucial—type of interoperability. The internet has shown us how fluidly information-based systems can affect one another if we want them to, and occasionally when we don't. Machine learning has made abundantly clear how inadequate most conceptual models of causal events—A causes B—are, for in a machine learning system, B may be brought about by the interrelationship of innumerable variables. Together, these two technologies are getting us used to the idea that causality is just one way things may interact.

This is changing how we think things happen in several crucial ways:

Working across kinds

A clockwork's gears work together causally because they are of the same kind: solid, scaled to fit with one another, shaped with the connecting gears in mind. Interoperability, on the other hand, allows things that are *different* in kind to interact.

That got much easier as we moved business and culture onto digital media, for, like metal gears, digital bits have much in common with one another: they are binary and can be manipulated by digital machines. But unlike clockwork gears, bits can do more than go around in circles. Bits can represent just about anything we want. We can then tell those bits to interoperate in particular ways simply by writing the rules—the code—governing their engagement. For example, a developer can often just write a couple of lines of code for an app to display digital images, whether the app is a word processor embedding a photo, a music player displaying an album cover, or an online game allowing the user to choose an avatar.

Interoperability's ability to work across different systems is important for more than technical reasons. As Palfrey and Gasser say in *Interop*, "There is an essential difference between making complex systems interoperable and simply making everything the same."[12] Making things the same works well when the units are relatively simple and neutral, such as mapping systems that use longitude and latitude to precisely position items on the map.[13] It gets much harder when the units carry human meaning, as when geographic systems disagree about whether Palestine is a country or what the exact boundaries of "the Wine District" are.

Interoperability, on the other hand, can enable interaction while preserving differences. For example, when you use your credit card to pay for a meal in a foreign land, the transaction is enabled by uniform standards for the transmission of financial data, connecting banks in different countries, each of which has its own laws, customs, and currencies. Similarly, you can share the photos you've tagged "Pat and Ari's Amazing Vacation 2019," even though the friends and relatives who receive them may view them on a different device and relabel them "Pat and Ari Go Somewhere Boring." Libraries and archives that disagree about which information about items is worth collecting can share what they have, transposing it into common categorization standards while maintaining their own, local way of thinking about things. A little bit of shared information can lead people to works that disagree about everything else. And a lot of shared information can enable machine learning systems to help us discover meaning in those differences and similarities.

Indeed, for the past twenty-five years, we've been getting accustomed to interoperability working not just across banking systems, image programs, and archives but across radically different sorts of devices—although anyone who has ever tried to connect this year's television to last year's laptop can attest that it's not always as easy as we would like. Nevertheless, the integration of different devices has been a part of our experience of the web at least since 1993 when scientists at Cambridge University hooked up a video camera to the web so they could use their browsers to see whether there was a fresh pot of coffee in the community kitchen.[14] That coffee pot became world famous, setting the tone for how we imagine the web's future: more and more disparate items and information connected across their differences. The Internet of Things is making this real. Your thermostat can interact with your smartphone, your smartphone can interact with your baby monitor, your baby monitor can send JPGs to your smartwatch, and all of them can tweet at you angrily behind your back. (Be sure to check your toaster's privacy statement.)

Classic causality lets things interoperate only if they are very much alike: two metal gears, nine billiard balls bounded by a pool table, a comet and two planets. Interoperability, on the other hand, bridges differences.

Adjustable rules

If you throw a rock against a wall, the consequences will occur according to the same laws of physics that govern what happens when an asteroid hits a planet. But if an email message contains a date, it may trigger a notice that automatically creates an event in your online calendar, it might ask if you want to add an item to a to-do list, and it might translate the event's time into your local time zone. It all depends on the rules of interoperability that you have set up—and there is no predetermined limit on those rules.

In the interoperable world, we get to decide the rules of engagement. Even something as straightforward as copying information from one app into another can have different rules. The designers of Twitter made it easy to embed a tweet into another page. If you paste text copied from Amazon Kindle, it automatically includes the bibliographic information about the source, as well as a note that it came from a Kindle. The German site Angst & Panik has created different rules of engagement for itself, which work out to rules of disengagement: the site does not let users even select text, much less copy and paste it.[15] Flickr has an API that lets users retrieve photos based on tags and comments, while the Google Photos API does not. Before long, an email app that lets you click on a date to add it to your calendar will provide a button to let you book an autonomous car to take you to any appointment not within walking distance.

Newton discovered a handful of fundamental laws that rule nature. Imagine if he had been able to invent new ones.

Action at any distance

In Newton's universe, if you bring two things close enough, they causally interact: an asteroid can collide with a planet or a cloud of dust; water vapor can condense on a cold surface and the surface can absorb some of the condensation; the moon can pull the oceans, wearing away at the coastlines that help shape the tides. In fact, as others have said, Newton's genius wasn't in figuring out that there is a gravitational force pulling the apple down to the earth but in realizing that the apple was also pulling up on the earth . . . and, infinitesimally, on every star.[16]

In our new world, interoperability does the job of gravity, connecting every object across every length. But the gravity of interoperability does not diminish over distance, the way Newton's gravity so rapidly does. The basic hyperlink—the technology that started the web era—is perhaps the best example of this: no matter how far away a page is in terms of real-world geography or topic, a hyperlink keeps it as close as a click.

Responses out of proportion

In Newton's world, effects are proportional to causes. How far the ball goes depends on how hard you've kicked it. There are, of course,

effects that seem disproportional to causes: a yodel causes a land-
slide, or a single stone melts and unleashes an earthquake. But in
Newton's world, we're confident that a closer look will reveal pent-
up forces at play; the accounts always balance. Such seemingly out-
of-scale events are the exceptions in Newton's world, where we far
more commonly turn to clockworks ticking, planets orbiting, or billiard balls clacking as our models of how things happen.[17]

The interoperable universe has gotten us more used to small
events triggering huge ones: the invention of hashtags turns Twitter into a new type of news medium, a video from a mobile phone
triggers weeks of demonstrations, a software program written by a
college student ends up connecting billions of people. Small causes
can trigger huge events because interoperability enables more pieces
to interact with more pieces more easily in a universe that is already
ineffably complex.

Everything affects everything

$$F = Ma$$

That's "Force equals mass times acceleration," one of Newton's most
important and well-known equations. But why is it expressed that
way by every high school textbook when the basic rules of algebra
tell us that it's exactly equivalent to $M = F/a$: mass equals force divided by acceleration, or $a = F/M$? W. Daniel Hillis, a polymath computer scientist, thinks he knows why: $F = Ma$ fits into a scientific
framework—causality—that Hillis argues is ready for retirement,
or at least needs a rest.[18]

A cause is something that changes something else, so in the relationship of force, mass, and acceleration, we informally think of the
cue ball as the force, the eight ball as the mass, and the change in
the eight ball's position and speed as the main effect. Hillis thinks
this is because most often we think of force as the thing we get to
choose to do: we can choose to aim the cue ball at the eight ball, but
we can't easily choose to change the eight ball's mass. Cause and effect thereby fit nicely with thinking of ourselves as active agents of

change who get to determine our fates by intervening in a universe of passive objects.

Hillis calls cause and effect an "illusion" and a "convenient creation of our minds." Causal explanations "do not exist in nature" and are "just our feeble attempts to force a storytelling framework onto systems that do not work like stories."

This is different from the critique provided by the eighteenth-century Scottish philosopher David Hume, who said that cause and effect is nothing but our mental association of one event with another that regularly, in our experience, follows it; Hillis supplies a motive for the narrative we add to these associations. But Hillis's account doesn't deny that there is more than a mere psychological association at work: if causality is "just a framework that we use to manipulate the world," we only use that framework because it works. In this way Hillis is not contradicting Judea Pearl's important recent argument for giving machine learning systems causal models so that they can make more useful predictions. Pearl argues against traditional statistics' unwillingness to acknowledge that in some correlations, one side is the cause and the other is an effect. For example, where I live, the appearance of the constellation Orion correlates with the coming of winter but does not cause winter to arrive. On the other hand, the appearance of the sun each morning not only correlates with a temperature rise but causes it. Pearl argues that machine learning systems need to be given models of causality, and not just left to suss out statistical correlations, if they are to become true engines of science. With an understanding of causality, we can ask counterfactual questions, which are the cornerstone of scientific understanding: Mosquitoes and tropical flowers both correlate with the presence of malaria, but if we got rid of the tropical flowers, would there still be malaria? If not, then flowers don't directly cause malaria.[19]

In his essay, Hillis does not dispute that some correlations are causal and some are not. He is instead pointing to our insistence on the simplification that causality can allow us. Hillis points to examples in which causality fails as a framework for our "storytelling": weird quantum effects and complex, dynamic systems "like the biochemical pathways of a living organism, the transactions of an economy, or the operation of the human mind." We have a motive for seeing cause and effect even in those systems, Hillis tells us: we get to continue to believe that we can control events by finding the single lever that will bring about the single result we want. Pearl wants to add a causal model to the purely correlative world of machine learning, and Hillis wants to limit simple causality as the primary model we bring to understanding every aspect of the real world.

Machine learning could benefit from having Pearl's sort of causal model available to it, even while machine learning and the chaos of the internet have begun reducing our reliance on the sort of simplified causality that Hillis is arguing against.

Our framing of what happens in terms of causality works for us, and it is difficult—or, if you're Immanuel Kant, impossible—to imagine experiencing the world as nothing but a series of events that have no connection beyond a probability of correlation. But I think Hillis's point is good, for simple causality can keep out of view the cascades and inverted cascades we step through every day. Cascades include inhaling a microorganism that puts us in bed for a week, which then disturbs the schedules of those with whom we live and work, causing more effects to sprawl outward. An inverted cascade occurs when an enormous amount of energy results in a relatively small effect. For example, the bus that arrives on time makes it seem as if the universe's clockwork is functioning well, but the bus driver could only count on the vehicle to move forward when she stepped on the accelerator because the tank was filled with gasoline that resulted from massive investments in extraction tools, pipelines, refineries, ocean shipping, and regulatory and taxation regimes.[20]

If we think in terms of cause and effect, we tend to narrow down what happens to the most immediate and tangible events. If we think about interoperability, the entire world is present in the most routine of our everyday acts.

————————

Every day, we experience the ways in which the interoperable world is different from the causal one: interactions among things of different sorts, rules that vary by domain, the ability to create new rules, an indifference to distance, and an apparent lack of proportionality between cause and effect. These daily demonstrations are tacitly leading us to a different idea about how things happen. Whether or not we have ever heard of Pierre-Simon Laplace, we have been living in his theoretically predictable universe because change, we've thought, generally ticks like a clock: a gear shoves the one to which it is connected, and so on, one gear tooth at a time.

When we instead think about causality as one facet of the interoperable universe, we experience what happens as the consequence of a wild network of causes in which everything affects everything everywhere, all at once but not all in the same way, across all distances, in ways that might upset our every prediction.

A Fruitful Unpredictability

Metaphors count.

When we think about the future—not our particular future, but how the future operates—it's not uncommon for us to envision a landscape that we are moving through. It is filled with possibilities. We choose our destination and move toward it. As we do, the possibilities fall away in the same way that when we drive through a wooded landscape, the distant trees approach us, trail off to the edges of our vision, and then vanish behind us. At the moment of the present—the Now—all that remains are the possibilities that have managed to survive. They are the ones that somehow become real. That's how things happen, at least according to the metaphors that have shaped our experience.

Being enabled to create new ways for parts and systems to interoperate reverses that flow. Rather than possibilities narrowing as they approach, when we take the world as interoperable, we create more possibility.

The *internet* does this by allowing networks to interoperate.

The *web* allows pages on the internet to interoperate with other pages through links.

Schema.org and *microformats* use the web to enable systems to recognize and reuse the elements of pages. So does the Semantic Web, a form of markup created by the inventor of the World Wide Web, Tim Berners-Lee, to enable websites to make the information on them available to the apps and services anyone might build.

Open APIs from social-networking sites, government agencies, libraries, media sites, and many more provide standard, documented ways for a new application to put data to use in unanticipated ways.

Applications, including games, databases, spreadsheets, and enterprise operations systems, often let us change the rules about how they integrate with other apps and data. Apps like IFTTT—If This Then That—let users specify triggers for cross-app integration.

Machine learning systems ingest piles of data, possibly from systems that might seem unrelated, and find hidden relationships that let us predict in domains that once seemed too random to do so.

Protocol by protocol, standard by standard, app by app, system by system, and network by network, we have created a richly layered ecosystem of interoperability, each layer enabling new types of interactions. The result can be diagrammed neatly in an abstract way: the internet rules for transporting data from one site to another go at the bottom, data interchange formats go above them, and the customer-facing applications and services go at the top.

But it is far messier than that. For example, programmers create libraries of functions that can be reused by other programmers to create services—which may themselves be interoperable—at various layers. It is not uncommon for gamers to create a mod that is not itself a game but is designed to enable other gamers to make new variations on the original game. Then there are the feedback loops that arise from this multilayer interoperability: Schema.org's standardization of airplane flight information already enables machine learning systems to find gaps in airline schedules, and that information can then be used to fill those gaps. The rise of interoperable banking data and services is enabling the world's poor to participate in the global economy, which is likely to require new banking services.[21] The introduction of the hashtag let tweets interoperate in terms of their human meaning, but it also changed the role of Twitter in the ecosystem of news and businesses, which has resulted in calls to change Twitter, the news media, politics, and even the core internet protocols in order to prevent the "fake news" that the hashtag ecosystem has supercharged.

Our daily engagement with the internet has brought us face to face with chaos, in all its ugliness and awesomeness. The success of AI's algorithms reveals complexity that we wrote off as not worth paying attention to because there was nothing we could do about it. Our experience with these two technologies is revealing interoperability as the basic enabling condition for the next moment not being exactly the same as the prior moment—the very definition of what it means for something to happen.

But the secret of interoperability is that even if it's created with a narrow purpose, people will find a broad and unpredictable range of things to do with it: a standard way to connect printers to a computer becomes a way to attach a braille reader or a sewing machine that embroiders hats with custom slogans. The more unexpected uses interoperability engenders, the more valuable it is.

Reducing the world to what we could understand and predict made sense when knowing our world was our best way of controlling it. Now machine learning is letting us manage more and better by not insisting that we understand exactly how it works. Likewise, our new online ecosystem brings us significant benefits by letting others build whatever they want using the resources openly available to them online, and generally without having to ask anyone for permission.

Yet we are living through an aching and demanding contradiction. We are accustomed to reading the past twenty years as a period in which governments have increased surveillance and businesses have extracted every scrap of personal data they need to micromanipulate our behavior. Indeed, a surprising number of us are quantifying and recording our own heartbeats, steps, sleep periods, and grams of food, always looking for clues for a better life. This boiling of chaos down into a controllable residue is happening at the same time as we are purposefully increasing unpredictability. This contradiction is part of the definition of our new age. We may not be able to resolve it any more than we were able to resolve the contradictions of reason and faith, free will and determinism, individualism and communitarianism, altruism and selfishness.

If I had to guess, I'd say that the ideas of connection, of collaborating while preserving differences, of openness, of enablement, of play, and of hope are going to be dominant in the long term. That's my preference, which undoubtedly affects my judgment.

I understand that my argument for this hope is far from ironclad because it is based on some abstract assumptions: control is isolating, but interoperability is connective. Control is fragile; interoperability is resilient. Control is the narrow path a flashlight shows. Interoperability is the way light illuminates, feeds, warms, and liberates, all depending on what it touches.

And the forest through which the lit path runs is the world that happens.

Coda: Signs and Causes

When a culture looks at a bird's entrails to predict the fate of a king, we snicker: bird guts have no causal relationship with whether the king lives or dies. But these cultures are not looking for causal relationships. For them, and for much of our own culture's history before Newton, the universe is not a clockwork of causes but a web of meaning.[22]

For example, we used to assume that plants that look like parts of the human body can cure diseases of those parts. We now know that that's wrong. But it is not as without sense as it at first sounds. In his book *The Order of Things*, the philosopher Michel Foucault quotes the fifteenth-century medical genius Paracelsus: "It is not God's will that what he creates for man's benefit and what he has given us should remain hidden. . . . And even though he has hidden certain things, he has allowed nothing to remain without exterior and visible signs in the form of special marks—just as a man who has buried a hoard of treasure marks the spot that he may find it again."[23]

And here's the twist ending: machine learning is making us comfortable again with relying on signs.

Despite its ethical shortcomings, Cambridge Analytica's promise about the 2016 US presidential election was not patently ridiculous: by analyzing Facebook data, its machine learning algorithms might have been able to predict which political ads would best work on users clustered by personality type. That analysis need not focus on, or even consider, overtly political information from Facebook. For example, in 2013, two psychologists at Cambridge University gave fifty-eight thousand volunteers a personality test and then correlated those psychological profiles with what the volunteers "liked" on Facebook. ("Liking" in this case means pressing the Like button.) For example, it turned out that being extroverted correlated strongly with liking Nicki Minaj, while openness correlated with liking Hello Kitty.[24]

We can perhaps make up stories about why that's so, but we can also imagine correlations that defy such attempts at explanation. For example, Cambridge Analytica may well have had access to more than what people liked on Facebook. Applying machine learning to all that data might reveal—hypothetically—that writing long posts on weekdays, responding quickly to posts by people whose pages the user infrequently visits, and using the word *etc.* in more than 12 percent of one's posts all correlate with being a moderate Republican. Maybe posting photos that often show a city skyline in the background and double-clicking on buttons that only need a single click correlate with liking cats over dogs and supporting the gold standard. It's also conceivable that very small changes might result in very different predictions. Clicking the Like button for Nicki Minaj might make it much more likely that you're an extrovert, but a tiny bit more likely that you overtip. Put those correlations into a web in which another thousand data points each make it slightly more likely that you're an overtipper, and the system might make a probabilistic prediction that you're 86 percent likely to tip your Starbucks server two dollars when fifty cents would be enough and zero would have been acceptable.

We often use machine learning systems because they can increase the accuracy of our predictions or classifications. But that doesn't mean the models they construct for themselves are based on causal relations—a lack that Judea Pearl hopes will be rectified. There is, as far as we know, no causal relationship between having an open personality and liking Hello Kitty. There is no causal relationship between double-clicking on buttons, preferring cats, and overtipping. Those turn out to be *signs* of a tendency to overtip, but not causes. Tracks in the snow didn't cause someone to walk up the hill, but those tracks can be reliable signs of the direction she's going. A friend's posture, microsecond hesitancy in talking, and choice of dessert are not causes of sadness, and may be only very indirectly caused by sadness, but may yet be reliable signs of sadness.

Likewise, the signs a machine learning system considers may spring from whatever causes overtipping as a trait. Maybe they are all expressions of a need to be liked, of a fear of embarrassment, or of a sense of compassion. If the correlations are statistically valid, there is presumably some reason why they are. But the causes may be a set of dependencies so manifold and subtle that it's possible we may never discover them. Nor do we need to, so long as the machines are giving us accurate enough results and are not reinforcing societal biases.

Now, a machine learning model based on signs is clearly not the same as the ancient system of signs that was designed by God or that was an expression of the fundamental symmetry of the universe. Our new system of signs can be more chaotic; if all were orderly and beautiful, we wouldn't need powerful computers to see the signs and to make inferences from them.

With machine learning, we have gained something much closer to the probabilistic truth, at the price of a universe simple enough for us to understand and beautiful enough to strike us dumb. But our new signs are far more reliable than a gutted bird and, taken together, are themselves a sign of an irreducible intricacy of connection that we may yet learn to love.

Chapter Five

Strategy and Possibility

As we become more comfortable accepting that much of what we thought were truths turn out to be shortcuts that let us deal with a world thoroughly beyond our understanding and control, the concepts we use to organize our behavior and ideas are being reframed. In this chapter we'll explore one of the most basic terms in the vocabulary we use to talk about the future: *possibility*. It's too fuzzy a term to approach head on, so we'll ask what the evolution of strategy making—business strategies in particular—reveals about our ideas about the nature of the possible.

Narrowing Possibilities

Even though Apple likes to keep its cards close to its chest, in 2014, as part of its patent lawsuit against Samsung, the company published a memo from Steve Jobs written a year before his death. Jobs had sent it to Apple's top one hundred executives, apparently outlining a presentation he was planning on giving.[1] It begins with a slide titled "2011 Strategy," followed by slides such as these:

> *2011: Holy War with Google*

and

2011: Year of the Cloud

Before ending this overview section by announcing that the company will be building a new campus, he writes,

> *tie all of our products together, so we further lock customers into our ecosystem.*

Jobs then goes through Apple's product lines, each with an opening statement of his strategy for it. For example, he writes,

> *2011 Strategy: ship iPad 2 with amazing hardware and software before our competitors even catch up with our current model.*

And about Apple's mobile operating system, he writes,

> *Strategy: catch up to Android where we are behind (notifications, tethering, speech, . . .) and leapfrog them (Siri, . . .).*

These are strategies in different senses. Announcing the "Year of the Cloud" marks out a broad, cross-product area Jobs wanted Apple to focus on. "Holy War with Google" designates the enemy against which the company will compete to the death. Tying "all of our products together" is a tactic in furtherance of the strategy of trying to "further lock customers into our ecosystem." (It is also a sterling example of using *intra*operability to *reduce* users' possibilities.)

Jobs may not have been entirely consistent in his use of the term *strategy*—as we'll see, the term's application to business is relatively new and not entirely settled—but his talk illustrates a shared, functional definition: a strategy is what leaders tell their lieutenants to focus on. When Scott McNealy, the CEO of Sun Microsystems, in 1990 said, "We're getting all our wood behind one arrow," the phrase caught on not just for Freudian reasons—"arrow," "wood"—but because we think about strategy as a way of focusing all of our organization's energy on a single goal.[2] A strategy is a way to marshal limited resources by making a decision that says yes to one path and no to all the others.

So, in an age as chaotic, uncontrollable, and unpredictable as the one we have entered, you'd think strategic focus—making the hard decisions about how to best use limited resources—would be more important than ever. Without a doubt, that is often the case. But as we have already seen, many organizations are instead beginning to think about strategy differently (adopting lean, agile, disruptive strategies, etc.), in part because of the volatility of our environment; in part because the digital elements of a strategy can be altered so much more quickly and inexpensively than, say, retooling a manufacturing process; and in part because our recent experiences with unanticipation have made obvious the hidden costs of the old anticipate-and-prepare strategy of strategies.

We will undoubtedly continue to use strategies that focus our resources by reducing possibilities, even while we're adopting elements of strategic interoperability that make more things possible. But just as how we predict reveals how we think the future happens, how we strategize reveals what sort of thing we think possibilities are.

The Invention of Strategy

In 1964, the publisher of management pioneer Peter Drucker's new book insisted that he change the title from *Business Strategies* to something that would make more sense to the business audience; Drucker published it as *Managing for Results*.[3] Strategy was still something that armies, not businesses, needed. In fact, even armies didn't think about strategies the way we do today until a few hundred years ago. Strategies only make sense when we think the future comes about in particular ways.

That's why in the eighth century BCE when Homer recounted the story of the Trojan War that had occurred four hundred to five hundred years earlier, King Menelaus did not present a slide deck that laid out the strategy for assaulting the walled city of Troy. Instead, his "strategy" consisted of showing up and doing some fighting.

It took another three hundred years for the distinction between strategy and tactics to emerge for the first time, at the hands of no less than Socrates.[4] But Socrates meant something very different by *strategy* than we do. He tells us a strategist is an "inventor of tricks," and compares strategic generals to musicians coming up with new songs—like Odysseus, who ended the Trojan War by stuffing warriors into a gift horse.[5] So, at this founding moment of the distinction between strategy and tactics, strategy isn't characterized by steadiness but by nimbleness, a term we today associate with agile development and companies that pivot.

That view was true to the Greek understanding of how things happen: moody Fates, self-absorbed gods, and unpredictable mortals set us on the dark, twisty path of our lives. For our modern idea of strategy to emerge, we needed a future that's orderly and predictable enough for long-term planning to make sense.

We didn't get that sort of future until around the time of Newton. Lawrence Freedman, in his sprawling work *Strategy: A History*, says this new definition of strategy reflected "an Enlightenment optimism that war—like all other spheres of human affairs—could benefit from the application of reason." Warfare became subject, or so it seemed, to laws not entirely unlike Newton's.[6]

The concept of martial strategy flowered in the first half of the nineteenth century, when books began to appear that explained the strategy of war the way a mathematician proves theorems in geometry or a clockmaker explains clocks.[7] The most renowned theoretician of war, Carl von Clausewitz, in his 1835 *On War*, certainly acknowledged the randomness and unpredictability of battle, but he also tried to find the rules that could generally be relied on.[8] Clausewitz sometimes expressed these in a Newtonian vocabulary of force, movement, friction, mass, and inertia, with occasional geometrical-style deductions that prove, for example, that grand battles are preferable to many smaller skirmishes.[9] Strategy thus became something subject to laws, although those laws interacted with battles so frenzied and desperate that only God or Laplace's demon could fully comprehend them.

Today we cannot imagine a publisher asking an author to remove the word *strategy* from the title of a business book, or a CEO responding to the question, "What's your company's strategy?" with a firm "I don't know." But the concept of strategy has gone through considerable and rapid churn over the past thirty years. In part this was intentional: consultants discovered they could charge a premium for explaining why the existing strategies were pathetically outmoded compared to the new, shiny ones they just happened to have a slide deck about—reengineering's call for senior management to "blow up the organization" being perhaps the poster child for this.[10] Other approaches to strategy making were far more consequential.

These different approaches have had at least two things in common. First, to varying degrees and in different ways, they work by enabling an organization to narrow the possibilities down to the ones that the organization is going to go after. Second, if how we predict tells us how we think about the future, how we strategize tells us how we think about possibility.

The Possibility That Strategy Reveals

Into the category of "possibility," we have traditionally crammed everything from wishes and fantasies to the choices of entrées on the menu we're holding. That's because in the West we have been so focused on the actual and the real that we treat possibilities as a broad category of things defined by their lack of reality. But possibility looks different in a universe characterized by interoperability.

Let's look at five not quite miscellaneous examples of conceptions of strategy from recent decades, then come back to see how each reveals the nature of possibility.

1. **Military.** In 1941, before the Pearl Harbor attack precipitated the United States' entry into World War II, the US and British militaries met in Washington, DC, and decided on a

joint strategic goal they termed "Europe First": they would focus on defeating Germany before turning to the Japanese.[11] This strategy would entail making strategic decisions about the theaters to commit resources to and which not to, whether to launch a massive invasion of Europe, and the balance of land and sea forces. Such decisions were guided by intensely pragmatic considerations about logistics, terrain, weather, the state of the troops, and so on.

2. **Cold War.** Named for "research and development," RAND was founded in 1946 by General Henry "Hap" Arnold, who believed America needed to collect its greatest minds to keep American science and technology ahead of everyone else's, especially the Russians. The US Air Force became its main client, and the group grew so rapidly that it was soon advertising jobs for hundreds of researchers, including in ads that bragged that RAND's president was a direct intellectual descendant of Isaac Newton.[12] Herman Kahn became the most famous of the RAND crew because he wrote best-selling books, because he was an eccentric character, and because he was one of the inspirations behind the crazed scientist in Stanley Kubrick's 1964 *Dr. Strangelove, or: How I Learned to Stop Worrying and Love the Bomb.* He developed nuclear war strategies by cold-bloodedly thinking through the various moves Russia and the United States might make in an extended exchange of nuclear missiles. This led him to calmly compare scenarios in which "only" five million people die with ones in which twenty million civilians are incinerated— rational discussions of the unthinkable.

3. **Scenario Planning.** Peter Schwartz credits Kahn with helping to inspire what seems like a very different approach to strategy making—scenario planning—invented in the 1960s at Royal Dutch Shell by Pierre Wack.[13] (Schwartz carried on Wack's work there.)[14] Schwartz describes the process this way: "In a scenario process, managers invent and then consider, in depth, several varied stories of equally plausible

futures. The stories are carefully researched, full of relevant detail, oriented toward real-life decisions, and designed (one hopes) to bring forward surprises and unexpected leaps of understanding. Together, the scenarios comprise a tool for ordering one's perceptions."[15]

As Wack himself wrote, the challenge was not to spin up imaginary scenes but rather to break managers out of the existing models that assumed the business environment would continue pretty much as it was at the moment. Wack feared that the grip of those models was too strong to let managers take seriously the process he was proposing. "[H]ow could our view be heard?" he wondered.[16]

The answer was by presenting rigorous, fact-based analyses that show that what happens next might be very, very different from the way things are now. Wack's group's voice was heard much more clearly after its analyses convinced Shell to prepare for the possibility of an oil crisis, a scenario that came to pass in 1973.[17] By 2006, Bain & Company reported that 70 percent of companies it surveyed were using scenario planning.[18]

4. **Transient Advantage.** In Rita Gunther McGrath's 2013 book, *The End of Competitive Advantage*, she distinguishes her ideas about the "strategy of continuous reconfiguration" from prior approaches, especially Michael Porter's "sustainable competitive advantage."[19] McGrath argues that competitive advantage is no longer sustainable and "no longer relevant for more and more companies" because digitalization, globalization, and other factors have made the environment far too dynamic. Even Porter's assumption that a strategy is devised for a single market can keep a company from creating strategies that address the entire "arena" in which the business operates, to use McGrath's term. So companies must be always alert to changes anywhere in their environment and have in place the organizational structure and the culture that enables them to disengage from the current strategy and to create a new one.

5. **Flip-Chart Strategies.** In a familiar ice-breaking exercise at management off-sites, designed to free up the imagination of the attendees, the participants are broken into small groups and asked to create a magazine cover story about their company ten or twenty years in the future. "Go wild!" they are instructed. The aim is distinctly not to point to the real possibilities looming but to imagine success beyond reason. Flip-chart strategies are designed not to be taken seriously.

If we turn inside out these five markers along the path that business strategy has followed, they become case studies in the perception of the nature of possibility. Let's go back over them with that in mind.

1. *During World War II,* the possible actions worth considering were the ones that worked within the physical limitations of moving soldiers, supplies, and equipment, and that responded to the ever-changing, unpredictable situations on the ground. Possibilities were rooted in earth and mired in mud.

2. *During the Cold War,* possibilities arrived in the nose cones of unstoppable missiles that didn't have to worry about fighting their way through enemy-held territory, about whether the rivers were swollen and the bridges intact, about how to get fresh water and canned rations to hungry soldiers. The missile launches in this model occurred in "turns"—retaliation for the enemy missiles that'd just been launched, followed by a counterretaliation—with nothing stopping the combatant nations except their willingness to press the button again. Never before had war seemed so much like playing chess.

    Indeed, RAND's approach removed the real world, with its mountains, rutted roads, and broken axles, from the "gameplay." Thus, the possibilities were dictated by the logic of the game, not by the physical impediments. That logic consisted of the set of assumptions the combatants had about the rationality of their opponents, their willingness to sacrifice their populations, and the like.[20] As you followed each possible branch of the tree of possibilities, you summed the costs and gains, the risks and rewards of this terrifying game of life, or more appropriately, game of Global Thermonuclear War.[21]

3. The *scenario planning* that began at Royal Dutch Shell treats possibilities as much more real. It does not assume that the movers are rational actors following relatively simple rules independent of what's happening on the ground. It instead looks at the ground and sees complex, potentially disruptive forces at play that can only be ascertained by taking a wide view anchored in deep factual analysis. It asks how the world might surprise us with changes in every dimension, from the climate to disease to the rise and fall of despots. This is much closer to the World War II military's on-the-ground understanding of possibilities than to the Cold War's gamelike logical possibilities, except Shell's scenario planning considers disruptions in the context itself and proceeds with less urgency, with more information, and from far more comfortable quarters.

4. McGrath's *transient competitive advantage* approach to strategy sees possibilities as real, imminent dangers and opportunities that come and go based on the constantly changing interactions among all the pieces in all of the domains in which business operates: markets, customers, suppliers, employees, management structures, and so on. Being alert to these possibilities requires avoiding the assumption of the fixity of any element of one's world. Where scenario planning looks out for planet-scale changes, McGrath urges us to be aware of the small changes that, because of the delicate interrelationship of every aspect of life, might push a business over the edge or give it a new handhold up. The possibilities that open up arise from the interactions of everything, which is to say, from the interoperability of all.

5. Finally, *flip-chart scenarios* treat possibilities as *mere* possibilities: whatever is imaginable and desirable should, for the duration of the exercise, also be considered possible. And because these exercises are intended to boost morale, the possibilities are always positive, so at the end, no group's *Time* magazine cover contains phrases such as "bankrupt," "doomed," or "prison time for CEO."

If strategies reveal how we think about possibility, then we ought to now see some strategic responses to interoperability's throwing possibility open.

Strategies Wide Open

Strategies facilitate decision making by telling an organization what to focus on, and what not to: focus on the iPhone by getting its operating system competitive with Android while—judging by Jobs's conspicuous silence on the topic in his slide deck—letting the Mac just glide along for a year or two. Strategizing has thus been typically conceived as a limiting operation. It identifies the possibilities and chooses the ones the organization wants to make real.

But now we're seeing some organizations think about strategies not in terms of winnowing and reducing possibilities. In an interoperable world, we can succeed at least in part by allowing others to make more of our offerings than we can anticipate. Here are three cases of organizations thinking differently about strategizing and possibility in a world of newfound complexity.

Drupal: Distributing Strategy

Dries Buytaert's slide deck for the annual Drupal conference outlines a very different type of strategy from the one Jobs did in his email to Apple's top one hundred.[22]

That's to be expected. Buytaert lists himself not as a CEO but as the "founder and project lead" of Drupal, an enterprise that in its structure is just about a perfect reverse image of Apple. Drupal is an open-source content management system developed by more than one hundred thousand loosely affiliated volunteers who share their work and enthusiasm.[23] Because of Drupal's ability to be modified and extended, it's used by over a million websites.

Buytaert's slides were intended for the 2017 DrupalCon, the annual gathering of thousands of Drupal developers, held that year in Vienna, Austria. As founder, his words are listened to carefully. But unlike with Jobs's presentations, the developers are perfectly free to ignore them. "People work on what they want to," Buytaert told me in the Boston headquarters of Acquia, his for-profit company that provides Drupal-based solutions.[24]

Buytaert could not compel the community of developers to march toward some goal even if he wanted to. They don't work for him. They work for the companies that are using Drupal. So, he says, "I don't give them a roadmap." What good is a map to a destination if you've got one hundred thousand people who want to go to their own happy places?

This, for Buytaert, is a feature, not a bug. "I open sourced Drupal," he says, "so other people would take it in directions I didn't expect." As an example, he cites the Howard Dean presidential campaign's use of it in 2004 to create DeanSpace, one of the first social networks for political campaigns. Since then Drupal has been used for everything from creating a community out of the fans of Spain's Sevilla soccer team to providing a self-service site for Australian taxpayers.

Even if Buytaert had the power, desire, and personality required to stand on a stage and dictate a strategy, he knows that doing so would only limit Drupal's possibilities, making it less able to address the particular needs of each particular site. So in 2017 he did what he does every year: in substantial detail—103 slides at the Vienna meeting—he described the current state of the distributed project that is Drupal (the 22 percent increase in the number of bugs that were fixed in 2016, the 28 percent increase in the number of contributors), how the businesses that provide Drupal services have been doing (they've been getting more deals at higher prices), and the competitive landscape (Drupal's market share is healthy but decreasing).

In his talk, Buytaert did discuss areas of the product he thinks the community should work on, just as Jobs did. But there are two major differences. First, Drupal developers will implement these changes only if they want to. They will not be punished for pursuing different goals. In fact, they are likely to be celebrated for it. Second, Buytaert and the attendees of DrupalCon do not assume the zero-sum approach to resources that is behind traditional strategies' aim of focusing the business on some possibilities at the expense of others. The Drupal ecosystem is one of abundance.

Buytaert uses the development of an image gallery feature for Drupal to illustrate his point. "There may be five good ways of doing that, but," he acknowledges, "only one or two will win." "Winning" in this case means being adopted by many other Drupal users and perhaps becoming a de facto standard for how image galleries are implemented. But that's not the only way the Drupal community measures success. The other attempts may well find a home with others who share their circumstances and needs; an ecosystem like Drupal's supports infinite biodiversity.

It's not easy to create such an ecosystem. "It's not 'If you build it, they will come,'" Buytaert says. But that ecosystem is of strategic importance, for it multiplies Drupal's value to its users. Building community and, at least as challenging, avoiding the many ways that online communities can go wrong require care and investment.

This was the topic of Lisa Welchman's 2013 keynote to the global conference, held in Prague that year. She asked, How do you manage growth of an open organization? Her answer: "This community is like a ginormous fungus." In particular, it's like a huge, underground fungus that had recently been discovered in Oregon. A *Scientific American* article explained the fungus's growth by saying, in Welchman's paraphrase, that it has "good genes and a stable environment." The Drupal community's good genes are its "standards-based framework," she explained. The stable environment is the community's set of social conventions and norms for conduct, ethics, collaboration, and decision making.[25] These conventions and norms enable technical and personal interoperability.

With that infrastructure in place, the project doesn't need a traditional strategy, for a strategy drives toward a particular goal. Far better to simultaneously drive at all the goals that segments of the community deem valuable.

While strategies typically are about removing possibilities to maximize the effort put behind the chosen ones, Buytaert eschews limiting the scope of Drupal developers' focus. He does so by executing his own personal strategy: "I try to get out of the way of the community." That facilitates independent developers opening possibilities made real by Drupal's architecture and that serve the real needs of users. These are, as we will discuss further, *real* possibilities.

Tesla and Google: Letting Go

On June 11, 2014, the walls of Tesla Motors' headquarters in Palo Alto were covered with more than one hundred patent awards. On June 12, they were gone, replaced by a wall graphic that paraphrased a meme based on a bad translation in an early video game: "OEMs [original equipment manufacturers]: All our patent are belong to you." Tesla's CEO, Elon Musk, had decided to open source the company's patents: anyone could use its inventions without asking permission or paying for the privilege.

In a blog post, Musk explained his reasoning: "Tesla Motors was created to accelerate the advent of sustainable transport. If we clear a path to the creation of compelling electric vehicles, but then lay intellectual property landmines behind us to inhibit others, we are acting in a manner contrary to that goal." Also, because the major automotive companies were making so few electric cars, Tesla probably did not feel threatened by them. Also, open-source projects draw many of the world's best engineers. Finally, a patent is "a lottery ticket to a lawsuit."[26] So Mr. Musk tore down that wall.

Tesla still takes out patents, including some highly valuable ones for battery technology, but it abides by its pledge not to sue any company that uses its technology in "good faith," which means that if a company uses Tesla's patents, it agrees to let Tesla use that company's own technology, creating an open-source environment for patented technology.[27] It also means that you agree not to use Tesla's patents to create a knockoff product; if you want to name your electric vehicle company Tessla Moters, you're going to have to invent your own technology.

Musk has claimed that some companies are using Tesla's open-source patents, but there are no details available about which companies and which tech. So Tesla's move may turn out to have been an empty gesture. Nevertheless, it was a gesture with a strategic intent. It is to Tesla's advantage to have a robust market for electric vehicles, both to create more customers and to advance the infrastructure required to support electric cars. Tesla's open sourcing of its patents can also help to establish its interfaces as standards.

Google has gone the same route with greater success with a technology not as much in the public eye: in 2015 it open sourced TensorFlow, its machine learning software. It did this even though machine learning is now essential to almost all that Google does, including how it searches, translates languages, sorts photographs, suggests responses to text messages, maps routes for cars, and drives its autonomous vehicles . . . not to mention beating the world's greatest go players.[28]

At a symposium in September 2017 put on by Google PAIR (People + AI Research),[29] Zak Stone, then the product manager for TensorFlow, told me why Google made such crucial software freely and openly available.[30] As with Tesla, the reasons mix self-interest and commitment to an ideal. By providing open access to the software, the community extends and debugs it for free, which lets Google serve its users better. As with a minimum viable product, Google learns what TensorFlow needs by seeing how people actually use it, and how they use it in ways that Google would not have thought of on its own. As with Tesla, TensorFlow's libraries and application programming interfaces (APIs) can become de facto standards, enabling Google's work to interoperate with products it did not create.

Uptake has been far better than with Tesla's open-sourced patents, in part because adopting a software library is far less expensive and risky than building a factory to produce cars that conform to particular specifications; also, Google does not demand a company reciprocate by opening up its tech.[31] Finally, Google understands the lesson expounded by Drupal's Dries Buytaert: open APIs and standards won't get adopted unless the organization works hard on building and maintaining a community.

It seems to be working. On the first anniversary of the open sourcing of TensorFlow, Stone posted at the *Google Research Blog* that 480 people had contributed to the software, including many outside Google; two years later, that number was up to 1,600.[32] In that first year, Google released substantial libraries of code for doing high-value tasks such as identifying the objects in images. Crucially, Google engineers and other members of the community had put in the time to answer thousands of questions on the public Q&A sites used by engineers—over 18,000 at Stack Overflow as of December 2018.[33] This concerted effort by Google is having the desired effect of jump-starting the AI market, making the work that's created interoperable and thus ever more useful, and establishing Google as a vital center of development even for work done outside Google.[34]

This has happened because Google adopted a strategy in the traditional sense: the leadership decided to put machine learning at the heart of the company's development efforts and turned resources toward that goal. But the forces this strategy is marshaling are not only Google's. And it's marshaling those forces not by giving them marching orders, or by pulling levers with known results, but by attracting others through the gravity that shapes networks.

In adopting these new strategic approaches to strategizing, all three of these organizations have decided to embrace the essential unpredictability of the interoperable universe, rather than resist it. Drupal carefully cultivates open software platforms and a community of developers so anyone on the planet can build something that adds value to the Drupal project; the interoperability of what gets built—a custom image browser that works for one installation is likely to work for all of them—then multiplies that added value. Tesla and Google are building ecosystems that make their products and services more widely usable, and they are doing so by releasing code and tools that will help others populate those ecosystems with value. The two companies understand that widely accepted standards create markets that attract more players, establishing those markets more rapidly. Of course, it also improves Tesla's and Google's market positions if their standards become these new industries' standards.

There are, as always, risks and downsides to these approaches. An open platform faces the same competitive pressures as any other offering; developers are unlikely to flock to the goods and services you're making openly available unless you're offering something of truly unique value. It also requires a commitment to maintaining the platform for the long haul; otherwise, developers that depended on your platform will find their work is now broken. And, of course, if you're not a Tesla or a Google, you may well not be able to drive standards for your industry. All of this costs money, with the risk that you'll back the wrong standards, or you'll be stuck maintaining an open API that only a few people have built anything with. Openness isn't free. But closedness has its own costs.

Step 2

Step 1. Collect underpants.
Step 2. ?
Step 3. PROFIT.

This "business plan" from a 1998 episode of *South Park* has been the subject of thousands of memes because, even so many years ago, it was clear that fresh-faced high-tech startups were failing to recognize how hard it is to get from a good idea—granted, "collect underpants" is not one—to a functioning, profitable business.

Part of the joke is its Newtonian framework: the missing step that connects the cause with the effect. It's not simply that the underpants entrepreneurs—who in this episode happen to be gnomes— don't know what Step 2 is. It's that they think there is a Step 2: something that will lead to profit as surely as propelling a cue ball at just the right speed and angle will sink the eight ball. But, as we have seen throughout this book, refusing to know can itself be a highly effective strategy.

———————

We have been confused about how to think about possibility for a long time. Actuality is easy: it's the stuff we stub our toes on. But possibilities can be many different sorts of things. They can be what has not happened yet. They can be what could be even if they never will never be. They can be fantasies, dreams, fears, predictions, desires, or delusions. But overall, possibilities have been defined by the single thing they have in common: they are the not-real, which can include the not-yet-real, the never-will-be-real, and the never-could-be-real.

Interoperability makes possibilities very real. We know this if only because we stub our toe on noninteroperable systems every time we buy the wrong charger for our phone or the wrong tip for our electric toothbrush.

The serious strategic approaches we've looked at—military, RAND game theory, scenario planning, transient competitive advantage—each go through a phase in which the range of possibilities is expanded, only to then be reduced to the single one that will be acted on—McGrath's less so. The aim is to winnow, to narrow, the future. Such is the tyranny of decisions.

This approach is right at home in the Age of Newton. You don't want to disperse your limited supply of energy. You want to focus it because the more force you put behind the arrow, the more energy it will travel forward with. So say Newton and McNealy. Likewise, when talking about changing a large organization's strategy, we sometimes say, "It's like turning a battleship," a direct application of Newton's first law: an object in motion will tend to remain in motion in its current direction. The more massive it is, the more energy it will take to alter its course. Strategies have been our corporate battleships because physical and organizational resources have been so difficult to reassign—sometimes because we've optimized logistical and organizational processes to support long-term, nonagile strategies because we have assumed the future will be orderly. That's the assumption that gave rise to the idea of strategy in the first place.

But now we are able to decouple decision making from strategy, at least to some degree. Drupal, Tesla, and Google are making this strategic move when they provide tools and services that enable people outside the company to *decide* to create things beyond the companies' anticipation. Likewise, companies that adopt some form of agile development, that structure their software around an internal API, that put minimum viable products into the market, or that adopt McGrath's advice, are using strategies that purposefully avoid or minimize the cost of making decisions, of saying yes to this and no to all the rest.

Such approaches to strategy are feasible now because our products and processes are so often mediated by digital networks. Their digital nature means that they can be altered just by typing. Not only are fingers far more agile than tired soldiers crossing faltering bridges, but code is pestered by mere bugs, not artillery shells. The networking of digital creation means that the boundaries drawn between users and cocreators are artificial; enabling those boundaries to be overstepped can be a strategic move toward radically increasing the value of one's products by reducing one's control over them. And now that machine learning is guiding everyday aspects of our lives, it is provoking inevitable but impossible questions about the ways in which the world surpasses our understanding. We may not be able to answer these questions finally, but strategies that act as if we have as much control as we used to imagine we did increasingly may look like they are in denial.

Possibilities in our new world are of a different sort than we're used to. In a clockwork universe, a thing will either happen or it won't; the possibilities that don't happen have thereby proved that they weren't really possible after all. But interoperability mints *real* possibilities that can be actualized, and can be actualized by people unknown to those who created the interoperable tools and re-sources: we can plug our thing into their thing, these services can be used with our data, we can mash our content up with that content and that data. We couldn't before, but now that these systems are interoperable, we *can*. That's what it means to say that interopera-bility creates *real* possibilities: possibilities that can be actualized without waiting for further technical changes, for permission, or for someone else to come up with the idea and choose to build it.

Of course, organizations will continue to pursue strategies that narrow the possibilities and will concentrate their resources on the achievement of the ones they've chosen. But over the past twenty years we have moved from assuming that the natural state of a busi-ness is to be a fort with a thick wall that firmly separates the inside from the outside. It is now quite common—the norm, even—for a business to think of itself as embedded in a messy network of sup-pliers, customers, partners, and even competitors.[35] Businesses have gone out of their way to open up their processes, welcoming customer input and engaging far more broadly with their ecosystems. It turns out that Fort Business was a social construction, not a formation decreed by nature.

Functionally, this shift toward a networked, or permeable, view of business can be characterized as an increase in interoperability. Systems that were once kept apart by narrow and formal channels have now been enabled to affect one another: product cocreation with customers; multiway marketing conversations rather than one-way broadcasting of messages; standards alliances with competi-tors. The knocking down of the old walls that were definitional of a business is better understood as a strategic and purposive commit-ment to increasing a business's interoperability with the rest of its environment. A business does this in order to make more possibili-ties real, knowing that this entails that those possibilities will be more unpredictable, for they may be actualized far outside the busi-ness's old, crumbling walls.

This is a far cry from our old anticipate-and-prepare strategy of strategies that relied on narrowing the possible possibilities and betting on the one that will actualize. In an interoperable world in which everything affects everything else, the strategic path forward may be to open as many paths as possible and enable everyone to charge down them all at once, together and apart.

Coda: Strategic Obscurity

Accumulate thickly, arise thinly.

That's a literal translation of the four Chinese characters that Ren Zhengfei, founder and chairman of Huawei, sent out to his 170,000 employees in 2016.[36] The four characters are a *chengyu*, a saying that often refers to a classic story in Chinese literature. This one traces back to Su Shi, an eleventh-century writer of the Northern Song dynasty.

Ren periodically sends out such poems. Because they are strategic communications from the chairman of the world's largest telecommunications equipment and services company, he works on finding exactly the right ones. But the right poem is not the one that explicitly and perfectly captures the corporate strategy. Rather, Ren chooses poems that are obscure. Every employee, at every level, is invited to join a study group to try to make sense of the four characters, each of which is rich with meaning.[37]

One can only imagine the online ridicule an American CEO who distributed poems would risk for trying to sound wise and superior. At Huawei it's different. The employees do not assume the poem has one clear and correct meaning that Ren could have instead just written out in a memo. It's not a secret message from the boss that they have to decipher. Rather, the practice requires employees to bring their experience, values, and feelings to the group discussions where shared ideas and values are developed. There they may discover new purposes for the group and the company, new directions, new ways of understanding what they are doing together.

If your strategy requires "putting all your wood behind the arrow," it is of the essence that the leader be clear at the very least about which way the arrow is to be pointed. But if the corporate goal includes more than hitting a small bull's-eye a manageable distance away, there's virtue in obscurity.

First the disclaimer: Of course, clarity is vital in many situations. If you're writing an airplane repair manual, you can't tell readers, "Go pull out that thingy on the left, under that other thing, and shake it until it sounds better." The CFO can't write in the annual report, "We lost a bunch of money," and leave it there. Clarity is often required.

But obscurity has some advantages that clarity just can't match.

Obscurity creates empowerment that clarity can take away. For example, if your boss lays out careful and clear instructions for launching a product, those instructions have power over you. If you decide to add a webinar series, or give an exclusive preview to an important outlet, you risk getting reprimanded for not following those clear, crisp directions. If, on the other hand, your boss tells you to launch a product but does not provide clear instructions about how to do it, she has empowered you to imagine, to decide, to create. Obscurity frees you.

Obscurity enables creativity. When all we see in the night sky is a black curtain randomly interrupted by dots of light, we start to imagine the lines that connect them into shapes that look like a ladle, a hunter, a crab. We become creative. In business the same thing can happen when a group brainstorms solutions to a difficult problem or finds itself in a new arena where their old assumptions may not hold.

Obscurity enables engagement. When everything is clear, the conversation tends to be pragmatic and operational. We hammer down the details and are guided by the gods of efficiency. But when the way forward is murky, and even more when we don't yet know where we should be going—which way the arrow is pointed—we will turn it over in our minds. We will wonder aloud to the person next to us, and then we will expand the possibilities together. What's clear is the same to everyone—that's part of the meaning of being clear. What's obscure looks different to each, and thus brings out what's unique about each.

Obscurity has these powers because clarity is not a natural state for humans. Our lives are uncertain. Our way forward is hard to discern. Clarity is a helpful tool, but there's often more truth in obscurity.

Chapter Six

Progress and Creativity

In 1954, Western Electric produced a five-minute video in which a perfectly coiffed redhead leads us step by step into the brave new world of rotary dials.[1] First, look up a number in the phone directory, she tells us in a cheerful voice that makes it seem as if it's all going to be OK. "It saves time to keep the number in front of you when you dial." Great tip! Now, pick up the handset and listen for the dial tone.

Things continue to go well as she demonstrates on a dial the size of a small pizza. "When dialing, notice that I brought my finger around until it firmly touched the finger stop. And now I remove my finger and let the dial go back by itself."

But then comes a moment of unexpected sternness: "A failure to bring your finger fully to the finger stop with each pull of the dial may cause you to dial a wrong number. The same can happen if you pull the dial back."

From this video we learn three things.

First, how to dial a phone.

Second, in warning us, with a steely conviction that her smile fails to mask, against pulling on the dial to speed its return, our host is anticipating that we humans will make the mistake of assuming that we are the agents of change. It's a natural mistake, for we create tools to bend the future toward our desires. But that's only half true about rotary telephone dials. Yes, we rotate the dial clockwise, but the actual dialing occurs on the counterclockwise return trip precisely because that trip is not under our control. The number we dialed is sent across the phone network as a series of timed electrical pulses. Monkeying with their tempo by pulling on the dial to hurry its return trip can throw the timing off. So inside the phone is a governor that makes pulling back on the dial feel like trying to drag your finger through wet corn starch (try it sometime). Our tutor has to warn us in a stern-friendly tone against even trying because the phone company has anticipated that we'll fight against the governor installed to prevent our anticipated urge to hurry the dial up. Misuse anticipated and prepared for.

Third, having to produce a video to instruct your users in how to use the latest feature you've added to your product is a sign that you may be taking a step that will merit its own tick mark on your product's time line. In this case, it's the beginning of requiring people to make their own calls instead of asking an operator to do it for them. The tick mark goes on a line that is the shape of the future as we imagine it: drawn left to right, slowly inclining upward, with marks for every achievement.

The next tick on the telephone's time line has its own lesson. The touch-tone keypad that replaced the rotary dial was introduced at the 1962 World's Fair, where the future was on display; AT&T didn't mention that its operators had been using buttons to dial since 1941. But between then and 1962, computers, with their push-button keyboards, had become the mark of modernity. At last the phone had joined the Computer Age, an achievement fully meriting a mark on the time line.

In truth, though, touch-tones were what we would today call a "hack." They seemed as digital as a computer, but they were actually as analog as Alexander Graham Bell's moustache. The telephone system from the start had been designed to convey the human voice. That *anticipation* meant that it was far easier to have the touch-tone keys send analog signals—audible tones within the range of the human voice—than to convert the underlying system to a digital network designed for the crisp on-offs of bits.

Still, touch-tone dialing was such a hit that even now our mobile devices default to a simulation of the old touch-tone keypad, right down to tones that are now meaningless to the system—a digital system simulating an analog system simulating a digital system.[2] And we still talk about *dialing* a keypad. That persistence justifies treating the introduction of the rotary dial and touch-tones as worthy of tick marks on the time line.

We get to choose what we count as tick marks because progress is a story we tell ourselves. That story narrows complex histories of innovation to a single line. For example, here's one reasonable time line of the telephone's history:

- **1876:** The phone is invented.

- **1877:** Bell Telephone is founded.

- **1930s:** The two-piece "candlestick" phone is replaced by a unit that combines the speaker and earpiece.

- **1950s:** Rotary phones are introduced.

- **1960s:** Touch-tone dialing is introduced.

- **1980s:** Cordless phones and fax machines become available.[3]

This is definitely progress. But even if we throw in the 1959 introduction of the Princess phone, a time line as spread out over time as this one is unthinkable—intolerable!—for the device in our pockets today. If there aren't new apps to look at every day, and a new model of our chosen phone every year, we feel bewildered, if not outraged.

But the most important change we're experiencing in the nature of progress is not in its pace but in its shape: a one-dimensional line that tells a one-dimensional story is now unwinding into its natural complexity. The new shape of progress reflects a change at the macro level—the top-down view from far away—not only in how we think things happen but also in what drives our story forward.

The Invention of Progress

In 1967, the famous teacher and scholar Charles Van Doren carefully articulated the essence of progress in four assertions: (1) A "definite pattern of change exists in the history of mankind." (2) That pattern is known to us. (3) It is, "in the long run, irreversible." (4) "The direction of the irreversible pattern of change in history is toward the better."[4]

There's a fifth assertion not on that list because Van Doren discusses it at length throughout his nearly five-hundred-page book: something causes that pattern to occur and persevere. If we thought it were all just an accident, a series of dice throws, we would call it luck, not progress. Van Doren notes eleven different forces behind progress, which he divides into two major categories: progress caused by something about the nature of the universe (God, natural principles) and progress caused by something about humans.[5]

As an example, the abolitionist Unitarian minister who originated the phrase "The arc of the moral universe is long but bends towards justice,"[6] famously invoked by Martin Luther King Jr., believed in a combination of the two drivers. In 1853 Theodore Parker thought that moral progress occurred because the divine principle in humans tends to win out. But why, he wondered, is that arc so long? Parker explained that while natural laws—Newton's laws—are reliable and predictable, the moral law only has an effect if we humans listen to our conscience. Too often we fail to hear and heed that quiet voice. The driver of moral progress is our paying attention (Van Doren's second sort of driver) to the divine law (the first driver).

So what do we think drives technological progress? Until relatively late in our history, the clear answer would have been, "Absolutely nothing," for the concept of progress didn't seem to apply to technology any more than we currently think it applies to fashion or to the movement of tectonic plates, albeit for different reasons. To see why it took so long to think of technology as subject to progress, we first have to take a quick look at the history of progress itself.

"All that the hand of man can make, is either overturned by the hand of man, or at length by standing and continuing consumed."[7] Thus wrote Sir Walter Raleigh in the preface to his incomplete million-word history of the world published in 1614.[8] Such pessimism ruffled no feathers because it was obvious to everyone—as obvious as the march of progress is to us—that the older a civilization grows, the weaker and more corrupt it becomes.[9] After all, a civilization is like a human body, isn't it? That's where we got the idea that it needs a *head* to run it and that there are *organs* of government. So it was assumed that, like a human body, once a civilization reaches adulthood, it begins to decline.[10] (This line of thought was part of a more encompassing strategy for understanding the universe by looking for analogies among its parts at every level.) Even the Greeks, who ever after were held up as the pinnacle of learning and art, had assumed that their own civilization was yet another step in the decline from the original Golden Age before Zeus took over.[11] Christian beliefs about the Fall of man and the upcoming Apocalypse added a decisive ending to this story. Even in the early nineteenth century, the Romantics lamented the lost innocence of childhood and praised the "noble savages" who resisted the corrupting influence of "civilization."

Sir Walter Raleigh's history wasn't an argument against progress, for there was no conception of progress to argue against. To be learned meant to be a scholar of the Greek and Roman sources of all wisdom and beauty: Aristotle, Cicero, Virgil, and their ilk. Even the geniuses of the Renaissance did not think they were making progress beyond the classics, but rather believed they were renewing them; *renaissance* means "rebirth." For example, when a 1509 book, illustrated by Leonardo da Vinci, described the glories of the golden ratio—a rectangle of particular proportions revered by Renaissance artists—it was presented as founded in Plato's theory of shapes and interpreted through a Christian understanding of God.[12] If it was true or beautiful, or preferably both, then the Greeks or Romans had discovered it.

So it was shocking when, in 1687, a poem by Charles Perrault—the creator of the genre we call fairy tales—was read out at a meeting of the Académie française, for it contained these audacious lines, among others:

> *Learned Antiquity, throughout all its stay,*
> *Was never as enlightened as we are today.*[13]

The arrogance! The horror! Outraged shouts from the audience demanded that the reading be stopped mid couplet.

That session was only the opening shot in what was called in France "the Quarrel between the Ancients and the Moderns."[14] Those advocating for the idea of progress maintained that the ancient world was based on superstitions, while the modern world was advancing our knowledge by means of the new scientific method pioneered by Sir Francis Bacon.

Five years later, the dispute had hopped across the English Channel. Sir William Temple, a statesman and hugely popular writer, wrote an essay in which he argued against progress in no uncertain terms.[15] Temple was what we might today call a science denier, questioning that the Earth revolves around the sun and that the heart pumps blood through our veins and arteries.[16] Embarrassingly for Temple, some of the examples of great ancient works he used to make his point turned out to be far more modern than he supposed, and one was an outright forgery.[17]

When Temple died, his former personal secretary, the young Jonathan Swift, took up the cause in 1704 by publishing an odd allegory in which ancient and modern books engage in a physical battle.[18] In the essay, "The Battle of the Books," Swift ridicules the moderns for overvaluing their own worth, for getting wrapped up in venomous squabbles, and for failing to recognize their indebtedness to the ancients.

"The Battle of the Books" was well received by the traditionalists, but victory was fleeting.[19] The modern idea of progress began to take root, bringing changes broad and deep.

But there was still no progress for tools.

The Progress of Things

A jump rope is just a rope. You have to make the jump thing happen.

—MITCH HEDBERG

Anne Robert Jacques Turgot is credited with formalizing the idea of progress in an essay he wrote in 1750 at the age of twenty-three. It's a beautiful essay, but a modern reader goes through it waiting for him to mention progress in the first place we look for it these days: technology.

After talking about progress in philosophy, politics, the conduct of nations, and more, he eventually does get to tech, citing advances such as the invention of paper, glass, windmills, clocks, eyeglasses, and the compass.[20] But he doesn't see progress in the improvement in technology itself or in how those improvements made our lives better. Rather, progress in technology—or "the mechanical arts," as he calls it—has to do with the knowledge we gained from those advances. For example, if a clockmaker discovered a new alloy for making a gear, the progress was not in the improved clock but rather in the metallurgical knowledge the clockmaker uncovered. In fact, the only invention that Turgot mentions for what it actually did for us is the printing press, but that's because its direct effect was to improve knowledge: "At once the treasures of antiquity, rescued from the dust, pass into all hands, penetrate to every part of the world . . . and summon genius from the depths of its retreats."[21]

Tools were just too humble to count for much in the reckoning of how civilization has advanced, for tools were assumed to have no value in themselves. Whatever value they have comes from our projects. Without us, a jump rope isn't even a rope. It's just a length of twisted fiber lying on the floor.

Tools gained more significance in the nineteenth century as big new technologies made changes with such broad and significant implications that we began to be willing to see progress in the tools themselves: the steam engine, trains, the telegraph, the early automobile.[22] These inventions were lauded—and in many cases, blamed—for large-scale changes in our lives. Yet, even so, tools were not important enough for anyone to bother writing a history of them.

This lack of interest in tools is evident in the series of wildly popular books begun in 1861 by Samuel Smiles about the great feats of engineering accomplished by Englishmen. Smiles tells ripping yarns of the Great Men who, through the force of their manly will, changed the course of the river Thames, drained the swamps of England, and engaged in other monumental struggles against the elemental forces of nature. But the tools these heroes used to accomplish their amazing feats are largely absent from these stories. Focusing on the tools would not only have missed the point, it would have demeaned the story. Tools are nothing. The courage and character of the Great Men who wield them are everything.

It seemed that to think that tools contributed anything to history would be like writing a history of Napoleon's military genius from the point of view of his saddle.

It took until the 1950s for a full history of tools to be written in English: the five-volume *History of Technology*. The academic journal *Technology and Culture* devoted an entire issue to it, hailing it as the very first history of technology, although there were some plausible predecessors.[23] Even so, this history did not do much more than list the small improvements that, over the centuries, made the wheelbarrow sturdier and easier to roll, the plow easier for oxen to pull through the land, and timepieces smaller and more accurate.[24] Histories like these are essentially a set of verbose time lines for each invention.

So, even once we gave our tools their due, we arranged their histories into simple lines with ticks. It would take computers to make those lines obsolete.

Engines of Generativity

Smiles focused on the steam engine as he did on no other technology, for it provides power "capable of being applied alike to the turning of mills, the raising of water, the rowing of ships, the driving of wheel-carriages, and the performance of labour in its severest forms."[25] That is, the steam engine is an *engine*: it drives other things. What things? Whatever can make use of the back-and-forth of a piston.

Waterwheels were engines that put circular motion to work grinding flour or sawing logs. Windmills, too. But these earlier engines had to be planted next to their energy sources. A steam engine you could put anywhere—including at the front of a moving train—and bring the energy source to it. This made possibilities real that in the past were mere dreams; Smiles thought Roger Bacon must have had steam engines in mind when, in the thirteenth century, he fantasized about chariots and sea ships being moved "with incalculable force, without any beast drawing them."[26]

What excited Smiles about steam engines is at the heart of the significance of computers, too. Both technologies are engines, and engines are a special sort of tool.

Typical tools exist in order to modify the world in some specific way so that we can achieve a particular goal. A saw is a tool because it cuts wood so we can build things. The spice shelf is a tool because it lets us organize our spices so we can find them. The Wenger 16999 Swiss Army knife is a tool with eighty-seven purposes in mind. Tools are integral to our traditional strategy of anticipating and preparing.

So if a can opener is for opening cans, and the steam engine is for doing work that can make use of a rod moving back and forth, what is a computer for?

Let's see. A computer is a tool for simulating the path of a space probe on its way to Pluto. A computer is a tool for calculating how much butter you need to make mashed potatoes for eight adults and five children. It's a tool for setting an alarm to remind you to cancel a trial subscription before it automatically starts billing you. It's a tool for drawing swirling fractal designs to amaze your friends when they're high. A computer does not have *a* purpose or eighty-seven purposes. It has whatever purpose one of us programs into it.

That makes computers special in our history. We can't bring much more to a rope beyond jump, pull, tie, and snap. Steam engines were initially limited to providing back-and-forth physical power for physical tasks. Computers, however, can do whatever can be done by representing the world as bits. This has caused the straight line of progress to sprout exponential curves. And if computers bent the line of progress upward in field after field, connecting those computers to one another is twisting it into knots.

Progress in the Wild

In *The Future of Ideas*, Lawrence Lessig tells of a piece of plastic invented in 1921 that a user could attach to a phone's mouthpiece to dampen room noise. Hush-a-Phone's only mistake was not having been invented by the phone company. It took a Supreme Court decision in 1956 to give customers permission to attach things not made by AT&T to their phones.[27] Before that, even something as slightly innovative as a nonblack phone, much less one in the shape of a sneaker or Fred Flintstone, was out of bounds, unless, of course, the phone company itself produced it. Innovation at the pace of the Supreme Court is not what we're looking for these days.[28]

This is closer to what we want:

As you might recall from chapter 3, GitHub manages the contributions made by teams of developers working simultaneously and independently—twenty-eight million developers, eighty-five million projects. Developers can reuse portions of other people's code or even "fork" their own version of other people's projects posted on the site. What people make out of other people's work can then become available to still others to fork, mod, and reuse.

The relationships among pieces of code can get complicated quickly, so GitHub provides a button that draws a map of the branches representing the use and reuse of a project's code. That's fine when a project's code is reused a few times, but when it comes to something like Google's TensorFlow machine learning software that was modded over twenty-four thousand times in 2017, GitHub gives up on diagramming it. As forks get forked and snippets get resnipped, the map would look like a jungle of bushes and vines so dense that to characterize its shape, we'd be driven to use words like *jungle, bushes, vines,* and, perhaps, *hairball.*

That shapeless shape is the new shape of progress—which is to say, of the future.

The difference between progress's old, sloping line and its new shape is the difference between incrementally improving a clock by coming up with a new way to fasten a balance wheel, and smashing the mechanism, throwing it into the air, and never knowing all the different ways the scattered parts have been picked up and reused . . . except in the digital world, you don't have to smash the clock to enable its pieces to be reused by someone for some purpose you never envisioned. After all, the internet is in the business of disrupting intentions.

If we were to absolutely insist on drawing an upward-sloping line of progress for the internet itself, many of the biggest tick marks would be for what was given away: the collections of ideas and images; the libraries of code to be reused freely; the application programming interfaces (APIs) that make services and data available; the standards and protocols that let all those pieces play well together.

Our traditional tools have had purposes that anticipate needs, from our prehistoric ancestors making their arrow tips, to the steam engine's repetitive thrusts. The perpetually startling fact of the internet, its most distinctive characteristic, is not its openness to every purpose, for disconnected computers are open in the same way. Rather, it's the interoperability it enables among everyone privileged with a connection to it. In effect, on the internet, just about anything can become—with varying degrees of difficulty—a general-purpose engine: a tool that enables other tools to be built. For example, even the very earliest web browsers had a "View Source" button to show you the HTML code that produces the formatted page users interact with, turning every web page into a learning experience for the curious and a source of reusable code. Overall, the internet is *generative* to a degree we have until now only experienced with language.

Generativity is the term Jonathan Zittrain uses in his book *The Future of the Internet, and How to Stop It* to express how easily we can use a tool for our own purposes, despite what it may have been designed for.[29] The tiny computer in your digital watch is not very generative because it's dedicated to a single set of tasks: show the time of day, work as a stopwatch, buzz you awake, and so on. The computer in your smartwatch is at least somewhat generative because it lets developers—perhaps even an open community of developers—create apps for it that the original designers did not anticipate. Your laptop is highly generative because it provides a wide range of powerful capabilities that can be put to use by anyone with the skills. At the system level, open APIs, open standards and protocols, open libraries of code, and open-licensed content are all generative. Generative of what? We can't know. That's what makes them generative.

While *interoperability* refers to the degree to which elements from different systems can work together, generativity is the ability of a tool or system to be used in unanticipated ways. Interoperable systems are generative. Interoperable systems that connect generative systems are especially generative, creative, and unpredictable. Generativity is the degree to which interoperability enables unanticipation.

Generativity on its own does a great job screwing up the simple, clear lines of progress, for every tick mark that represents a new generative tool earned its place by enabling untold and unanticipated uses to spray from it like water bursting through a hole in a high-pressure hose.

This is the environment we've been living in since big computers became essential tools for business, and even more so since the personal computer became a standard appliance. Generativity has been supercharged by the constant availability of the ever-interoperable internet. Even if we don't engage in this environment as coders or remixers, we benefit from it and we're aware of it. Even if we're curmudgeons who refuse to use that newfangled Internament or are principled abstainers on the grounds that the net is destroying privacy and is taking civilization down with it, we nevertheless hear the electric crackle as pieces meet other pieces and give rise to new things.

For those of us for whom the internet is our *where* for much of the day, we feel this in what we take for granted. We expect to be able to comment and to post links. We expect to be able to copy, paste, and reuse. We expect to be surprised. We expect to be confronted with more than we could ever manage. We expect to be able to share with others what we have found. We expect to find ways to make some sense of what we found online or off, settling or unsettling its meaning. We expect that others will put work done by others to surprising uses. We expect to be able to recontextualize what we have found, for the enlightenment or amusement of strangers. We expect, overall, this new environment to enable reuse, plasticity, reframing, and sharing at levels never before experienced in our species' long tool-using history. And we expect to do all this with the phone in our pocket.

———————

Our newly interoperable, generative present is undoing our traditional idea of progress.

Traditional progress assumes one thing leads to another: clocks that were pendulum based get windup springs so they can keep time on tilting surfaces such as wrists and the decks of ships. *Generativity* assumes that one thing leads to an uncountable and unpredictable set of anothers: the GitHub platform gives rise to unmappable interrelationships among its projects; game modding puts gangsters in tutus and turns a first-person shooter into a physics simulator.

Traditional progress assumes there are tick marks, and that each will be improved by the next invention that warrants one. Tick marks are thus like stepping-stones leading up a grassy hill. *Generativity* certainly understands that some inventions are more tick-mark-worthy than others, and that there are chains of inventions that build on predecessors; developers sometimes call those tick marks "version numbers." But overall the generative future does not much feel like a sequence of stepping-stones. The most important tick marks are the generative ones that lead in thousands of other directions.

Traditional progress is a line drawn between tick marks. *Generativity* understands that straight lines are in denial.

Traditional progress assumes a forward thrust: the upward sloping line is going to keep on going. In the realm of technology, which is where these days we generally are most confident that progress is going to continue, this is due at least in part to the fact that, short of an apocalypse, technological advances are irreversible, as Braden R. Allenby and Daniel Sarewitz point out in *The Techno-Human Condition*: the world's second smartphone built on the world's first one, and we won't forget what we now know about them.[30] *Generativity* shares that optimism, but not because there is some logical and inevitable path for technological items to follow. The historian of science Thomas Kuhn said scientific progress should be seen, like evolution, as "a process driven from behind, not pulled from ahead."[31] What drives generative progress is not a final destination dragging us along an inevitable uphill path but rather the lowering of the barriers to invention—by interoperability, generativity, and an open network of collaborators—so that human ingenuity can be applied to needs, desires, and whims that otherwise would have gone unnoticed and unaddressed.

Traditional progress has been hard. If I say that *generativity* makes it easy, I don't mean that we don't need geniuses devoting years of their lives to breakthroughs that make life better for all of us or that redo our core scientific understanding of how the universe works. Progress still benefits from the "Great Men" of yore, except without the gender bigotry. When progress is so hard, the tick marks are hard-won and spaced out. But the generativity of the networked world has made it so much easier to collaborate with colleagues or strangers, to collaborate iteratively, to collaborate at scale. It has made today's advances available to billions of people to be put to new uses tomorrow. Where once there were lonely geniuses standing on the shoulders of giants all looking up and to the right, now there are networks of people alive with ideas keeping one another up late at night.

The result is that the inventor rolling the boulder up the hill of progress is no longer our sole paradigm of progress. Much innovation (but by no means all) is now incredibly easy, and if the results are not worth the flick of our finger across our phone's screen, so what? With the barriers down, inventing has become fun, even an idle pastime.

Finally, *traditional progress* has felt like a story because that's what we wanted it to be. "You see, the first mechanical clocks had no faces and would toll the time to let monks know when to pray, but then . . . ," and so on until we get to reprogrammable, networked digital watches. But such stories are told by those gazing back from atop the slope. What looks like a path connecting two points on the old time line was actually a storm cloud of trials, errors, frustrations, near misses, and fruitful mistakes. Further, tick marks are often part of their own intersecting time line: the development of pendulum-driven clocks is an important tick mark in the history of timepieces, but pendulums are not just parts of old clocks. They were used to draw beautiful shapes in sand that proved that the Earth rotates on its axis. The invariance of their swing led to an exploration of harmonic motion important to our understanding of the movement of the planets and the behavior of ions.[32] The pendulum makes a cameo in the story of the watch, but it is the star of its own movie. Our insistence on seeing progress as a line hides our world's aversion to straight lines.

Why have we so insisted on turning complex histories into simple stories? Marshall McLuhan was right: the medium is the message. We shrank our ideas to fit on pages sewn in a sequence that we then glued between cardboard stops. Books are good at telling stories and bad at guiding us through knowledge that bursts out in every conceivable direction, as all knowledge does when we let it.

But now the medium of our daily experience—the internet—has the capacity, the connections, and the engine needed to express the richly chaotic nature of the world. This comes at the price of the comforting illusion of comprehension, as artificial intelligence has been teaching us. Indeed, when it comes to AI, the stages of innovation now sometimes seem to mirror the stages of grief: denial, anger, bargaining, depression, and acceptance. Before long, AI will be the fully accepted norm. In fact, it already is for many of the services we already rely on.

Our acceptance of machine learning is likely to shape our idea of progress as much as computers themselves did. In some domains we may, for good reason, decide to require AI to produce conclusions only through processes that we can understand, much as Samuel Butler's 1872 novel *Erewhon* prophesied that we would stop the development of new machines for fear that they would supplant us.[33] But in most domains we are likely to continue to embrace machines that make recommendations based on data and relationships that surpass our understanding.

The line of progress is not an arrow pointing up a hill. It looks much more like the densely branched maps of machine learning's model of the world. Those models may be impenetrable to our will to understand, but they are nevertheless enabling us to see that the world, its people, its things, and its history are like those models but ever so much more so.

The Shape of Surprise

Bob: I can can I I everything else.
Alice: Balls have zero to me to me to me to me to me to me
to me to me to.

These are two Facebook bots talking to one another in a language they invented. They started out with English, but as they negotiated with one another in what's known as a "generative adversarial network," they invented their own pidgin English.[34] Or recall the two AlphaGo programs we encountered in this book's introduction that played each other and came up with what seemed like nonhuman strategies. In another case, Antonio Torralba, a computer science professor at MIT, was seeing whether he could train a machine learning system to differentiate photos of residential bedrooms from those of motel rooms without telling the system what to look for.

When he examined how the system was making the distinction, he found to his amazement that it had taught itself to identify wall sconces, and was using their presence as a strong indicator of a motel room.[35] It's a little bit like a machine learning system that's designed to distinguish human voices from traffic noise beginning to understand what the humans are saying.

Tick marks on a time line don't seem to do justice to this sort of autonomous generativity. These machines don't necessarily proceed step by step. The mass of deeply related data points can give rise to unexpected, emergent phenomena, the way dead-simple starting configurations of John Conway's Game of Life can result in blocky creatures that grow wings and fly off the grid.

When a machine learning system goes not from A to B but from A to G or perhaps from A to mauve, we have tick marks but no lines. We have advances but no story.

We are already familiar with this type of lineless movement. On the net, a click can take us to a subworld we did not anticipate and that may be related in ways we do not understand. We've built a world together in which anything can be connected in any way that one of us imagines. We do this online, and we are doing it now with connections that machines on their own make among the real-world data we provide them. The densely linked structure of the net seems to be reflected in the picture of the world machine learning is constructing from the data we feed it.

———————

The idea of progress was first applied to knowledge and our moral nature. In both of those domains, there is a perfect end to which we can aspire. Our knowledge can edge toward complete and error-free understanding. Our souls and behavior can move closer to their divine purpose. When we began to apply progress to our tools and technology, it too could be seen as advancing toward a perfect end: the train tracks stretch across the nation, and the train engines run faster, with fewer breakdowns, and require less fuel. Clocks keep better time, work on rocking ships, and then on rocket ships.

The pull of that perfect endpoint made sense of progress. It still does. Each version number of a product should make it better or cheaper, and occasionally both. That's old-school progress. And it's powerful enough to get Apple fanboys to line up for days waiting for the latest iProduct.

But if tech progress suddenly meant only that we get upgrades to our products, we would feel that we were in fact in an age of decline. We instead now measure technological progress not by its movement closer to perfection but by its generativity, its left turns, its disruption of expectations. As I write, virtual reality systems are making rapid and traditional-style progress in their quality—screen resolution, sound, weight, ease of set up—and price. But quality and price now seem simply like rather boring inhibitions we have to overcome in order to unleash the imagination of creators who will do things with VR that will startle us. Even before most of us have played a VR game, we cannot wait to see how VR will be deployed as a platform for everything from therapy sessions to interactive storytelling to new ways to engage socially. VR holds promise as a generative tick mark from which will emanate lines that lead to ideas in expected domains and to domains we never ever expected we'd be strapping on silly-looking goggles to experience.

What drives this type of progress does not compel it to move in a particular direction. There is no perfection pulling it forward. Interoperability isn't directional. It can't be, for we are not the animators of the cold metal of the world, bending it to our will. Our relationship to technology is far more complex than that. Our will—our being—has been shaped from its beginnings by what the world offers us. We and our things work each other out in mutual play. That we will do so is inevitable. How we do so in an interoperable world is unpredictable.[36]

Generative progress leaves lines that sprout, rush forward, twist back, abruptly stop, and then perhaps suddenly start again sprouting new branches with their own convolutions. Generativity turns what had been laborious into child's play, sometimes literally. There is no Newtonian force driving this. Often even looking backward we cannot see even a trace of inevitability. The motive force of this new type of progress may be commercial or social, but more often is—perhaps simultaneously—someone feeling in her heart that playing with some thing or system will reveal more of what it is, what she is, what we are, and what we could be.

We have a word for the shape formed when movement rapidly emanates from a single point in myriad directions. It's not an inclined line.

It's an explosion.

Coda: What We Learn from Things

I declare the global social space we are building to be natu-rally independent of the tyrannies you seek to impose on us. You have no moral right to rule us nor do you possess any methods of enforcement we have true reason to fear.

When John Perry Barlow wrote these words in his "Declaration of the Independence of Cyberspace" in 1996, they captured the sense many of us early enthusiasts had that not only would the World Wide Web give us a second chance at creating the era of peace, love, and understanding we'd tried for in the 1960s, but that this new world would arrive inevitably.

We may have been wrong about the opportunity, but we were definitely wrong about the inevitability of the outcome.

While more of the transformation occurred than we often acknowledge, and more of that transformation has been positive than we allow ourselves to believe, there's no denying that the net hasn't worked out the way we'd thought. There are many reasons why my cohort went so wrong about it. We vastly underestimated the tenacity and power of the existing institutions. We didn't foresee the centralization of online power. While the open web had connected people to pages, we didn't anticipate commercial entities being the ones that connect people to people. Perhaps most humiliating for me is the extent to which my vision was blurred by my privileged position as a middle-class, Western, white man. You mean not everyone would have the leisure time to browse, or the freedom and confidence to blog their views? Shocking—or at least an inconvenient truth. And those in more vulnerable positions might find their comments overrun by racist, sexist threats? That was worse than shocking, and remains appalling.

The sense of inevitability with which the web's early cohort, including me, greeted its supposed triumph is harder to understand. It seems to be a classic case of falling for technodeterminism, but I was aware of that trap. So why did I, at least, seem to walk straight into it?

Technodeterminism is the belief that technology causes changes in a culture and society. How wide and deep those changes are, and how inevitable they are, determines just how much of a technodeterminist you are. For example, in 1962 the historian Lynn White Jr. wrote, "Few inventions have been so simple as the stirrup, but have had so catalytic an influence on history."[37] By putting the full thrust of a horse behind a lance, stirrups changed warfare, which then changed the social structure required to support horse-borne soldiers, eventually resulting in feudalism.[38] In the case of the internet, technodeterminists say things like, "The internet will transform politics! The internet will make us free!"

Technodeterminism has fallen so far into disrepute that just about the only people who seem to be technodeterminists are those who think the internet is a threat to civilization. When Nicholas Carr says that using the internet damages our ability to engage in long-form thought, he is being a technodeterminist.[39] When Sherry Turkle says that using mobile phones is turning our children into narcissists, she is being a technodeterminist.[40] Perhaps correctly.

It took me an embarrassingly long time to realize the source of my assumption of the inevitability of the net's triumph. It wasn't technology that was the driver but rather my idealistic conviction that given an opportunity, people would rush to satisfy their human yearning to connect, to create, to speak in their own voices about what matters to them. Give us the means to do those things, and we will not let anything stop us. The determinacy I sensed was coming not from the tech but from our deep human need to connect and to create.

But that is too simple an answer. If technodeterminism attributes too much power over us to our tools, attributing all of tech's effect to our humanity undervalues the role of tools in shaping us.

Around the same time that my cohort was initially besotted with the internet, a Scottish philosopher named Andy Clark was coming up with an insight that helps explain how technology affects us: we think out in the world with tools.

Clark means this quite literally. Take the whiteboard away from the physicist and she can no longer do the math that is her work. Take the graph paper away from the architect and she can no longer think about exactly where to place the stairs, and probably won't come up with the idea of moving the closet to the left so the stairway can take an extra turn.

As soon as I read the idea, I felt as if I had known it all along—the sign of a powerful idea. Nor am I alone in this: Clark's article on the topic is the most cited philosophy paper of the 1990s.[41]

Clark's idea seems novel because in the West we've been brought up to think that our minds are radically separate from our bodies. Our bodies are physical objects, subject to the same physical laws as the clothes they wear and the ground they tread. But our minds escape those laws, at least according to thousands of years of Western tradition. Our minds are immaterial, and, as souls, are possibly eternal.

There is beauty to that vision, but also terrible problems with it. Once you've decided the physical and mental realms are separate, you have to go through philosophical contortions to explain how the two can in fact affect each other. Morally, you may well end up denigrating the body not only as a mere vessel but as the source of desires that degrade our minds.

Clark instead asks us to consider how we actually think. We figure out seating charts by shuffling name cards on a diagram of the tables. We figure out what we think about a topic by using an outliner—or PowerPoint—that lets us see how our ideas flow and fit together. We count coins by making physical stacks of them. We confirm the existence of the Higgs boson by building a particle collider 16.8 miles long. We know more than Socrates did because, despite his objections, we became literate and wrote down what we learned.[42] We think not just with our heads but also with our hands and the tools they hold.

In fact, all of our experience exists in our engagement in the world outside our heads; knowledge is just a special case of this.

Walking by the water's edge, we see a flat rock and heft it. The stone suggests a project. We jiggle it slightly, our hand assessing its suitability. But for this project to have presented itself to us, we need more than stones and ponds. We need to have learned the nature of water's ever-changing surface by having had to drink quickly from our cupped hands. Only then could our older cousin's skipping of a rock on a lake make us laugh with the discovery of water's hard top. We need fingers that can find the stone's thinner edge that now shows itself as its front. We need a moment free of chores and countdown timers, and access to water that isn't barricaded by wire fencing. We need everything to be ready for the plink of a stone marking with circles where it forgot to sink.

The whole world is in this experience of our body's engagement with a flat rock. We learn about ourselves by playing with things. We learn how the world works by playing with things.

That is why technodeterminism is too simple to accept or to refute. We are not an effect of things, and things are not simply caused by us. Our purposes are shaped by what the things of the world allow, and those purposes reveal things in their relevant facets: the smoothness of the stone, the resistance of the water's surface.[43]

If we think out in the world with tools, and if our use of those tools shows us what sort of place the world is, and if our new tools are substantially different from the old ones, then perhaps we are beginning to understand our world differently.

Perhaps very differently. We can disassemble a car engine to see how it works, and while no single person understands everything about the Large Hadron Collider, we can inquire about any aspect of it and expect to be able to find the answer. But not always with machine learning. Machine learning works, yet we cannot always interrogate it about why it works.

Machine learning thereby undoes a founding idea of Western civilization: The Agreement that the human mind is uniquely attuned to the truth of the universe. For the ancient Hebrews, this was expressed by God's making us in His image, not physically but in giving us minds that within our mortal limits can understand and appreciate His creation. For the ancient Greeks, the *Logos* was both the beautiful order of the universe and the rationality by which we mortals can apprehend that order. The Agreement has meant that our attempts to understand how things happen are not futile. It has meant that we belong in this universe. It has meant that we are special in this universe.

The fact that a new technology is leading us to recognize that our ancient agreement is broken is not itself technodeterminist, any more than saying the flat stone reveals the pond as having a hidden surface is technodeterminist. We think out in the world with things in our hands. We experience out in the world with things in our hands. Each revelation is mutual. Each revelation is of the whole.

Now we have a new tool in our hands.

Chapter Seven

Make. More. Meaning.

Our success with the internet and machine learning is changing our minds about how things happen.

As our tools head toward having the power to model dust in all its particularity, we are more willingly accepting the overwhelming complexity of our world.

We are learning this first through our engaged hands. Our heads are lagging, as is to be expected.

We are in transition. We are confused.

Good.

———————

Yes, it's odd for a book to have a coda for every chapter, an essay different in style of writing and thought. That oddness is intentional. The codas are there to signal that this book does not intend to encapsulate its topics but to open them up. How could it be otherwise when the Twitter version of this book's imperative is "Make. More. Future."?

A new paradigm for something as fundamental as how things happen affects not just business, government, education, and the other large-scale domains into which we traditionally divide our world. It pervades our understanding of everything.

This last chapter—a coda of codas—attempts to trace some of the ways our embrace of complexity, even as it overwhelms our understanding, is enabling us to discover more of what our under-standing aims at: a sense of meaning.

Explanations

My friend Timo Hannay was forty-six when he gave in to his wife's counsel and went for his first physical exam in about ten years. He was told that all his systems were in good shape, although he could stand to lose a little weight.

Three months later, he woke up on a Saturday morning feeling ill enough that his wife took him to the Royal Free Hospital in north London. "I ended up spending a week there," he told me in an email. "They gave me an angiogram (thus diagnosing it formally as a myo-cardial infarction), inserted three stents and put me on a cocktail of drugs (anti-platelets, beta-blockers and statins), some of which I'll continue to take for life." He's been following the regimen of meds, exercise, and diet, and feels healthier than he has in years.

There's nothing extraordinary about this story. From the checkup through the postoperative treatment, Timo received excellent health care. All has gone as well as he and his medical team hoped. But we should be at least curious about the everyday fact that while Timo's initial checkup did not lead to a *prediction* of a heart attack, once the event occurred, the same evidence was read backward as an *explanation* of that event.

Pierre-Simon Laplace would have been pleased. His omniscient demon that can predict everything that will happen based on its complete knowledge about any one moment can just as easily "post-dict" everything that has happened. For the demon, explanations are exactly the same as predictions, except the predictions look for-ward and the explanations look backward.

We humans, of course, don't know now what we will know later, so predictions and explanations are different for us.[1] In Timo's case, the most important difference between what the physicians knew before and after his heart attack was that a heart attack had occurred. Once we know that, we can see the path to the attack. We can reconstruct it.

Or at least we think we can. It should concern us that when we look backward, we find reasons for just about everything. The stock market fell yesterday because of fears about the Middle East. Our town voted down the school tax increase because people think the town government is fiscally irresponsible. The car ahead of us sat through the entire green light because the driver was probably texting. If something happens, we envision the path that led up to it. We are a species that explains things even when we're just making it up.

We can do this because we've decided that usually an explanation need only point to the *sine qua non* cause, or the "but for *x*" cause, as in, "But for the want of a nail, a kingdom was lost"—or, more likely for the rest of us, "But for that nail, I wouldn't have gotten a flat tire."

"We ran over a nail" is a fine explanation of a flat tire, especially if the nail is still sticking in the tire, but in truth there are many other *but for*s that apply to that situation: but for our being late and having to take the Gardner Street shortcut, where the nail was; but for tires being made out of a material softer than iron; but for pointy objects being able to penetrate materials as stiff as tires; but for our having been born after pneumatic tires were invented; but for rust-based extraterrestrials not using space magnets to pull all iron objects off the surface of the earth . . . and so on until we, demon-like, are done listing everything that had to happen and not happen for us to find ourselves pulled over on a dark road thumbing through a manual to find out where we're supposed to attach the car jack.

The sine qua non form of explanation has such deep roots in our thinking in part because of the social role of explanations. Outside of scientific research, we generally want explanations for events that vary from our expectations: Why did we get a flat? Why did I get a stomachache? Why did the guy in the car ahead of me sit through an entire green light even though I honked? For each of these special cases, we find the "but for *x*" explanation that points to what was unique in each case: the exceptional, differentiating fact.

Sine qua nons work well when the exceptional case is a problem: the nail in the tire is the explanation because the nail is the thing we can change that will fix the problem. We can't go back in time and take a different road or change the relative hardness of rubber and metal. But we can take the nail out of the tire. Explanations are tools, as we discussed back in chapter 2. They are not a picture of how the world works; more often, they are a picture of how the world went wrong. By isolating one factor, they enable us to address problems—pull the nail out of the tire, put stents into Timo—which is no small thing, but the world is not a single-cause sort of place. In focusing on what's unusual, explanations can mask the usual in all its enormous richness and complexity.

Then there's the unsettling truth that machine learning is putting before our reluctant eyes: in some instances, there may be no dominant unusual fact that can serve as a useful explanation. A machine learning diagnostic system's conclusion that there is a 73 percent chance that Aunt Ida will have a heart attack within the next five years might be based on a particular constellation of variables. Changing any of those variables may only minutely affect the percentage probability. There may be no dominant "but for x" in this case.

This can make machine learning "explanations" more like how we think about our own lives when we pause to marvel—in joy or regret—at how we got wherever we are at the moment. All the *ifs*, too many to count! If Dad hadn't been so supportive, or so angry. If you hadn't mistakenly signed up for that college course that changed your life. If you had looked right instead of left when stepping off that curb. If you hadn't walked into that one bar of all the gin joints in all the towns in all the world. We got to here—wherever we are—because of countless things that happened and a larger number of things that did not. We got here because of everything.

In moments like that, we remember what explanations hide from us.

Levers without Explanations

In 2008 the editor of *Wired* magazine, Chris Anderson, angered many scientists by declaring the "end of theory."[2] The anger came in part from the post's subtitle, which declared the scientific method to be "obsolete," a claim not made or discussed in the article itself. Apparently even editors of magazines don't get to write the headlines for their stories.

Anderson in fact maintained that models are always simplifications and pointed to areas where we've succeeded without them: Google can translate one language to another based only on statistical correlations among word-usage patterns, geneticists can find correlations between genes and biological effects without having a hypothesis about why the correlations hold, and so on.

Massimo Pigliucci, a philosophy professor, summarized many scientists' objections in a report published for molecular biologists: "[I]f we stop looking for models and hypotheses, are we still really doing science? Science . . . is not about finding patterns—although that is certainly part of the process—it is about finding explanations for those patterns."[3]

Not all scientists agreed. A 2009 book of essays by scientists argued for using Big Data analysis to find patterns, titling the approach "the Fourth Paradigm," a phrase coined by Jim Gray, a Microsoft researcher who had disappeared at sea two years before.[4] Many but not all of the contributors assumed those patterns would yield theories and explanations, but now, as claims about the power of Big Data have morphed into claims about inexplicable deep learning, Anderson's claim is again being debated.

In one particular field, though, the practice of model-free explanations is outrunning that debate. When it comes to understanding human motivation—how we decide what to make happen—we are getting accustomed to the notion that much of what we do may not have, and does not need, an explanation.

In 2008, the highly acclaimed academics Richard Thaler and Cass Sunstein opened their best seller, *Nudge*, with a hypothetical example of a school system that discovers that arbitrary changes in the placement of food items on the cafeteria counter can dramatically change the choices students make.[5] "[S]mall and apparently insignificant details can have major impacts on people's behavior," the book concludes[6]—a lesson we learned in the introduction of this book when we looked at A/B testing. Since all design decisions affect our behavior—"there is no such thing as a 'neutral' design"— *Nudge* argues we should engineer systems to nudge people toward the behavior we want.[7]

This is a powerful idea that is being widely deployed by businesses and governments—Sunstein worked in the Obama White House— because we've gotten better at it. And we've gotten better at it because we've largely given up on trying to find explanations of how it works. But it is not the first time our culture has heard that there are surprising, and surprisingly effective, nonrational levers for changing behavior.

You can see the distance this idea has traveled by comparing *Nudge* to Vance Packard's 1957 *Hidden Persuaders*, a best seller that today is best remembered for its warnings about subliminal advertising: flashing an image of an ice cream bar onto a movie screen so briefly that it does not consciously register was said to increase ice cream sales at the concession stand. In truth, Packard's book spends less than two pages on the topic, most of it casting doubt on it.[8] Nowadays, other than the occasional crank who finds the word *sex* written in the nighttime stars over Simba's head in *The Lion King*, one does not hear much about subliminal advertising of this sort.[9]

Packard's real concern was the way advertisers were short-circuiting our decision-making processes through what was then called motivational research, or MR. MR assumed the Freudian model that said our unconscious mind is a cauldron of desires, fears, and memories suppressed by our higher levels of consciousness. By using coded words and images to appeal to those repressed urges, advertisers could stimulate powerful associations. For example, since smoking cigarettes is "really" a way of assuaging men's anxieties about their virility, ads should show manly men smoking as sexy ladies look on. Likewise, cars express aggression, and home freezers represent "security, warmth, and safety." Air conditioners are for people "yearning for a return to the security of the womb." Shaving "is a kind of daily castration." Those associations may sound outlandish now, but *Fortune* magazine in 1956 estimated that $1 billion—worth $9 billion today—spent on advertising in 1955 came from firms using MR to guide them.[10]

Both nudges and MR-based ads aim at influencing our choices without our knowing it, but the theories behind them are very different. *Nudge* is based on a well-supported modern theory of the brain: beneath the Reflective Brain is the Automatic System that we share with lizards . . . and, as Thaler and Sunstein playfully point out, also with puppies.[11] The Automatic System responds so quickly that it often leaps to the wrong conclusion. By appealing to it, advertisers can nudge us in ways that our Reflective Brain would not have agreed to. In contrast, MR is based on an out-of-favor psychological theory that assumes that even the nonrational parts of our minds are still understandable in terms of human desires, fears, anxieties, and the like. We can give a Freudian explanation of why men prefer razors with thick, meaty handles, but the explanation of why a nudge works—in the cases where an explanation is even offered—will be more like the explanation of why giraffes have long necks: What about our evolutionary history might have led to our being susceptible to being nudged in that direction? We have moved so far from explaining our behavior based on our rationality that we don't even point to our irrational psychology.

Theories, of course, still have value, but if there's a way to influence a shopper's behavior or to cure a genetic disease, we're not waiting for a theory before we give the lever a pull.

Unlevered

I'm just a bill. Yes I am only a bill. And I'm sitting here on Capitol Hill.

If those words have invoked a melody in your head that you will not be able to extricate until tomorrow afternoon, then it's highly likely you were either a child or had young children sometime between 1976 and 1983 when ABC's *Schoolhouse Rock!* aired its most famous educational music video.[12]

In the unlikely event you've never heard it, it's about how the levers of government work. Or, in its many parodies, how they don't work.[13] Even so, complaining that a machine doesn't work as well as it should accepts that it should be working like a machine. That has been our model.

The Occupy movement disagreed. A loose confederation of people who established communal camps at institutions they thought had too much power, Occupy sought to bring change but refused to pull on any of the known levers. It rejected the idea that it was a citizens' lobbying group. It didn't try to raise money or circulate petitions. It resisted even coming up with a list of the changes it wanted to bring about.

Occupy was about gravity, not levers.

Granted, Occupy was weird. And one might certainly argue that it failed. But that assumes a particular definition of success. Gravity—or "pull," as John Hagel, John Seely Brown, and Lang Davison call it—works differently from how levers do.[14]

The essence of a lever is that it has a direct effect on something. If it doesn't, it's a broken lever. Or possibly it's not attached to anything, in which case it's like a child's pretend steering wheel mounted on the dashboard of a real car. If Occupy thought that a bunch of young people hanging out in tents for several months was going to bring about legislative change, then Occupy was pretend politics. If the aim of Occupy was to directly bring about government reform or a more equitable society, it failed.

That's how it looks if we take Occupy as an attempt to pull on a lever. In fact, Occupy and many protest movements are like gravity in Einstein's sense: space-time is reshaped by objects with mass. The more people who are pulled into the gravity well, the greater the movement's mass. As its gravity grows, it starts to affect the environment more widely and more powerfully, sometimes at such a distance that people don't always know they are being pulled by it. If you now think about tax and budget proposals in terms of what they mean for the 1 percent, then Occupy has shaped your space-time with its one-percenter rhetoric.

Occupy's rejection of the lever-based theory of change is espoused not just by activists camping out in city squares but also by every marketing professional or individual with a Facebook or Twitter account. We now talk about social influencers shaping their environments. We measure our likes, our followers, and our upvotes as a type of mass that increases our gravity the more followers we attract.

Public relations agencies used to try to manage a client's brand by managing its communications. Now they are likely to talk about reaching the influencers by giving them something to talk about, free products, or cash. This is very unlike the MR approach that for decades assumed customers could be manipulated by putting words and images in front of them that would trigger their unconscious Freudian fears and desires. It is not even as direct as nudges that use evolutionary accidents of our brain to move us in the desired direction. It is instead about increasing the gravitational pull of the people who populate our online universe.

Even the functional elements of online tools frequently work gravitationally. For example, in a literal sense, a hashtag on Twitter is nothing but a label: a # followed by a word or a spaceless phrase that acts as a searchable ID for disconnected tweets on the same topic. But that misses what's significant about them: hashtags exert more influence the more often they're used. For example, the #MeToo hashtag took on mass in 2018, attracting more women (and some men) to attach their story to it, and more people of every gender to retweet it. It became a massive comet dense with stories, anger, pain, and commitment. Its pull was so strong that it reached beyond the internet and deep into culture, business, politics, and personal lives. The significance of Occupy is arguable; the significance of #MeToo is not.

Levers are for machines. Gravity is for worlds held together by interests, attention, ideas, words, and every other driver of connection.

Stories

Tweets scroll past at a pace that would dismay Laplace's demon. A news site that hasn't changed since we visited it ten minutes ago feels as if it's printed on yellowing paper. There's no point in pretending we're keeping up with every friend's post on Facebook and every colleague's latest job news on LinkedIn. News used to come in diurnal cycles, the paper thumping onto our archetypal porch each morning, and the nightly news showing up on our televisions at dinnertime. Now you can't step into the same network twice.

In his provocative book *Present Shock,* Douglas Rushkoff argues that the net is wiping out our sense of the future and the past.[15] As one piece of evidence for this "presentism," as he calls it, Rushkoff points to our impatience with stories. We don't have the attention span for anything but the quickest hit off of YouTube, and then it's time to carom to the next shiny online object.

Rushkoff's book talks about something we all feel, but there's a second phenomenon that points in the opposite direction: we love long narratives more than ever.[16] When people talk about the "new golden age of television," they almost always point first to series with scores of characters, and arcs that stretch over years: *Game of Thrones, The Sopranos, Breaking Bad.* We are in the age of hundred-hour stories, as Steven Johnson points out in *Everything Bad Is Good for You.*[17] He presents evidence that our television series have become far more complex over time, perhaps not coincidentally as the internet has come to prominence—far more complex than a Dickens novel, although with six hundred characters, *War and Peace* still sets a high water mark. Even beyond the blockbuster long narratives, storytelling is entrenching itself just about everywhere we look. Podcasts that tell stories are a rising cultural force, whether it's fiction (*Welcome to Night Vale, Fruit*), journalistic investigations (*Serial, S-Town*), personal stories (*The Moth Radio Hour*), or the storifying of ideas (*This American Life, Radiolab*). There are courses on storytelling and conferences about the future of storytelling, including one with exactly that name. Our story these days is all about storytelling.

How can we be simultaneously approaching Peak Storytelling and Peak Distraction?

————————

> Any ordinary person of two centuries ago could expect to die in the bed in which he had been born. He lived on a virtually changeless diet, eating from a bowl that would be passed on to his grandchildren.
>
> **—BERNARD STIEGLER, *TECHNICS AND TIME*, VOL. 2**[18]

> There are eight million stories in the naked city. This has been one of them.
>
> **—*NAKED CITY* (1958–1963)**

Stories make sense *as* a whole and *of* a whole: they unfold so that the end makes sense of the beginning. That's why the very first commandment sworn to by the members of the Detection Club founded in 1931 by Agatha Christie, Dorothy Sayers, and other legends of British mystery writing was, "The criminal must be someone mentioned in the early part of the story."[19] Imagine the outcry if at the end of *The Usual Suspects* Keyser Söze turned out to be a shop teacher who had not yet been mentioned in the movie. Stories, like strategies, generally work by providing a carefully limited set of possibilities and then narrowing them down to one. In a mystery, the possibilities are the suspects and their sneaky behavior; in a Jane Austen novel, the possibilities are the paths that are open to the hero, framed by the paths that, by convention and character, are not. Stories operate within closed worlds of possibility.

But now more than ever, we feel that we are in an open world. Our ever-growing global network creates new possibilities—and new possibilities for creating new possibilities—every day. The history we are creating together no longer feels much like a story, although we'll undoubtedly make one up when we're looking backward.

But the fact that we tell (or listen to) one-hundred-hour narratives and also sniff the air with our lizard tongues, ready to dart in a new direction, is not a contradiction that needs resolution. Because these long narratives occur within constantly connected publics, they have had to take on the lizard's ability to turn quickly. After all, it cannot be merely an accident that multiseason sagas have arisen at the same time that the "[SPOILER]" label has become a crucial piece of metadata. We need that tag because we now watch these shows together, even when we do not watch them at the same time or in the same place. Talking with friends and strangers about who will be the next person the creators will kill off or who the mysterious stranger will turn out to be helps us make sense of the sprawling plots, keeps us engaged, and gives us a sense of participation in the creation of the work.

This means, though, that with crowds anticipating every move, long narratives have to disrupt the expectations central to traditional stories. *Game of Thrones*—the books and television series—without fanfare killed off popular characters that viewers had assumed were following an arc to the end. The author, George R. R. Martin, has said that he feels a moral obligation not to reinforce the calming notion that some lives are protected in wars because they happen to be the protagonists. Literature should reflect the truth that our lives are equally precarious, and that war is a horrific waste of them. Readers and viewers may have taken to Martin's work not because of its moral stance but because never knowing which character might die keeps the long series surprising, but either way, it changes our notion of how a narrative works, as well as what we should expect from our own story.

So it is a mistake to see our constant distraction and our absorption in long-form stories as a contradiction. Rather, they are ends of the same pool of complexity and randomness. Distractions are at the shallow end; long-form storytelling is the deep end. Both recognize the overwhelming detail and arbitrariness of the waters we're in.

Both are affecting the narratives we tell ourselves about our own lives.

The assumption that we embark on careers has been in disrepute for at least a generation. The causes of this change are multiple: economic factors that tip businesses toward hiring temps and free-

lancers, a business landscape marked by disruption, the globalization of the workforce, the disintermediation of business functions,
the availability of platforms that match a global workforce to atom-
ized tasks, and more. Call it the gig economy, Free Agent Nation, or
"taskification," but careers no longer seem like a natural way to organize one's life and tell one's story.[20]

The alternative is not necessarily aimlessly wandering about, our
careers emulating Jack Kerouac's cross-country drives or the car-
oming of a silver ball in a pinball machine. A better paradigm might
be starting a family, the primordial generative activity. Much of its
joy—and worry—comes from watching each member step into Her-
aclitus's river. If our careers seem less like a discernible, narrow
path we're following and more like the interdependent movement
that happens when everything affects everything all at once, at least
we have positive models for understanding it. If the business we
launch seems less like a carefully crafted timepiece and more like
our child in its complex, interdependent generativity, that would not
be the worst imaginable way of reframing our understanding.

Stories are a crucial tool but an inadequate architecture for understanding the future. There's no harm in telling those stories to
ourselves. There's only harm in thinking that they are the whole or
highest truth.

Morality

Just as we saw in the coda to chapter 1 that the Kingdom of the Normal and the Kingdom of Accidents are changing their relationship,
so are the Land of Is and the Land of Ought.

The Land of Is, with its sinners, slouches, and villains, suffers in
comparison to the perfect Land of Ought, where the ruler is wise,
the citizenry is noble, and everybody does exactly what they should.
And they do so precisely and only because one ought to do what one
ought. No self-congratulation or luxuriating in a sense of moral
righteousness mars the purity of motives in the Land of Ought. So
when we mortals are wondering what is the morally right thing for

us to do—a question always present, if in the background—we look up to see what goes on in the Land of Ought. But because we are mere mortals, we don't always do what we see there—which is why, as we've seen, the arc of the moral universe is so long.

In the history of Western philosophy, the question of what goes on in the Land of Ought has often turned into an argument over principles. For example, in the Land of Ought, the citizens follow the principle "Thou shalt not steal." So should you steal an apple to save your dying grandmother? No, unless there's a higher principle that says, "Thou shalt sacrifice property rights to save lives." (Ought's wise ruler would undoubtedly express it more elegantly.)

This principled approach to moral philosophy is called *deontology* by the professionals. While it has several important competitors, the best known is *consequentialism* because it looks to the consequences of actions to determine their morality. A consequentialist would very likely feel morally OK about stealing the apple for Grandma, assuming that the theft's only negative effect is its negligible cost to the grocer.

These days, one particular type of consequentialism has come to dominate our moral thinking. Utilitarianism traces back to the early part of the nineteenth century when the philosopher Jeremy Bentham looked across the social stratification of English society and proclaimed that the pain and pleasure of an uneducated chimney sweep is as important as that of the finest snuff-sniffing, sherry-slurping lord. So, said Bentham, to determine if an act is moral, we should simply add up the pleasure and pain that would be felt by everyone affected, treating each person's pain and pleasure equally. Then we should do that which will cause the least aggregate pain or the most aggregate pleasure.

Utilitarianism for a long time felt like a betrayal of morality, for we had assumed that moral action is what you ought to do regardless of the pain or pleasure it brings; we need morality, we thought, precisely because doing what's right often entails self-sacrifice or pain. Utilitarianism removes everything from the Ought *except* its calculation of pain and pleasure. In looking solely to outcomes, it obviates much of the moral vocabulary about intentions that we have traditionally employed.

You can see this in the change in how we think about the Trolley Problem, first proposed in a 1967 philosophical article by Philippa Foot.[21] In the article, Foot explores a Catholic teaching called the Doctrine of Double Effect that says that it's permissible to do something otherwise morally wrong in order to support a higher moral principle, but only if the bad side effect is not your intent. To explore this, Foot asks us to imagine the now famous situation: You are a passerby who sees a trolley careening toward five people on its track. You can pull a lever to switch the trolley to a track that has only one person on it, or you can take no action, knowing that it will result in five deaths. Should you pull the lever?

If you say yes on utilitarian grounds, then Foot asks, why shouldn't a surgeon kill and carve up a healthy patient in order to harvest organs that would save five other patients? The utilitarian calculus is the same: five lives for one. But—and it's about to get tricky—the Doctrine of Double Effect says that it's wrong to kill someone as a *means* to save others, as when the five patients are saved *by means of* the organs harvested from the one. But the five on the track are saved by your diverting the trolley to the track where there just *happens to be* one unfortunate person. If you could somehow yank the single person off the track, you still would have saved the five. But there's no way to save the five patients except by killing the one healthy person; they are saved directly by that person's death. The distinction between these direct and indirect intentions is essential to the original Trolley Problem argument.

Yes, this now sounds not only confusing but trivial, but that's the point.[22] In the fifty years since Foot towed the Trolley Problem into view, our culture has rapidly migrated to utilitarianism as the default, so we spend less time looking up to the Land of Ought, where intentions count greatly, and more time assessing pure consequences. Intentions, blame, and guilt now feel like interior states and thus distinct from the consequences that need weighing. Principles aren't entirely gone from our moral conversations, but they can feel archaic

or worse: letting five people die to maintain the purity of your intentions can seem self-indulgent.

The decline of principle-based morality has been hastened by our
assigning moral decisions to AI systems. Because those systems are
not conscious, they don't themselves have intentions, and thus they
don't make distinctions between direct and indirect intents. The *operationalizing* of morality—turning it into programming code—is
affecting our idea of morality.

Consider Isaac Asimov's Three Laws of Robotics from a short
story he wrote in 1942. (That story was included in the 1950 book *I
Robot*, on which the 2004 movie was based.)

> *A robot may not injure a human being or, through inaction,
> allow a human being to come to harm.*
>
> *A robot must obey orders given it by human beings except
> where such orders would conflict with the First Law.*
>
> *A robot must protect its own existence as long as such pro-
> tection does not conflict with the First or Second Law.*

These operationalize moral principles by organizing them into a
hierarchy that enables the robot to know whether it should steal an
apple to save a human—yes, it should—without having to engage
in endless arguments about the contradictory mandates of moral
principles.

This approach skirts around the problems we humans have with
applying principles. For example, we all agree that killing is wrong,
but few of us believe that that rule is absolute. That's why we can't
come to agreement about the merits of capital punishment, abortion,
drone strikes, the use of lethal force against unarmed offenders,
steering a trolley into five people instead of one, or going back
in time to kill baby Hitler. Deciding these cases would require a
Laplace's demon that thoroughly understands human history, psychology, cultural values, personal histories, social norms, and the
particularities of each case. Even then we'd probably argue against

the demon the way Abraham argued with God to spare Sodom and Gomorrah.

So we can't expect our machines to be better than we are at applying moral principles to particular cases. We can only instruct them on what outputs should follow from particular inputs. That's what Asimov's Three Laws do.[23] For example, we're going to want our system of self-driving cars to lower the number of traffic fatalities compared to today's rates. If there's some unexpected event on a highway—a deer leaps the fence, lightning strikes the car ahead of us—rather than giving the autonomous vehicles principles they have to apply, we're going to instruct them to network with the other autonomous cars on the road to figure out the collective behaviors that would result in the fewest deaths. That's an engineering problem, not a moral one.

Behind the engineering design, there are of course values: we program autonomous cars to minimize fatalities because we value life. But the AI only has the instructions, not the values or principles. It's like training a junkyard dog to bark when strangers enter the yard: the dog may follow your instructions but is unlikely to know that behind them is your principled commitment to the sanctity of private property.

But here we hit a knotty problem. Operationalizing values means getting as specific and exact as computers require. Deciding on the application of values entails messy, inexact, and never-ending discussions. For example, we talked in the coda to chapter 2 about the need to rein in AI so that in attempting to achieve the consequentialist goals we've given it—for example, above all, save lives on the highway, then reduce environmental impacts—these systems don't override our moral principles, especially of fairness.[24] Good. We don't want AI to repeat or, worse, amplify historic inequities.

But how do we wrangle our values into the precision computers require? For example, if a machine learning system is going through job applications looking for people who should be interviewed, what percentage of women would count as fair? Fifty percent seems like a good starting point, but suppose the pool of women applicants is significantly lower than that because gender bias has minimized their presence in that field. Should we require 50 percent anyway? Should we start out at, say, 30 percent and commit to heading up to 50 percent over time? Perhaps we should start at, say, 70 percent to make up for the historical inequity. What's the right number? How do we decide?

And it quickly gets far more complex. Machine learning experts are still coming up with variations on fairness that are couched in the operational terms that computers understand. For example, "Equal Opportunity" fairness, as its originator Moritz Hardt calls it, says that it's not enough that the people a machine learning system recommends be granted loans (for example) represent the general demographic breakdown, or the breakdown of those who applied for a loan. If that's all that fairness requires, then you could stuff the acceptance pool with randomly chosen demographic members, including people the machine learning system thinks are terrible risks for loans. Instead, Hardt argues, you want to try to make sure that the same percentage of men and women who are likely to succeed at loans are given loans.[25] Others have suggested that this doesn't go far enough: fairness requires that the percentage of men and women who succeed *and* the percentage who were wrongly denied loans (wrongly because they would have paid them back) be the same for the genders. And from there the conversation gets *really* complex.

Those are just some of the types of fairness that machine learning experts are discussing. There are many more. In fact, one talk at a conference on fairness and machine learning was titled "21 Definitions of Fairness and Their Politics," although it was mischievously overstating the situation.[26]

Whatever particular flavor of fairness we decide is appropriate in this or that case, computers' need for precise instructions is forcing us to confront a truth we have generally been able to avoid: we humans are far more clear and certain about what is unfair than what is fair.

That sort of imbalance is far from unusual. The British philosopher J. L. Austin made the same sort of point when he argued against the usefulness of "reality" as a philosophical concept.[27] We use the word *real* mainly when we need to distinguish something from the many ways in which it can be unreal: a real car and not a toy, a counterfeit, a phantasm, a hallucination, a stage prop, a wish, and so many more. We have a large and quite clear vocabulary for the ways in which things can be unreal. But from this we should not conclude that there must be a clear and distinct way in which something can be real.

Similarly, there are many ways a situation can be unfair. We are quite good at spotting them. But that does not mean that the meaning of *fair* is anywhere near as clear. That's not to say that fairness is a useless concept. On the contrary. But it plays a different role from unfairness. When we declare something to be unfair, we are not merely stating a fact. We declare unfairness as a way to initiate the sense of outrage that generates solidarity—those who agree are your cohort—and action. On the other hand, we rarely yell, "That's fair!" Far more often, it's said with a shrug intended to end a discussion, not to open one.

AI is going to force us to make decisions about fairness at levels of precision that we previously could ignore or gloss over. It will take contentious political and judicial processes to resolve these issues. Operationalized fairness's demand for precision can make fairness look more like a deal than an ideal. Not that there's anything wrong with that.

But we may learn another lesson as well, one that further diminishes our impulse to consult the Land of Ought for moral guidance. In her 1982 book, *In a Different Voice,* Carol Gilligan argues that men tend to look for what is the principled thing to do, while women tend to do that which cares for the person in need; men's eyes look up to the Land of Ought, while women look into the eyes of the people affected. Gilligan of course knows she's generalizing, and it's entirely possible that the generalization holds less well than it did forty years ago. But the distinction is real and goes beyond gender.

The upward glance to moral principles turns away from the concrete particularities of a case, locating moral value in the principle those particularities get subsumed under. In a similar way, when utilitarians sum up the aggregate pleasure and pain an action will bring, they are locating moral goodness in that aggregate, not in the particularities of each case. Now, utilitarians would properly push back that the sum in fact reflects each person's pleasure or pain, but to do their calculations the utilitarians have to at least momentarily turn away from the individuals they're quantifying; one of the complaints against Robert McNamara's leadership of the Department of Defense during the Vietnam War was the use of "body counts" as a metric of success. So both deontologists and utilitarians honor the Ought as something above and beyond the individuals affected, albeit in different ways.

This might remind us of our traditional confidence in the universality of laws governing the physical universe and its many subdomains, and remind us as well of the difficulty of applying general laws to a contingent, interoperating, generative universe of spinning dust, some of which happens to have motives and loved ones. We may be learning that the particulars that generalities whisk off their shoulders like dandruff turn out to count for everything.

The most important recent movement in philosophical ethics accords with this as well. Virtue ethics notes the problems with deontological and utilitarian approaches and instead asks what Aristotle took to be the fundamental question of ethics: What does it mean to lead a good life? The answer does not lay out the principles to be followed or the calculus to be computed. Modern virtue ethics instead says that the good life is one in which we flourish. Flourishing by its nature is open ended. How you flourish depends on the particularities of who you are and which virtues—"excellences" in the ancient Greek sense—you cultivate. Flourishing is not an end state but a response to the unpredictable opportunities and obstacles that happen to face us. The fact that modern virtue ethics was initiated by a woman—Elizabeth Anscombe in a famous 1958 paper[28]—and that much of the most important work on it (especially on the ethics of care) has been done by women is not an accident.[29]

These movements away from principles and from a cold calculus of pleasure and pain brings morality more in line with the transformations we have seen under way in realm after realm: a turn from reducing complex phenomena to instances of general rules and laws, and toward acknowledging the particulars that make each case unique.

Machine learning systems are profoundly nonmoral. They are just machines, not Just machines. But the need to operationalize our morality for them is leading us ever further down the path away from the principle-based morality that governs the Land of Ought. This can lead, perhaps simultaneously, to two contradictory outcomes. If we outsource morality to AI unchecked, the vulnerable can be tyrannized by faceless statistical engines that literally do not hear their voices. We could also lazily cede control to AI in cases where fairness and flourishing would be better served by insisting that the decisions be left up to us. At the same time, our machines' ability to process individual cases according to models that account for more detail and particularity than the human brain can follow may shift our own model, encouraging us to attend more closely to the particular and personal details that make moral situations as unique and real as each inhabitant of the Land of Is.

Meaning

[T]he network failed to completely distill the essence of a dumbbell.

That's the conclusion reached by the Google computer scientists who fed images of dumbbells into a deep-learning system and then asked it to draw an image of what it thinks a dumbbell is.[30] As we noted in chapter 2, the system succeeded in putting together images showing dumbbells at different orientations, but many of the images had a weight lifter's detached arm eerily gripping the dumbbell. The results were greeted as an amusing failure.

But was it a failure? That depends on what "meaning" means. . . .

We have long tried to understand meanings with something akin to the sine qua non approach to explanation. Aristotle helped set us down this road by telling us that what a thing is—its essence—is the category it's in plus what distinguishes it from other items in that category. For example, we human beings are in the category of animals, but we're distinguished from other animals by our ability to reason. We are the rational animals.

For a couple of millennia, we found comfort in this idea of meaning: not only was there an order, but the principle of order was simple and consistent. For example, in the eighteenth century, Carl Linnaeus placed each animal, vegetable, or mineral in a category and placed each category in a hierarchy that looked like the Org Chart of Everything. Scientific genus-species names still reflect Linnaeus's Aristotelian-style classification.[31]

But in the late nineteenth century, a different idea began to emerge. The Swiss linguist Ferdinand de Saussure proposed that every word exists in a web of words that are related to it but that are different from it. The meaning of *sneaker* is its similarity to, and difference from, *shoe*, *boot*, *high heel*, and so forth. Each of those words is at the center of its own web of similarities and differences.

The notion of meaning as a messy relational context—a web or network—has become quite pervasive, in part because it's become possible to put this context to work. For example, Facebook's social graph and Google's Knowledge Graph connect atoms of information without regard for what single categories they should be filed under. A graph can connect information about, say, the Apple Watch to snippets about other smartwatches, digital watches, analog watches, descriptions of how digital watches are manufactured, histories of timepieces, philosophies of the clockwork universe, the physics of time, maps of the sources of the raw materials required, the sources that use forced labor, literary references to digital watches, photos of people wearing watches, the science of digital displays, the way high school boys used to try to get their calculators' LCD displays to display 80085 because it looks like it spells "BOOBS" . . . anything related in any way. Each of those nodes is itself connected to many more pieces, like words in Saussure's webs of meaning, like hyperlinked pages on the web, and like data in the models machine learning systems build for themselves.

Our old technology was not nearly as generous with meaning. The beatniks of the 1950s were on to something when they insisted, "I am not a number," in between bongo solos. The first generations of computers indeed reduced things—employees, inventory, processes—to the handful of fields that the technology could manage. Now we worry not that computers have reduced us to what fits onto punch cards but that they know far too much about us and how we're connected. We at times, understandably, yearn for the good old reductive days.

Being overly inclusive in the data we collect and connect raises obvious issues about the loss of privacy, but we are at the same time gaining galaxies of meaning. Aristotle and Linnaeus tried to describe what a thing essentially is by referencing exactly two relationships: how it is like the other things in its category and how it is distinguished from them. At its heart, this approach assumes that each thing is essentially distinguishable from all the rest of creation that is not that thing. Our new view expresses meaning in the overwhelming and unsystematic connections of things to everything else in every way imaginable, including some that only our machine learning systems see. In a connected world, the boundaries between things are drawn not by those things' essential essence but by our intentions.

So did Google's AI fail at the task of identifying dumbbells? Yes, if we take things to be what they are only when they're apart from everything else. But if you were an alien, which photo would give you a better idea of what a dumbbell is, a dumbbell in isolation or Google AI's image? Is a dumbbell a dumbbell apart from its complex web of relations to human bodies, exercise equipment, health, mortality, and vanity?

There are, of course, times when we want the pared-down meaning—for example, when you're trying to check out a dumbbell's handgrip in a product catalog. But you are checking out handgrips presumably because you already know that a dumbbell is a weight intended to be grasped and lifted in order to become strong, to become attractive, or to finally win the approval of your mother, the competitive weight lifter. The pared-down meaning only makes sense within the thing's place in the messy, generative set of implicit and explicit connections of everything to everything else. Precision comes at the cost of meaning. Messiness is the root of all.

In this way, the internet's collaborative, cacophonous chaos of links and machine learning's model of models unrestrained by complexity are far more representative of what things are than Aristotle's or Linnaeus's attempt to clarify meaning with the edge of a scalpel.

The Future

If the globe that ornaments your desk has ridges where there are mountains, that globe is bumpier than the Earth it represents. In fact, if your globe is the size of a billiard ball, to be accurate it should be smoother than a billiard ball.[32]

Our calculators assume we need only so many digits of magnitude or precision, and make us trade off between the two.

We've been able to program traditional computers only because we've been willing to specify a relative handful of stepwise rules, load in readouts from the dials we've planted across the planet, and handcraft the exceptions we can anticipate.

From these sorts of peeks through the slats at our overwhelming world, we have confronted the future by ascertaining its possibilities and relentlessly reducing them as best we could.

Now we have new tools. They sometimes come to conclusions that surpass our ability to comprehend them. They express their truths in probabilities and percentages; certainty has come to flag that an error is about to be committed. They create a place of connection and creativity that thrives on particularity. They open a world in which every mote depends on every other in ways that explanations insult.

These new tools are far from infallible. In fact, unchecked they can visit unfairness with especial ferocity on the most vulnerable.

But we built these tools because, overall and most of the time, they work. They have shown us that we no longer have to reduce the future to survive it. We thrive in our new future by making more of it.

This future isn't going to settle down, resolve itself, or yield to simple rules and expectations. Feeling overwhelmed, confused, surprised, and uncertain is our new baseline stance toward the world because that expresses the human truth about the world.

We are at the beginning of a new paradox: We can control more of our future than ever, but our means of doing so reveals the world as further beyond our understanding than we've let ourselves believe.

We have a category for this sort of paradox: the awe that first roused humans to look up and to begin to grow into what we are.

Awe abides. It can be a gracious awe that gives thanks for a gift we did nothing to deserve. It can be awe at the preposterous improbability that billions of years would lead to this exact us standing at this precise here. It can be awe at the privilege of understanding so little, or so much, in the face of all there is to know. But awe always opens outward, letting the unthought ground our ideas and the winds wash through our words. One way or another, awe opens the *more* of the world.

Now, at last, our tools are complicit in our awe.

NOTES

Introduction

1. Riccardo Miotto, Li Li, Brian A. Kidd, and Joel T. Dudley, "Deep Patient: An Unsupervised Representation to Predict the Future of Patients from the Electronic Health Records," *Scientific Reports* 6 (2016): article 26094, https://perma.cc/R2GY-YBQQ.

2. There are many ways of computing this, but one calculation says that there are 10^{800} possible moves, which works out to 10^{720} for every atom in the universe. "Number of Possible Go Games," Sensei's Library, last modified June 25, 2018, https://perma.cc/2JPY-KMVF. Some estimates put the number of chess moves at 10^{120}. The number of atoms in the universe is generally estimated at around 10^{80}. To get a sense of how vast these numbers are, keep in mind that 10^{81} is ten times larger than 10^{80}.

3. Cade Metz, "The Sadness and Beauty of Watching Google's AI Play Go," *Wired*, Mar. 11, 2016, https://perma.cc/UPD4-KVUR.

4. Big Grammar has declared that *Internet* is no longer to be capitalized. That is, I believe, a mistake. Likewise for the *Net* and for the *Web*. But I have lost this battle with my culture. So, in this book the Internet and the Web—capitalized here for the last time in this text—will be treated as if they were just pieces of technology and not unique, lived-in domains.

5. Dan Siroker, "How Obama Raised $60 Million by Running a Simple Experiment," *Optimizely Blog*, Nov. 29, 2010, https://perma.cc/TW5M-PHJ5. See also Richard E. Nisbett, "What Your Team Can Learn from Team Obama about A/B Testing," *Fortune*, Aug. 18, 2015, http://perma.cc/922Z-5PMA.

6. Brian Christian, "The A/B Test: Inside the Technology That's Changing the Rules of Business," *Wired*, Apr. 25, 2012, http://perma.cc/H35M-ENAA.

7. For example, "Baltimore after Freddie Gray: The 'Mind-Set Has Changed'" increased readership by 1,677 over "Soul-Searching in Baltimore, a Year after Freddie Gray's Death." Mark Bulik, "Which Headlines Attract More Readers," *Times Insider*, June 13, 2016, https://www.nytimes.com/2016/06/13/insider/which-headlines-attract-most-readers.html.

8. Katja Kevic et al., "Characterizing Experimentation in Continuous Deployment: A Case Study on Bing," *ICSE-SEIP '17: Proceedings of the 39th International Conference on Software Engineering: Software Engineering in Practice Track* (2017): 123–132, https://doi.org/10.1109/ICSE-SEIP.2017.19.

9. Sean Hollister, "Here's Why Samsung Note 7 Phones Are Catching Fire," CNET, Oct. 10, 2016, https://perma.cc/HKM2-VQBB; Kate Samuelson,

"A Brief History of Samsung's Troubled Galaxy Note 7 Smartphone," *Time*, Oct. 11, 2016, https://perma.cc/NQ7F-9ZCT.

10. See Elizabeth Landay, "From a Tree, a 'Miracle' Called Aspirin," CNN, Dec. 22, 2010, http://perma.cc/HTT2-FR5C; and J. M. S. Pearce, "The Controversial Story of Aspirin," *World Neurology*, Dec. 2, 2014, http://perma.cc/2TAJ-RC2T.

11. Josefina Casas, "5 Tricks for Writing Great Headlines on Twitter and Facebook as Awesome and Clickable as Buzzfeed's," Postcron, accessed Nov. 2, 2018, https://perma.cc/JE59-CLT8.

12. "Every Drop Adds Up," ALS Association site, https://perma.cc/V8T7-XSAN.

13. Braden R. Allenby and Daniel Sarewitz, *The Techno-Human Condition* (Cambridge, MA: MIT Press, 2010).

14. Edward Lorenz, "Predictability: Does the Flap of a Butterfly's Wing in Brazil Set Off a Tornado in Texas?," address at the American Association for the Advancement of Science, Dec. 29, 1972, https://perma.cc/L5J3-BSF7. Also see Christian Oestreicher, "A History of Chaos Theory," *Dialogues in Clinical Neuroscience* 9, no. 3 (Sep. 2007): 279–289, https://perma.cc/6U5L-QKXH. Here are two excellent explanations and explorations: James Gleick, *Chaos: Making a New Science* (New York: Penguin, 1987); and Steven Johnson, *Emergence* (New York: Simon and Schuster, 2001).

15. See *Jurassic Park*. No, really, you should see it. We watch it every year at Thanksgiving.

16. Rachel Carson, *Silent Spring* (New York: Houghton Mifflin, 1962). On the term *ecosystem*, see A. J. Willis, "Forum," *Functional Ecology* 11 (1997): 268–271, 268.

17. Roger Abrantes, "How Wolves Change Rivers," Ethology Institute Cambridge, Jan. 13, 2017, https://perma.cc/3364-BUSZ.

18. Nassim Nicholas Taleb, *The Black Swan: The Impact of the Highly Improbable* (New York: Random House, 2007).

19. Daniel Pink, *Free Agent Nation* (New York: Warner Business Books, 2001).

20. Obviously, what I say in this book does not necessarily represent the opinions or ideas of any of those groups.

Chapter One

1. Kasha Patel, "Since Katrina: NASA Advances Storm Models, Science," NASA, Aug. 21, 2015, http://perma.cc/RFN4-94NZ. See also Kelsey Campbell-Dollaghan, "Here's How Much Better NASA's Weather Models Have Gotten since Katrina," Gizmodo, Aug. 24, 2015, https://perma.cc/A7QU-RWTK.

2. Patel, "Since Katrina."

3. Progress is being made in earthquake prediction. For example, a team led by researchers at Los Alamos National Laboratory has successfully used machine learning to analyze acoustic signals to predict when an earthquake will occur . . . in the laboratory. Bertrand Rouet-Leduc et al., "Machine Learning Predicts Laboratory Earthquakes," *Geophysical Research Letters* 44, no. 18, Sept. 28, 2017, 9276–9282, https://perma.cc/566D-JAB4. There's also been progress in using deep learning to predict when an earthquake's aftershocks will occur. See James Vincent, "Google and Harvard Team Up to Use Deep Learn-

ing to Predict Earthquake Aftershocks," The Verge, Aug. 20, 2018, https://perma.cc/RJX5-DUCX.

4. Statisticians distinguish between predictions and forecasts, using tomorrow's weather and long-term climate change as their standard example, but for our purposes here we don't need to. See Nate Silver, *The Signal and the Noise* (New York: Penguin Books, 2012), for an excellent discussion.

5. G. J. Whitrow, *Time in History* (New York: Barnes and Noble, 1988), 25.

6. In an article in the *Atlantic*, Eric Weiner says of Athens in particular, "[I]n their efforts to nourish their minds, the Athenians built the world's first global city. Master shipbuilders and sailors, they journeyed to Egypt, Mesopotamia, and beyond, bringing back the alphabet from the Phoenicians, medicine and sculpture from the Egyptians, mathematics from the Babylonians, literature from the Sumerians." Eric Weiner, "What Made Ancient Athens a City of Genius?," *Atlantic*, Feb. 10, 2016, https://perma.cc/QE9X-TSZV.

7. Actually, maybe not so literally, since the ancient Greeks didn't have a word for *blue* and there is debate about their perception of color. See Ananda Triulzi, "Ancient Greek Color Vision," Serendip Studio, Nov. 27, 2006, https://perma.cc/XDU7-LDFJ. Also, *RadioLab* has an excellent podcast episode about the perception of the color of the sky: "Why Isn't the Sky Blue?," *RadioLab*, May 20, 2012, podcast, 22:23, https://perma.cc/239Y-L2C6.

8. According to Lisa Raphals, the gods couldn't reverse the Fates' decrees, but they could at times postpone them. See her "Fate, Fortune, Chance, and Luck in Chinese and Greek: A Comparative Semantic History," *Philosophy East and West* 53, no. 4 (Oct. 2003): 537–574, https://perma.cc/6WGB-7H5T. On the broader question of the forces affecting ancient Greek life, see Martha C. Nussbaum, *The Fragility of Goodness: Luck and Ethics in Greek Tragedy and Philosophy*, 2nd ed. (Cambridge: Cambridge University Press, 2001).

9. Daniel C. Schlenoff, "The Future: A History of Prediction from the Archives of *Scientific American*," *Scientific American*, Jan. 1, 2013, https://perma.cc/UHD4-EVPG.

10. Bernard Knox, *Backing into the Future* (New York: W. W. Norton, 1994), 11.

11. Thorleif Boman, *Hebrew Thought Compared with Greek* (New York: W. W. Norton, 1960), 149.

12. John S. Mbiti, *African Religions and Philosophy* (Oxford: Heinemann Educational, 1969), 17. James Gleick mentions other cultures that do not think about the future as lying in front of them in his book *Time Travel* (New York: Pantheon, 2016), 137–138.

13. Anthony Sudbery, "The Future's Not Ours to See," preprint, submitted May 2, 2016, 2, https://perma.cc/P3J6-CYRM.

14. See the superb, detailed account in Paul N. Edwards, *A Vast Machine* (Cambridge, MA: MIT Press, 2013), 85.

15. For a fascinating, and readable, exploration of the role of divinatory prognostication in the ancient Greek understanding of cognition, see Peter T. Struck, "A Cognitive History of Divination in Ancient Greece," University of Pennsylvania Scholarly Commons, Jan. 2016, https://perma.cc/FG36-2YYP.

16. "Laplace's Demon," Information Philosopher, accessed Aug. 6, 2018, https://perma.cc/S89N-P4BB. On Laplace, see Martin S. Staum, review of *Pierre Simon Laplace, 1749–1827: A Determined Scientist*, by Roger Hahn,

American Historical Review 111, no. 4 (Oct. 1, 2006): 1254, https://perma.cc /2RYA-9AFP. Pierre-Simone Laplace, *A Philosophical Essay on Probabilities*, trans. Frederick Wilson Truscott and Frederick Lincoln Emory (New York: John Wiley and Sons, 1902), https://perma.cc/Z6MX-T5J5.

17. Miles Mathis, "On Laplace and the 3-Body Problem," Miles Mathis's website, Aug. 6, 2009, https://perma.cc/F32C-9CD8.

18. See Herb Gruning, "Divine Elbow Room," in *Polyphonic Thinking and the Divine*, ed. Jim Kanaris (Amsterdam: Rodopi, 2013), 43. Also, the winter 2015 issue of the *New Atlantis* has excellent articles on Newton's religiosity: *New Atlantis* 44 (Winter 2015), https://perma.cc/544V-UN3F. Of particular use here is Stephen D. Snobelen's "Cosmos and Apocalypse," *New Atlantis* 44 (Winter 2015): 76–94, https://perma.cc/X3UC-CJBK; and a 1967 paper that he cites: David Kubrin, "Newton and the Cyclical Cosmos: Providence and the Mechanical Philosophy," *Journal of the History of Ideas* 28, no. 3 (July–Sept. 1967): 325–346. Snobelen writes, "Newton's so-called clockwork universe is hardly timeless, regular, and machine-like. . . . [I]nstead, it acts more like an organism that is subject to ongoing growth, decay, and renewal."

19. Laplace, *A Philosophical Essay on Probabilities*, 3.

20. Jamie L. Vernon, "On the Shoulders of Giants," *American Scientist*, July–Aug. 2017, 194, https://perma.cc/DE9Q-PPYJ.

21. Isaac Newton, *Newton's Principia*, trans. Andrew Motte (New York: Daniel Adee, 1846), lxvii, https://archive.org/details/100878576/page/n7.

22. From Julie Wakefield's fascinating biography, *Halley's Quest* (Washington, DC: Joseph Henry, 2005), 76.

23. All of this account comes from David Alan Grier's *When Computers Were People* (Princeton, NJ: Princeton University Press, 2005), 11–25.

24. Incremental steps: Monique Gros Lalande, "Lepaute, Nicole-Reine," in *Biographical Encyclopedia of Astronomers*, ed. Thomas Hockey et al. (New York: Springer Science and Business Media, 2007), 690–691. Ardor: Grier, *When Computers Were People*, 22. Removed acknowledgment: Lalande, "Lepaute, Nicole-Reine," 690–691. Unacknowledged for later work: Catherine M. C. Haines, *International Women in Science: A Biographical Dictionary to 1950* (Santa Barbara: ABC-CLIO, 2001), 174. Canceled errors: Grier, *When Computers Were People*, 23.

25. "[N]ot one word of proof or demonstration do you offer. All is probability with you, and yet surely you and Theodorus had better reflect whether you are disposed to admit of probability and figures of speech in matters of such importance. He or any other mathematician who argued from probabilities and likelihoods in geometry, would not be worth an ace." *The Thaetetus*, trans. Benjamin Jowett, https://perma.cc/U55R-3ZUE.

26. Leonard Mlodinow, *The Drunkard's Walk: How Randomness Rules Our Lives* (New York: Pantheon Books, 2008), 122.

27. I talk about the history of "information overload" in *Too Big to Know* (New York: Times Books, 2011), 5–6, with more detail in the endnotes.

28. Siobhan Roberts, "John Horton Conway: The World's Most Charismatic Mathematician," *Guardian*, July 23, 2015, https://perma.cc/64WC-9JRG.

29. You can read the rules and try it out at https://playgameoflife.com/ (https://perma.cc/WXB4-KREA).

30. Martin Gardner, "The Fantastic Combinations of John Conway's New Solitaire Game 'Life,'" *Scientific American*, Oct. 1970, 120–123, https://perma.cc/ER58 -TGV3. While encouraging readers to play the game manually, Gardner notes that some colleagues of Conway's had programmed a PDP-7 "minicomputer"—"mini" because you could have fit one into a large laundry room—to run the game.

31. Alexy Nigin, "New Spaceship Speed in Conway's Game of Life," *Nigin's Blog*, Mar. 7, 2016, https://perma.cc/WY2D-5KRF.

32. Daniel C. Dennett, *Darwin's Dangerous Idea: Evolution and the Meaning of Life* (New York: Simon and Schuster, 2014), 166ff.

33. Raymond Kurzweil, *The Singularity Is Near* (New York: Penguin Books, 2006).

34. Stephen Wolfram, *A New Kind of Science* (Champaign, IL: Wolfram Media, 2002).

Chapter Two

1. Alexandra Gibbs, "Chick Sexer: The $60K a Year Job Nobody Wants," NBC News, Mar. 4, 2015, https://perma.cc/7FYE-6KZR.

2. Richard Horsey, "The Art of Chicken Sexing," *UCL Working Papers in Linguistics* 14 (2002): 107–117, https://perma.cc/98MF-4YZM.

3. "What Does a Chicken Sexer Do?," Sokanu, accessed Sept. 30, 2018, https://perma.cc/XYP5-FZVN.

4. This idea is usually traced back to Plato's *Theaetetus*, although as Richard Polt reminds me in an email, Socrates's interlocutors fail to come up with an explanation of what constitutes justification, and the dialogue ends without a resolution to the question of what is knowledge.

5. For example, see Robert B. Brandom, "Insights and Blindspots of Reliabilism," *The Monist* 1, no. 3 (June 1998): 371–393. Brandom offers a sophisticated analysis of this question.

6. You could argue that the machine learning system's working model is also a conceptual model, but in fact there is no intelligence that has the concept, so I prefer not to.

7. See, for example, the excellent introduction to machine learning by Adam Geitgey, "Machine Learning Is Fun!," Medium, May 5, 2014, https:// perma.cc/FQ8X-K2KQ.

8. Richard Dunley, "Machines Reading the Archive: Handwritten Text Recognition Software," *National Archives Blog*, Mar. 19, 2018, https://perma.cc /NQ9R-NCZR.

9. Sidney Kennedy, "How AI Is Helping to Predict and Prevent Suicide," The Conversation, Mar. 27, 2018, https://perma.cc/D8K4-ERZV. For an excellent and highly accessible discussion of these issues, see Cathy O'Neil's *Weapons of Math Destruction* (New York: Crown, 2016) and the upcoming work *Smart Enough Cities*, by Ben Green (Cambridge, MA: MIT Press, 2019). (Disclosure: I edit the book series publishing Green's book.)

10. Nate Silver, *The Signal and the Noise* (New York: Penguin Books, 2012).

11. Paul N. Edwards, *A Vast Machine* (Cambridge, MA: MIT Press, 2013), 85.

12. Ibid., 94–96.

13. Ibid., 123.

14. Silver, *Signal and the Noise*, 386.

15. Jonathan M. Gitlin, "Krakatoa's Chilling Effect," Ars Technica, Jan. 9, 2006, https://perma.cc/XET2-GY9K.

16. Richard Mattessich, a professor at University of California, Berkeley, and two grad students created the Budget Computer Program for mainframes in the early 1960s. See Paul Young, "VisiCalc and the Growth of Spreadsheets," RBV Web Solutions, last updated May 7, 2000, https://perma.cc/2HRF-73RZ.

17. Steven Levy, "A Spreadsheet Way of Knowledge," *Wired*, Oct. 24, 2014, https://perma.cc/YQ8H-CCRK.

18. Dan Bricklin, "The Idea," Dan Bricklin's Web Site, accessed Sept. 30, 2018, https://perma.cc/55SU-NBSM.

19. Dan Bricklin, "Patenting VisiCalc," Dan Bricklin's Web Site, accessed Sept. 30, 2018, https://perma.cc/3UF9-UPAW.

20. Levy, "Spreadsheet Way of Knowledge."

21. George E. P. Box, *Robustness in the Strategy of Scientific Model Building* (Madison: Wisconsin University Mathematics Research Center, 1979), 2, https://perma.cc/7E54-AGVG.

22. "Armillary Sphere," Museo Galileo, accessed Sept. 30, 2018, https://perma.cc/9Y3G-V42C.

23. Oxford Museum of the History of Science, "Armillary Sphere," Epact: Scientific Instruments of Medieval and Renaissance Europe, accessed Sept. 30, 2018, https://perma.cc/6ZPN-LPK6.

24. Martin Kemp, "Moving in Elevated Circles," *Nature*, July 2010, 33, https://perma.cc/GW3N-VY6Y.

25. My friend John Frank, a computer scientist, read an early draft of this and commented in an email (Oct. 10, 2018),

> As a beautiful example, perhaps the canonical example, of a model foreshadowing its successor in a deeply technical manner, these many circles were approximating the Fourier components of the ellipses of the real orbits. A change of coordinates allows these Fourier components to become their simpler equivalent.
>
> Machine learning models provide a principled procedure for discovering those better coordinates that have not yet been articulated in an explanatory form.

26. C. H. Claudy, "A Great Brass Brain," *Scientific American*, Mar. 7, 2014, 197–198, https://perma.cc/7CQL-G5XG.

27. Ibid., 197.

28. Jonathan White, *Tides: The Science and Spirit of the Ocean* (San Antonio, TX: Trinity University Press, 2017): "hundreds of these eccentricities," 5–6; never saw an ocean: 115–116, 120.

29. Ibid., 152.

30. "History of Tidal Analysis and Prediction," NOAA Tides & Currents, last revised Aug. 8, 2018, https://perma.cc/XMZ2-6KD2.

31. Claudy, "Great Brass Brain," 198.

32. White, *Tides*, 202.

33. Dylan, "The Mississippi River Basin Model," Atlas Obscura, accessed Sept. 30, 2018, https://perma.cc/WL52-R2MG. The source of the $65 million fig-

ure seems to be J. E. Foster, *History and Description of the Mississippi Basin Model*, Mississippi Basin Model Report 1-6 (Vicksburg, MS: US Army Engineer Waterways Experiment Station, 1971), 2; this is according to Kristi Dykema Cheramie, "The Scale of Nature: Modeling the Mississippi River," *Places Journal*, Mar. 2011, https://perma.cc/DR5X-3Y34. If we assume, based on nothing, that the $65 million figure had already been translated into 1971 dollars, the current equivalent would be $386 million.

34. "America's Last Top Model," *99% Invisible*, July 19, 2016, podcast, 21:25, http://99percentinvisible.org/episode/americas-last-top-model/.

35. A. G. Gleeman, "The Phillips Curve: A Rushed Job?," *Journal of Economic Perspectives* 25, no. 1 (Winter 2011): 223–238, 225.

36. "A Pioneering Economic Computer," Reserve Bank Museum, https://perma.cc/W7MH-5HLK.

37. Larry Elliot, "The Computer Model that Once Explained the British Economy," *The Guardian*, May 8, 2008, https://perma.cc/T88G-RQDB.

38. "America's Last Top Model."

39. See the "Scales" subhead on this page from the US Army Corps of Engineers: "The Technical Side of the Bay Model," US Army Corps of Engineers, accessed Sept. 30, 2018, https://perma.cc/WXZ3-3DSQ.

40. The history of this disruption goes back at least to Peter Brown's work in the early 1990s at IBM, where he pioneered translating texts through the statistical analysis of existing translations, without providing the computer with linguistic models of the grammar, syntax, or semantics of either language.

41. Dave Gershgorn, "Google Is Using 46 Billion Data Points to Predict the Medical Outcomes of Hospital Patients," Quartz, Jan. 27, 2018, https://perma.cc/NHS2-HU2G.

42. Riccardo Miotto et al., "Deep Patient: An Unsupervised Representation to Predict the Future of Patients from the Electronic Health Records," *Scientific Reports* 6 (2016): article 26094, https://perma.cc/L8YL-6Q69.

43. Julian Mitchell, "This A.I. Search Engine Delivers Tailored Data to Companies in Real-Time," *Forbes*, May 11, 2014, https://perma.cc/L3JP-8D38.

44. Jeff Curie and Greg Bolcer, email exchange with the author, July 17, 2017. See also Mitchell, "This A.I. Search Engine Delivers Tailored Data to Companies in Real-Time."

45. As quoted in David Weinberger, "Our Machines Now Have Knowledge We'll Never Understand," *Wired*, Apr. 18, 2017, https://perma.cc/SP4T-AKZP.

46. There is a great deal of work and discussion about whether all machine learning implementations will always resist explanation. See Cynthia Rudin's ten-minute video from a webinar on Oct. 2, 2018: "Please Stop Doing Explainable ML," webcast, Oct. 2, 2018, https://perma.cc/CWG3-4HUK. (It's the second talk in the video.) Here is a suggestion for how to make machine learning's "decisions" understandable without having to understand exactly how those decisions were arrived at: Finale Doshi-Velez and Mason Kortz, "Accountability of AI under the Law: The Role of Explanation" (paper presented at the Privacy Law Scholars Conference, George Washington University, Washington, DC, 2018), https://perma.cc/L275-MH4N. Also see Finale Doshi-Velez and Been Kim, "Towards a Rigorous Science of Interpretable Machine Learning," preprint, submitted Feb. 28. 2017, https://perma.cc/2PSA-NZR4.

47. David Sutcliffe, "Could Counterfactuals Explain Algorithmic Decisions without Opening the Black Box?," Oxford Internet Institute, Jan. 15, 2018, https://perma.cc/HT5X-CV4L.

48. Deep learning systems are not the first computer programs to create their own models. John Frank, in his comments on a draft of this chapter, observed in an email dated Oct. 10, 2018, "This idea started with Leslie Valiant's 'Theory of the Learnable' which contributed to his winning the Turing Prize [https://perma.cc/H9DR-TP3H]. It was subsequently realized in a variety of fields by different domain-specific experts, such as Peter Brown et al. in 1991 for machine translation."

49. Jessica Birkett, "What the Dog-Fish and Camel-Bird Can Tell Us about How Our Brains Work," The Conversation, July 6, 2015, https://perma.cc/W28T-EERD.

50. Julia Angwin et al., "Machine Bias," ProPublica, May 23, 2016, https://perma.cc/249Q-7XCQ.

51. Dave Gershgorn, "By Sparring with AlphaGo, Researchers Are Learning How an Algorithm Thinks," Quartz, Feb. 16, 2017, https://perma.cc/V9YY-RTWQ.

52. Mix, "Google Is Teaming Up Its AlphaGo AI with Humans So They Can Learn from It," TNW, Apr. 10, 2017, https://perma.cc/5MMZ-5FXL.

53. Rory Cellan-Jones, "Google DeepMind: AI Becomes More Alien," BBC, Oct. 18, 2017, https://perma.cc/EEC4-N859.

54. Dawn Chan, "The AI That Has Nothing to Learn from Humans," *Atlantic*, Oct. 20, 2017, https://perma.cc/4EQ8-Z73X.

55. Kuhn actually talks about paradigm in many different ways. See my essay on the fiftieth anniversary of *The Structure of Scientific Revolutions*: "Shift Happens," *Chronicle of Higher Education: Chronicle Review*, Apr. 22, 2012, https://perma.cc/8XPS-84WN.

56. Nicholas Faith, *Black Box* (Minneapolis: Motorbooks International, 1997), 100–105.

57. Ibid., 103.

58. Jecelyn Yeen, "AI Translate: Bias? Sexist? Or This Is the Way It Should Be?," Hackernoon, Oct. 6, 2017, https://perma.cc/2A7N-KKSX.

59. Momin M. Malik and Hemank Lamba, "When 'False' Models Predict Better Than 'True' Ones: Paradoxes of the Bias-Variance Tradeoff" (unpublished manuscript, version 1.6, Dec. 2017), https://www.mominmalik.com/false_models_in_progress.pdf.

60. Parts of this coda are adapted from an article published on the Harvard Berkman Klein Center's page at Medium under a Creative Commons BY license: "Optimization over Explanation: Maximizing the Benefits of Machine Learning without Sacrificing Its Intelligence," Medium, Jan. 28, 2018, https://perma.cc/H538-3Q2G. A version of that article by agreement was simultaneously posted by *Wired* under the title "Don't Make AI Artificially Stupid in the Name of Transparency," https://perma.cc/X9N4-8RBT.

61. The McKinsey data comes from Michele Bertoncello and Dominik Wee, "Ten Ways Autonomous Driving Could Redefine the Automotive World," McKinsey&Company, June 2015, https://perma.cc/G8CT-JTTD. The Tesla information is from the Tesla Team, "An Update on Last Week's Accident," *Tesla Blog*, Mar. 20, 2018, https://perma.cc/Q8CH-7HLP. It's commonly said that the

National Highway Traffic Safety Administration says that 93 percent of traffic accidents are caused by human error, but it's hard to track down the source of that figure. See Bryant Walker Smith, "Human Error as a Cause of Vehicle Crashes," Stanford Center for Internet and Society, Dec. 18, 2013, https://perma.cc/9DR3-6EVC.

62. Brett Frischmann and Evan Selinger, *Re-engineering Humanity* (Cambridge: Cambridge University Press, 2018), 137.

63. Sam Levin and Julia Carrie Wong, "Self-driving Uber Kills Arizona Woman in First Fatal Crash Involving Pedestrian," *The Guardian*, Mar. 19, 2018, https://perma.cc/VB4P-27HG.

64. Devin Coldewey, "Uber in Fatal Crash Detected Pedestrian but Had Emergency Braking Disabled," TechCrunch, Apr. 24, 2018, https://perma.cc/W4L3-SVCM.

Chapter Three

1. The information about Ford's design of the Model T comes from John Duncan, *Any Colour—So Long as It's Black* (Titirangi, New Zealand: Exisle, 2008), Kindle edition.

2. Ibid., chapter 1.

3. Kate Wong, "Oldest Arrowheads Hint at How Modern Humans Overtook Neandertals," *Scientific American*, Nov. 7, 2012, https://perma.cc/7H9E-V8G2. Stone spear tips believed to be five hundred thousand years old have been found in Spain. See Kate Wong, "Human Ancestors Made Deadly Stone-Tipped Spears 500,000 Years Ago," *Scientific American*, Nov. 15, 2012, https://perma.cc/ET3R-3KRJ.

4. Dana Gunders, "Wasted: How America Is Losing up to 40 Percent of Its Food from Farm to Fork to Landfill," NRDC Issue Paper 12-06-B, National Resources Defense Council, Aug. 2012, https://perma.cc/DF6M-FECX. Food packages have only had dates attached to them for about the last hundred years, a result of the distribution of food far removed from its sources. See Rosetta Newsome et al., "Applications and Perceptions of Date Labeling of Food," *Comprehensive Reviews in Food Science and Food Safety* 13 (2014): 745–769, https://perma.cc/Q3JR-PPJE.

5. Gianpaolo Callioni, Xavier de Montgros, Regine Slagmulder, Luk N. Van Wassenhover, and Linda Wright, "Inventory-Driven Costs," *Harvard Business Review*, Mar. 2005.

6. Eric Ries, *The Lean Startup* (New York: Crown Business, 2011), 3–4.

7. Ibid., 107.

8. Ibid., 108–109.

9. Confirmed via email from Frank Robinson, Aug. 15, 2014.

10. Ries, *Lean Startup*, 97–99.

11. "From 0 to $1B—Slack's Founder Shares Their Epic Launch Strategy," First Round Review, accessed Aug. 21, 2018, https://perma.cc/73XZ-C3B7.

12. There are different formulations of this motto. This one is from Khurram Hashmi, "Introduction and Implementation of Total Quality Management (TQM)," iSixSigma.com, accessed Aug. 21, 2018, https://perma.cc/W2HT-8CWX. Another is "Do the right thing the first and every time," as in Hesbon Ondiek Yala, Harry Ododa, and Chelang'a James, "The Impact of Total Quality

Management (TQM) Policy on Customer Satisfaction at Kenya Power and Lighting Company (KPLC) in Uasin Gishu County, Kenya (2010–2012)," *International Journal of Academic Research and Development* 3, no. 2 (Mar. 2018): 187–193, 187, https://perma.cc/ZC5L-BG5L.

13. Tom Peters, "Leadership for the 'I-Cubed Economy,'" *Tom Peters's Blog*, Oct. 11, 2006, https://perma.cc/M3UQ-8EKD.

14. Aneesh Chopra, interview by the author, March 9, 2014.

15. Adrianne Jeffries, "Why Obama's Healthcare.gov Launch Was Doomed to Fail," The Verge, Oct. 8, 2013, https://perma.cc/LJ7Z-Z9BN. CGI, the main contractor charged with creating the site, claimed to have used agile techniques, but it's widely disputed that what CGI thought was agile met any reasonable definition of it.

16. Frank Thorp, "Only 6 Able to Sign Up on Healthcare.gov's First Day, Documents Show," NBC News, Oct. 31, 2013, https://perma.cc/574A-VLNV.

17. Evelyn Rusli, "Behind Healthcare.gov: How Washington Is Drawing Inspiration from Silicon Valley, Twitter," TechCrunch, Aug. 6, 2010, https://perma.cc/L6QY-3RL9.

18. Robinson Meyer, "The Secret Startup That Saved the Worst Website in America," *Atlantic*, July 9, 2015, https://perma.cc/3X7S-5A8Q.

19. Rusty Foster, "Don't Go Chasing Waterfalls: A More Agile Healthcare .gov," *New Yorker*, Oct. 28, 2013, https://perma.cc/M4SG-JS7S.

20. Peter Varhol, "To Agility and Beyond: The History—and Legacy—of Agile Development," TechBeacon, accessed Aug. 21, 2018, https://perma.cc/3U6A-2J2D.

21. VerionOne, *10th Annual State of Agile Report* (VersionOne, 2016), https://perma.cc/BP34-54YK; Kerby Ferris, "Duck Typing the Gender Gap," Media Temple, Feb. 17, 2016, https://perma.cc/394U-XVQY.

22. Aneesh Chopra, "From Silicon Valley to Main Street Virginia," *White House Blog*, Aug. 11, 2011, https://perma.cc/EE6Q-W94G. The number of employees Chopra cites seems high. David Kirkpatrick in *The Facebook Effect* (New York: Simon and Schuster, 2010) says that in 2010 Facebook only employed 1,400 people.

23. Kirkpatrick, *Facebook Effect*, 19.

24. Ibid., 23.

25. Information in this and the next two paragraphs about the success of Facebook's open platform comes from ibid., 226–232.

26. Ibid., 11.

27. The information in this and the next section comes from a paper I wrote as a fellow at the Harvard Shorenstein Center on Media, Politics and Public Policy: "The Rise, Fall, and Possible Rise of Open News Platforms," Shorenstein Center on Media, Politics and Public Policy, July 10, 2015, https://perma.cc/34CU-F7KD.

28. "The First 'Official' Castle Smurfenstein Home Page," accessed Aug. 21, 2018, https://perma.cc/9AL3-T7S4. There's uncertainty about whether the first of the Smurfing mods was *Wolfenstein* or *Dragon Egg*. I contacted David H. Schroeder, the creator of *Dino Eggs*, a similar hack of *Dragon Egg*, but he wasn't sure which came first. He did say, however, "My estimate is that—of folks who played games on Apple II's—perhaps 25% of them played Dino Eggs" (personal email, Dec. 26, 2013). See also Wagner James Au, "The Triumph of

the Mod," *Salon*, Apr. 16, 2002; and "History of Modding," *From Pacman to Pool* (blog), accessed Oct. 7, 2018, https://perma.cc/R94H-FEMS. For more on id Software's support of mods, see David Kushner, *Masters of Doom* (New York: Penguin, 2003).

29. "Sales of Grand Theft Auto Products Have Generated $2.3 Billion for Take Two since GTA5 Launch," *ZhugeEx Blog*, Jan. 3, 2016, https://perma.cc /VHE9-KSX8.

30. "Showing Pebblers Love with Longer Device Support," Fitbit Developer, Jan. 24, 2018, https://perma.cc/SLE8-NV8F.

31. "The Slack Platform Launch," *Slack Blog*, Dec. 15, 2014, https://perma.cc /4AC2-W5ZT.

32. Jennifer Pahlka, interview by the author, June 29, 2014.

33. Sorrel Moseley-Williams, "Adopt a Siren, Avert Disaster," Atlas of the Future, Oct. 10, 2015, https://perma.cc/SFZ9-JUB9.

34. Tim O'Reilly, "Gov. 2.9: It's All about the Platform," TechCrunch, Sept. 4, 2009, https://perma.cc/N39K-CDTQ.

35. Matt Apuzzo, "War Gear Flows to Police Departments," *New York Times*, June 8, 2014, https://www.nytimes.com/2014/06/09/us/war-gear-flows-to-police -departments.html.

36. Tom Giratikanon, Erin Kissane, and Jeremy Singer-Vine, "When the News Calls for Raw Data," Source, Aug. 21, 2014, https://perma.cc/D9MR -HJQE.

37. "About," GitHub, accessed Sept. 30, 2018, https://perma.cc/P4MD-9DYZ.

38. Arfon Smith, interview by the author, Dec. 3, 2014.

39. Sara Winge, email to the author, Nov. 14, 2017.

40. John Hagel, John Seely Brown, and Lang Davison, *The Power of Pull* (New York: Basic Books, 2010), 34.

41. Kevin Kelly, *The Inevitable: 12 Inevitable Forces That Will Shape Our Future* (New York: Viking, 2016).

42. Jerome H. Saltzer, David Reed, and David Clark, "End-to-End Arguments in System Design," *ACM Transactions on Computer Systems* 2, no. 4 (Nov. 1984): 277–284, https://perma.cc/77H4-WRES.

43. Personal email, Oct. 15, 2017.

44. "Searching the Web," *PC Magazine*, Dec. 5, 1995, 55.

45. Ibid.

46. The Wayback Machine at the Internet Archive (www.archive.org) has versions of Yahoo going back to 1996. All hail the Internet Archive! For the Yahoo! page from 1996, see https://perma.cc/G837-LJ8W.

47. The number is a little hard to figure. The library reported that in 2013, 733,890 of its 18.9 million items "circulated," but a high percentage of these are likely to be the same work circulated more than once, given that the students in the same class generally read the same books. On the other hand, not all of its 18.9 million items are available to be checked out. "Harvard Library Annual Report FY 2013," Harvard Library, accessed Aug. 21, 2018, https://perma .cc/JZM2-YQYZ.

48. "Harvard University Library," Wikipedia (no source for that figure is given), https://perma.cc/7QN5-RW4U.

49. I talk about this in *Everything Is Miscellaneous* (New York: Times Books, 2007).

Chapter Four

1. Sean Hollister, "After Two Weeks of Anarchy, 100,000 Simultaneous 'Pokémon' Players May Actually Beat the Game," The Verge, Feb. 26, 2014, https://perma.cc/6EWB-2QCG; Akimitsu Hamamuro, "Gravity Points," accessed Aug. 27, 2018, https://perma.cc/MFT6-8UN7.

2. John Palfrey and Urs Gasser, *Interop* (New York: Basic Books, 2012).

3. Emily Payne, "Do You Speak 'Pilot'? The 300-Word Language That Senior Air Crew Must Speak—WHATEVER Their Nationality," *Sun*, Oct. 16, 2017, https://perma.cc/X3SM-2HGW.

4. "A Brief History of Spreadsheets," *DataDeck Blog*, Jan. 31, 2018, https://perma.cc/U3DQ-CU4R.

5. GlobalData Healthcare, "Six Tech Giants Sign Health Data Interoperability Pledge," Verdict Medical Devices, Aug. 20, 2018, https://perma.cc/B5L7 -QRZW.

6. Judea Pearl, *The Book of Why* (New York: Basic Books, 2018), 353.

7. "Organization of Schemas," Schema.org, accessed Aug. 27, 2018, https://perma.cc/Y9RU-N8GW.

8. Evan Sandhaus, phone interview by the author, 2012.

9. Marc Ferrentino, telephone call, Nov. 28, 2018. Disclosure: I heard about this example from our son who works at Yext.

10. Microsoft, "Cortana and Structured Data Markup," Cortana Dev Center, Feb. 8, 2017, https://perma.cc/Z76L-CFJ6.

11. H2O from Harvard's Berkman Klein Center for Internet & Society is an example of this. See "H2O," Berkman Klein Center for Internet & Society, last updated June 21, 2018, https://perma.cc/FBR6-KAUM. The Open Syllabus Project at Columbia University aims at increasing the interoperability of syllabi by encouraging their open licensing and making their elements more identifiable. https://perma.cc/P6JJ-96WL.

12. Palfrey and Gasser, *Interop*, 49.

13. Even standardizing what would count as the prime meridian of longitude was once controversial, with England and France fighting for the honor. See Clark Blaise, *Time Lord: Sir Sandford Fleming and the Creation of Standard Time* (New York: Vintage, 2002).

14. Rebecca Kesby, "How the World's First Webcam Made a Coffee Pot Famous," BBC News, Nov. 22, 2012, https://perma.cc/DNF7-PTA6.

15. Doris Wolf, "Psychopharmaka, die in der Behandlung von Angst und Panikstörungen eingesetzt werden," Angst & Panik, accessed Nov. 7, 2018, https://www.angst-panik-hilfe.de/medikamente-angstbehandlung.html.

16. There's an interesting argument about whether Newton thought that if there were just one body in the universe, it would exert gravity, or if gravity is a relationship between two objects. See Eric Schliesser, "Without God: Gravity as a Relational Property of Matter in Newton," PhilSci Archive, Oct. 2008, https://perma.cc/4Y2X-4E78.

17. Stephen Snobelen, who, as mentioned in chapter 1, says that Newton viewed the universe as being more like an organism than a mechanism, also notes that Newton speculated that comets were God's way of pulling the planets back into their perfect elliptical orbits. Stephen D. Snobelen, "Cosmos and Apocalypse," *New Atlantis* 44 (Winter 2015): 76–94, https://perma.cc/X3UC-CJBK.

18. W. Daniel Hillis, "2014: What Scientific Idea Is Ready for Retirement?," *The Edge*, accessed Aug. 27, 2018, https://perma.cc/X9JT-SE55.

19. Pearl, *Book of Why*.

20. Kurt Vonnegut's *Slaughterhouse Five* has a wonderful example of this, tracking a bullet backward in time from its entry into a soldier to the mining of the minerals that made it.

21. Massimo Cirasino, Thomas Lammer, and Harish Natarajan, "Solving Payments Interoperability for Universal Financial Access," World Bank, Feb. 25, 2016, https://perma.cc/79D6-E9RQ.

22. For a particularly insightful exploration of the order of the world that divination relies on and reveals, see Elena Esposito, "A Time of Divination and a Time of Risk: Social Preconditions for Prophecy and Prediction," *Fate*, no. 5 (Aug. 2011), https://perma.cc/UNH6-US2Q.

23. Michel Foucault, *The Order of Things* (New York: Pantheon, 1971), 29. The translator is not listed, but seems to be Alan Sheridan: see "Philosophy— Translations," Alan Sheridan's website, accessed Oct. 7, 2018, https://perma.cc /8ZLF-GX53.

24. Elizabeth Gibney, "The Scant Science behind Cambridge Analytica's Controversial Marketing Techniques," *Nature*, Mar. 29, 2018, https://perma.cc /8LR5-LCLG.

Chapter Five

1. Zachary M. Seward, "The Steve Jobs Email That Outlined Apple's Strat-egy a Year before His Death," Quartz, Apr. 5, 2014, https://perma.cc/A5CV -SVL5.

2. Brenton R. Schlender, "Who's Ahead in the Computer Wars?," *Fortune*, Feb. 12, 1990, https://perma.cc/J9SA-JQKH. But he probably said it earlier; see Garson O'Toole, "Phrase: More Wood behind, All the Wood behind One Arrow," LinguistList listserv, Sept. 4, 2011, https://perma.cc/8W8H-A7PQ.

3. Lawrence Freedman, *Strategy: A History* (Oxford: Oxford University Press, 2013), 498.

4. Ibid., 69–70.

5. Burkhard Meißner, "Strategy, Strategic Leadership and Strategic Con-trol in Ancient Greece," *Journal of Military and Strategic Studies* 13, no. 1 (Fall 2010): 3–27, 12–14, 13.

6. Freedman, *Strategy*, xii–xiii.

7. For example, in 1805 Dietrich Heinrich von Bülow explained the strategy of war the way a mathematician proves theorems in geometry, and Antoine Henri Jomini in his 1838 treatise *The Art of War* looked for the timeless princi-ples of military strategy. Freedman, *Strategy*, 75–84.

8. Freedman, *Strategy*, 85–91.

9. Carl von Clausewitz, *On War*, 1832, trans. J. J. Graham (London, 1874), vol. 1, bk. 4, chap. 11, https://perma.cc/3GTU-XPGY.

10. Michael Hammer and James Champy, *Reeingineering the Corporation* (New York: HarperCollins, 1993).

11. Maurice Matloff, *US Army in WW2: War Department, Strategic Planning for Coalition Warfare* (Washington, DC: Government Printing Office, 1959), 9, http://history.army.mil/html/books/001/1-4/CMH_Pub_1-4.pdf.

12. See Alex Abella, "The Rand Corporation: The Think Tank That Controls America," *Mental Floss,* June 30, 2009, https://perma.cc/B5LR-88CF.

13. "The Evolution of Scenario Planning," Jisc, Feb. 20, 2008, https://perma .cc/KAB9-HG3S.

14. Angela Wilkinson and Roland Kupers, "Living in the Futures," *Harvard Business Review,* May 2013, https://perma.cc/L96E-5M9H.

15. Peter Schwartz, *The Art of the Long View: Planning for the Future in an Uncertain World* (New York: Doubleday, 1995), 71–72.

16. Pierre Wack, "Scenarios: Uncharted Waters Ahead," *Harvard Business Review,* Sept. 1985, 80, https://perma.cc/KAB9-HG3S.

17. Ibid.

18. Tim Hindle, "Scenario Planning," *Economist,* Sept. 1, 2008, https:// perma.cc/TFF7-VAYT.

19. Rita Gunther McGrath, *The End of Competitive Advantage: How to Keep Your Strategy Moving as Fast as Your Business* (Boston: Harvard Business Review Press, 2013). For an excellent interview about that book, see Theodore Kinni, "Rita Gunther McGrath on the End of Competitive Advantage," *Strategy+Business,* Feb. 17, 2014, https://perma.cc/D78W-YH37.

20. This shearing of the earth of possibilities so that they become mere formal representations tracks the view of Information Theory, which was gaining currency at the time that Kahn was working.

21. Obligatory references to the 1983 movie *WarGames.*

22. Dries Buytaert, "Driesnote," slide deck, DrupalCon, Vienna, Sept. 2017, https://perma.cc/6SKS-4XWS.

23. Drupal home page, accessed Sept. 21, 2017, https://perma.cc/2VJ8-8EW8.

24. Dries Buytaert, interview by the author, Acquia, Boston, July 22, 2015.

25. Lisa Welchman, "Keynote: The Paradox of Open Growth," slide deck, DrupalCon, Prague, Sept. 25, 2013, https://perma.cc/7WNS-VAN6.

26. Elon Musk, "All Our Patent Are Belong to You," *Tesla Blog,* June 12, 2014, https://perma.cc/CYS7-V5ZP.

27. For a highly critical view of the company's battery patents, see Steve Brachmann, "Tesla Battery Patents Further Proof of Elon Musk's Duplicitous Views on Patents," IPWatchdog, May 11, 2017, https://perma.cc/SL2X-S6T3. Fred Lambert, "A Number of Companies Are Now Using Tesla's Open-Source Patents and It Has Some Interesting Implications," Electrek, Nov. 10, 2015, https://perma.cc/49GJ-SZCF.

28. See Steven Levy, "How Google Is Remaking Itself as a 'Machine Learning First' Company," *Backchannel,* June 22, 2016, https://perma.cc/N6T7-DDT2.

29. As I completed writing this book, I began a six-month engagement as writer-in-residence at Google PAIR.

30. Conversation with Zak Stone at Google's Cambridge, Massachusetts, office, Sept. 2017.

31. Open Source licensing is complex. For example, here's a useful (but complicated) discussion: "Can I use open source software commercially? Will I have to face any legal consequences?," Quora, July 6, 2013, https://perma.cc /3GDT-AHC4.

32. Email from Zak Stone, Nov. 30, 2018.

33. On Dec. 1, 2018, Stack Overflow reported 36,311 questions tagged "tensorflow" had been asked, and 17,888 had been answered. Questions tagged:

https://perma.cc/NF5A-ZM5S. Questions answered: https://perma.cc/PV6K
-4D4S. (Thanks to Zak Stone for these links.)

34. Zak Stone, "Celebrating Google TensorFlow's First Year," *Google AI Blog*, Nov. 9, 2016, https://perma.cc/NYU6-HDY8.

35. I wrote about "Fort Business" in Christopher Locke, Rick Levine, Doc Searls, and David Weinberger, *The Cluetrain Manifesto* (Boston: Basic Books, 2000).

36. This section has been adapted from David Weinberger, "On the Merits of Obscurity," *Rhapsody*, Summer 2016.

37. Information from Walter Jennings, a public relations person with Ogilvy agency, confirmed with Huawei corporate, May 2016.

Chapter Six

1. "'Now You Can Dial,' Western Electric, 1954 or 1955," YouTube video, 9:51, posted June 9, 2011, https://perma.cc/W5TX-J23A. The film was released once dials became mandatory. An earlier set of "how to dial" films were released in the late 1920s when dials were first introduced as an option.

2. It is complicated, because everything is. First, according to Brough Turner, a provider of wireless connectivity, the analog sounds generated by touch-tone systems do have meaning once you've connected to an automated system that asks you to "Press 1 to talk with . . . ," etc. Brough Turner, email to the author, June 2018. Second, according to David Isenberg, a telecommunications expert, "Touch tones that are generated by old-style phones that only plug into the phone line and don't have an electrical connection or a battery are sensed and decoded at their central office," where they are converted into digital data. David Isenberg, email to the author, June 2018.

3. Because time is a flat circle, some hotels now have QR codes that lead to online videos explaining how to use the dial phone in the room. Based on a tweet, with photos, by David Schiffman (@WhySharksMatter), "Our hotel room has a rotary phone . . . and there's a QR code on the wall to download a video that explains how to use it," Twitter, May 19, 2018, http://perma.cc/W7Y2 -U3TP.

4. Charles Van Doren, *The Idea of Progress* (New York: Frederick A. Praeger, 1967), 4–6.

5. Ibid., 26ff.

6. Parker actually wrote, "Look at the facts of the world. You see a continual and progressive triumph of the right. I do not pretend to understand the moral universe, the arc is a long one, my eye reaches but little ways. I cannot calculate the curve and complete the figure by the experience of sight; I can divine it by conscience. But from what I see I am sure it bends towards justice." See my "Does the Moral Universe Arc?," Medium, June 18, 2015, https://perma .cc/7TMJ-HGUE.

7. Charles William Eliot, *Prefaces and Prologues to Famous Books* (New York: P.F. Collier and Son, 1910), 71, http://www.gutenberg.org/ebooks/13182.

8. The word count comes from Robert McCrum, "The 100 Best Nonfiction Books: No 99—The History of the World by Walter Raleigh (1614)," *Guardian*, Dec. 25, 2017, https://perma.cc/49YC-MMGZ.

9. G. J. Whitrow, *Time in History* (New York: Barnes and Noble, 1988), 46.

10. Franklin L. Baumer, M*odern European Thought: Continuity and Change in Ideas, 1600–1950* (New York: Macmillan, 1977), 118.

11. "[T]he typical Greek tended to be backward-looking, since the future appeared to him to be the domain of total uncertainty. . . . As for the philosophers, Plato thought that all progress consisted in trying to approximate to a pre-existing model in the timeless world of transcendental forms and Aristotle believed that it was the realization of a form which was already present potentially. Thus, for both of them the theory of forms excluded all possibility of evolution." Whitrow, *Time in History*, 46.

12. See Jane Gleeson-White, "Mathematics, Art and God: The Divine Proportion of Luca Pacioli with Drawings by Leonardo da Vinci," *Bookish Girl* (blog), Feb. 15, 2012, https://perma.cc/KW8M-YANT.

13. This is my lousy translation of "La docte Antiquité dans toute sa durée: A l'égal de nos jours ne fut point éclairée." At least it rhymes. The full poem is here: M. Perrault, *Le siècle de Louis le Grand* (Paris: chez Jean-Baptiste Coignard, 1687), https://perma.cc/V8RJ-2KLB. (It was read to the academy not by Perrault but by the abbot of Lavau.) Perrault went on to write a book about the superiority of contemporary literature to that of the ancients: *Parallèle des Anciens et des Modernes (The Parallel between Ancients and Moderns)*.

14. Some trace the debate considerably further back. See Douglas Lane Patey, "Ancients and Moderns," in *The Cambridge History of Literary Criticism*, vol. 4, *The Eighteenth Century*, ed. H. B. Nisbet and Claude Rawson (Cambridge: Cambridge University Press, 2005).

15. James Henry Monk, *The Life of Richard Bentley* (London: C. J. G. and F. Rivington, 1830), 1:45, https://perma.cc/N5MN-JMZ6.

16. Richard N. Ramsey, "Swift's Strategy in *The Battle of the Books*," *Papers on Language and Literature* 20, no. 4 (Fall 1984): 382–389, 384.

17. Monk, *Life of Richard Bentley*, 48.

18. The full title: "A Full and True Account of the Battel Fought Last Friday, between the Antient and the Modern Books in St. James's Library," in *A Tale of a Tub, to Which Is Added "The Battle of the Books" and "The Mechanical Operation of the Spirit,"* ed. A. C. Guthkelch and D. Nichol Smith (Oxford: Clarendon, 1920), https://perma.cc/4TCC-SNPS.

19. Ramsey, "Swift's Strategy," 382.

20. David Gordon, ed., *The Turgot Collection* (Auburn, AL: Ludwig von Mises Institute, 2011), 339. The book is openly available thanks to the Mises Foundation: https://perma.cc/858Q-2WV7.

21. Ibid., 340.

22. Regarding the telegraph, see Tom Standage, *The Victorian Internet* (London: Bloomsbury, 1998).

23. In 1974, Robert Multhauf wrote an article for that same journal that suggests both that *The History of Technology* was perhaps not quite as pivotal in the development of the field and that the discipline was only then, almost twenty years later, coming into its own. Multhauf says that the "literature of the history of technology" goes "back at least to Polydore Vergil's *De rerem inventoribus* of 1499" (1), acknowledging that this is not exactly what we mean by a history of technology since it covers things like rites of the church and adultery. Johann Beckman at Gottingen University wrote a book called *History of*

Inventions, published in 1805, but "did not actually write a history of technology as such" (1). One of his students, J. H. M. von Poppe, published a book called *History of Technology* in 1811. "Poppe's book remained almost unique for a century and a half, during which nearly everyone forgot that it existed." Multhauf adds, "It was simply a retrospective book on technology," lacking the contextualization we want in a modern history (1–2). Robert P. Multhauf, "Some Observations on the State of the History of Technology," *Technology and Culture*, Jan. 1974, 1–12. Also, here's a fun fact about Louis Figuier's 1870 history of technology: it was not translated into English, but his book on the "science" of the afterlife was. In it he claims that once we are done with our cycle of reincarnation, our soul goes to live on the sun, where we emanate rays of sunlight. He apparently meant this quite literally. Louis Figuier, *Les grandes inventions anciennes et modernes dans les sciences, l'industrie et les arts* (Paris: Hachette, 1870); Louis Figuier, *The Tomorrow of Death*, trans. S. R. Crocker (Boston: Roberts Brothers, 1872), 169 (chapter summary).

24. The history of the history of technology is far more complex than I'm letting on. For example, any such history should at least mention Lewis Mumford's influential 1934 book *Technics and Civilization*, in which he argues against thinking that inventions are responsible for the big turns in history: clocks did not impose a new, more rigorous sense of time on us, and the steam engine did not lead to us becoming machinelike cogs in the economy; we instead have to ask why we were ready to invent and be molded by these tools. Lewis Mumford, *Technics and Civilization* (San Diego: Harcourt Brace, 1934). Mumford was one of the contributors to the issue of *Technology and Culture* devoted to *A History of Technology*; he strongly criticized that work for not looking at the context and cultural meaning of the tools. Lewis Mumford, "Tools and the Man," review of *A History of Technology*, by Charles Singer, E. J. Holmyard, A. R. Hall, and Trevor I. Williams, *Technology and Culture* 1, no. 4 (Autumn 1960): 320–334. In the *New Yorker* that same year, Mumford criticized the volumes as perpetuating our "over-commitment to technology," as if it is "the source of a new kind of life, independent of human purposes." Lewis Mumford, "From Erewhon to Nowhere," *New Yorker*, Oct. 8, 1960, 180–197.

25. Samuel Smiles, *The Lives of the Engineers* (London: Murray, 1865), 4:4.

26. Ibid.

27. Lawrence Lessig, *The Future of Ideas* (New York: Random House, 2001), 30, http://www.the-future-of-ideas.com. See also Lauren Young, "The Battle over Net Neutrality Started with the 1920s-Era 'Hush-a-Phone,'" Atlas Obscura, Aug. 16, 2016, https://perma.cc/YY8K-VV5X.

28. Lessig is superb on (among many other things) the forces that shape the openness of systems. See Lawrence Lessig, *The Future of Ideas* (New York: Random House, 2001), available openly at http://www. the-future-or-ideas.com. (Lessig is a founder of Creative Commons, so of course he made the book openly available online.) p. 30.

29. Jonathan Zittrain, *The Future of the Internet, and How to Stop It* (New Haven: Yale University Press, 2008). Zittrain is the faculty director of Harvard's Berkman Klein Center for Internet & Society where I am a senior researcher.

30. Allenby and Sarewitz, *The Techno-Human Condition*.

31. Thomas Kuhn, "The Road since *Structure*," 1990 presidential address to the Philosophy of Science Association, in *The Road since Structure: Philosophical Essays, 1970–1993, with an Autobiographical Interview*, ed. James Conant and John Haugeland, 90–104 (Chicago: University of Chicago Press, 2002), 96.

32. Giovanni Lanzani, "A Brief History about the Pendulum," *EP Magazine*, Aug. 1, 2006, https://perma.cc/3K2L-YD5Q.

33. "I learnt that about four hundred years previously, the state of mechanical knowledge was far beyond our own, and was advancing with prodigious rapidity, until one of the most learned professors of hypothetics wrote an extraordinary book . . . proving that the machines were ultimately destined to supplant the race of man. . . . So convincing was his reasoning, or unreasoning, to this effect, that he carried the country with him; and they made a clean sweep of all machinery that had not been in use for more than two hundred and seventy-one years . . . and strictly forbade all further improvements and inventions." Samuel Butler, *Erewhon*, 2nd ed. (n.p.: A. C. Fifield, 1910), https://perma.cc/L2JR-6YQQ.

34. Mark Wilson, "AI Is Inventing Languages Humans Can't Understand. Should We Stop It?," *Fast Company*, July 14, 2017, https://perma.cc/LS5L-85Q7.

35. See my liveblogging of Antonio Torralba's take at a Google PAIR event, Sept. 26, 2017: "[liveblog][PAIR] Antonio Torralba on Machine Vision, Human Vision," *Joho the Blog*, Sept. 26, 2017, https://perma.cc/E9HB-DQQH.

36. Brett Frischmann and Evan Selinger argue cogently against the open-endedness implied by my characterization of the human-technology relationship as "play." They maintain that we are on a genuine slippery slope that leads us to cede too much of our autonomy to technology. *Re-engineering Humanity* (Cambridge: Cambridge University Press, 2018). They may turn out to be right; it would not be the first time I've been wrong.

37. Lynn White Jr., *Medieval Technology and Social Change* (Oxford: Oxford University Press, 1962), 38.

38. Because White saw the stirrup as simply a catalyst, not as a cause with an inevitable effect, he's arguably not as technodeterminist as it might seem. On the other hand, he is sometimes used as the very model of a technodeterminist historian. For example, see Matthew Fuller, "The Forbidden Pleasures of Media Determining," in *Media after Kittler*, ed. Eleni Ikoniadou and Scott Wilson, 95–110 (London: Rowan & Littlefield, 2015), 96.

39. Nicholas Carr, *The Shallows* (New York: Atlantic Books, 2011).

40. Sherry Turkle, *Alone Together* (New York: Basic Books, 2011).

41. Larissa MacFarquhar, "The Mind-Expanding Ideas of Andy Clark," *New Yorker*, Apr. 2, 2018, https://perma.cc/MW93-6HUN.

42. Plato, *Phaedrus* 274c–275b.

43. Martin Heidegger says this most famously about technology in "The Question Concerning Technology." His work on what he calls the Fourfold makes a similar claim. The French philosopher Bernard Stiegler's three-volume work *Technics and Time* investigates the way we and things form each other. Other people to explore include Bruno Latour on the role of scientific instrumentation and institutional processes in scientific thinking, and Don Ihde on the phenomenology of technology.

Chapter Seven

1. For a good discussion of the two big complications of this idea—chaos and entropy—see Cesar Hildalgo, *Why Information Grows* (New York: Basic Books, 2015).

2. Chris Anderson, "The End of Theory: The Data Deluge Makes the Scientific Method Obsolete," *Wired*, June 23, 2008, https://perma.cc/5PX9-ZMY9.

3. Massimo Pigliucci, "The End of Theory in Science?," *EMBO Reports* 10, no. 6 (June 2009): 534, https://perma.cc/7BQE-TT79.

4. Tony Hey, Stewart Tansley, and Kristin Tolle, eds., *The Fourth Paradigm: Data-Intensive Scientific Discovery* (Redmond, WA: Microsoft Research, 2009).

5. Richard Thaler and Cass Sunstein, *Nudge* (New Haven, CT: Yale University Press, 2008), 1–3.

6. Ibid., 3.

7. Ibid.

8. Vance Packard, *The Hidden Persuaders* (Philadelphia: David McKay, 1957), 61–62.

9. Surprisingly, letters were indeed purposefully added to the scene, but they spell out not "SEX" but "SFX," a shout-out to the special effects folks. See Bill Bradley, "Finally, the Truth about Disney's 'Hidden Sexual Messages' Revealed," Huffington Post, Jan. 14, 2015, https://perma.cc/R3N9-WA7Z.

10. Packard, *Hidden Persuaders*, 75, 84, 86, 100, 63.

11. Thaler and Sunstein, *Nudge*, 7.

12. Wikipedia, s.v. "I'm Just a Bill," last modified Sept. 8, 2018, https://perma.cc/86QJ-KDE3.

13. For example, *Saturday Night Live*'s 2014 "How a Bill Does Not Become a Law," YouTube video, 3:30, posted Nov. 23, 2014, https://perma.cc/2S7M-MVM3.

14. John Hagel III, John Seely Brown, and Lang Davison, *The Power of Pull* (New York: Basic Books, 2010).

15. Douglas Rushkoff, *Present Shock* (New York: Current, 2013).

16. I moderated a book talk he gave at Harvard, and we talked about these two interpretations of the rise of long-form narratives. David Weinberger, "Present Shock: When Everything Happens Now—Douglas Rushkoff, author of *Present Shock*, in Conversation with David Weinberger," Harvard Law School, June 18, 2013, https://perma.cc/9N8Y-TD2Y.

17. Steven Johnson, *Everything Bad Is Good for You* (New York: Riverhead Books, 2005), 131–135.

18. Bernard Stiegler, *Technics and Time*, vol. 2, *Disorientation* (Stanford, CA: Stanford University Press, 2009), 1.

19. See Jenny Crusie, "Rules for Golden Age Mystery Writing: Thank God It's Not 1928 Anymore," *Argh Ink* (blog), Jan. 8, 2016, https://perma.cc/G4CA-PSKQ.

20. Daniel Pink, *Free Agent Nation* (New York: Warner Business Books, 2001); Mary L. Grey, "Your Job Is About to Get 'Taskified,'" *Los Angeles Times*, Jan. 8, 2016, https://perma.cc/DM9X-C9F6.

21. Philippa Foot, "The Problem of Abortion and the Doctrine of the Double Effect," *Oxford Review*, no. 5 (1967): 1–7, https://perma.cc/GT2D-GVFN.

22. For a look at the shift in what the Trolley Problem means to us, see Ian Bogost, "Enough with the Trolley Problem," *Atlantic*, Mar. 30, 2018, https://perma.cc/YX3C-ZZGQ.

23. Asimov eventually added a "zeroth" law—"A robot may not harm humanity, or, by inaction, allow humanity to come to harm"—to cover some of the problematic cases that his short stories uncovered.

24. Among many others, see Frank Pasquale, *The Black Box Society* (Cambridge, MA: Harvard University Press, 2015); and Kate Crawford, "Artificial Intelligence's White Guy Problem," *New York Times*, June 25, 2016, https://perma.cc/WJ4Q-Q2R3. Also see Cathy O'Neil, *Weapons of Math Destruction* (New York: Crown, 2016).

25. Moritz Hardt, "Equality of Opportunity in Machine Learning," *Google AI Blog*, Oct. 7, 2016, https://perma.cc/6L8P-USQZ.

26. Arvind Narayanan, "FAT* 2018 Translation Tutorial: 21 Definitions of Fairness and Their Politics" (paper presented at the Conference on Fairness, Accountability, and Transparency [FAT*], New York University, New York, Feb. 23–24, 2018), https://perma.cc/8NLE-XKVU.

27. J. L. Austin, *Sense and Sensibilia* (London: Oxford University Press, 1962). Also see J. L. Austin, "A Plea for Excuses," *Proceedings of the Aristotelian Society*, n.s., 57 (1956–1957): 1–30, https://perma.cc/6QHH-J5E9. I wrote about this many years ago when I was an assistant professor of philosophy: "Austin's Flying Arrow: A Missing Metaphysics of Language and World," *Man and World* 17, no. 2 (1984): 175–195.

28. G. E. M. Anscombe, "Modern Moral Philosophy," *Philosophy* 3, no. 124 (Jan. 1958): 1–19, https://perma.cc/CJQ7-F58C.

29. To pick just one work of note because of its particular relevance to technology, Shannon Vallor, a professor of philosophy at Santa Clara University, has written an excellent book on virtue ethics: *Technology and the Virtues: A Philosophical Guide to a Future Worth Wanting* (Oxford: Oxford University Press, 2016).

30. Alexander Mordvintsev, Christopher Olah, and Mike Tyka, "Inceptionism: Going Deeper into Neural Networks," *Google Research Blog*, June 17, 2015, https://perma.cc/RU2C-58DH.

31. The effect of the connected digital realm on how we think about order and meaning is the topic of my book *Everything Is Miscellaneous* (New York: Times Books, 2007).

32. You can see the math for this at a discussion at Stack Exchange, "Is Earth as Smooth as a Billiard Ball?," question posed on Sept. 6, 2012, https://perma.cc/PN3X-SUFH.

BIBLIOGRAPHY

This bibliography lists all sources cited and a selected set of resources consulted but not cited. An inclusive list can be found at https://bit.ly/EverydayChaosBib.

Abella, Alex. "The Rand Corporation: The Think Tank That Controls America." *Mental Floss*, Jun. 30, 2009. https://perma.cc/B5LR-88CF.

"About." GitHub. Accessed Sept. 30, 2018. https://perma.cc/P4MD-9DYZ.

Abrantes, Roger. "How Wolves Change Rivers." Ethology Institute Cambridge, Jan. 13, 2017. https://perma.cc/3364-BUSZ.

Adrian, Bardon. *A Brief History of Time.* Oxford: Oxford University Press, 2013.

Allenby, Braden R., and Daniel Sarewitz. *The Techno-human Condition.* Cambridge, MA: MIT Press, 2010.

"America's Last Top Model." *99% Invisible*, July 19, 2016. Podcast, 21:25. https://perma.cc/UF6S-GMB3.

Anderson, Chris. "The End of Theory: The Data Deluge Makes the Scientific Method Obsolete." *Wired*, June 23, 2008. https://perma.cc/5PX9-ZMY9.

Angwin, Julia, Jeff Larson, Surya Mattu, and Lauren Kirchner. "Machine Bias." ProPublica, May 23, 2016. https://perma.cc/249Q-7XCQ.

Anscombe, G. E. M. "Modern Moral Philosophy." *Philosophy* 3, no. 124 (Jan. 1958): 1–19. https://perma.cc/CJQ7-F58C.

Apuzzo, Matt. "War Gear Flows to Police Departments." *New York Times*, June 8, 2014. https://www.nytimes.com/2014/06/09/us/war-gear-flows-to -police-departments.html?_r=0.

"Armillary Sphere." Museo Galileo. Accessed Sept. 30, 2018. https://perma.cc /9Y3G-V42C.

Au, Wagner James. "The Triumph of the Mod." *Salon*, Apr. 16, 2002.

Austin, J. L. "A Plea for Excuses." *Proceedings of the Aristotelian Society*, n.s., 57 (1956–1957): 1–30. https://perma.cc/6QHH-J5E9.

———. *Sense and Sensibilia.* London: Oxford University Press, 1962.

Barak, On. *On Time: Technology and Temporality in Modern Egypt.* Berkeley: University of California Press, 2013.

Barocas, Solon, and Andrew D. Selbst. "Big Data's Disparate Impact." *California Law Review* 104 (2016): 671–732. http://dx.doi.org/10.15779/Z38BG31.

Baumer, Franklin L. *Modern European Thought: Continuity and Change in Ideas, 1600–1950.* New York: Macmillan, 1977.

Berlinski, David. *Newton's Gift: How Sir Isaac Newton Unlocked the System of the World.* New York: Free Press, 2000.

Bertoncello, Michele, and Dominik Wee. "Ten Ways Autonomous Driving Could Redefine the Automotive World." McKinsey&Company, June 2015. https://perma.cc/G8CT-JTTD.

Bialik, Carl. "Isaac Newton Calculates the Apocalypse." *The Numbers* (blog), *Wall Street Journal,* June 20, 2007. https://blogs.wsj.com/numbers/isaac -newton-calculates-the-apocalypse-130/.

Birkett, Jessica. "What the Dog-Fish and Camel-Bird Can Tell Us about How Our Brains Work." The Conversation, July 6, 2015. https://perma.cc/W28T -EERD.

Blaise, Clark. *Time Lord: Sir Sandford Fleming and the Creation of Standard Time.* New York: Vintage, 2002.

Bochi, Patricia A. "Time in the Art of Ancient Egypt: From Ideological Concept to Visual Construct." *KronoScope* 3, no. 1 (2003): 51–82.

Bogost, Ian. "Enough with the Trolley Problem." *Atlantic*, Mar. 30, 2018. https://perma.cc/YX3C-ZZGQ.

Boman, Thorleif. *Hebrew Thought Compared with Greek.* New York: W. W. Norton, 1960.

Box, George E. P. *Robustness in the Strategy of Scientific Model Building.* Madison: Wisconsin University Mathematics Research Center, 1979. https:// perma.cc/7E54-AGVG.

Boyd, James P. *Triumphs and Wonders of the 19th Century: The True Mirror of a Phenomenal Era.* Philadelphia: A. J. Holman, 1899. https://perma.cc/AVS5 -7A88.

Brachmann, Steve. "Tesla Battery Patents Further Proof of Elon Musk's Duplicitous Views on Patents." IPWatchdog, May 11, 2017. https://perma.cc /SL2X-S6T3.

Bradford, Craig. "Schema.org—Why You're Behind If You're Not Using It . . ." *Moz Blog*, Nov. 13, 2011. https://perma.cc/W67A-VGXP.

Bradley, Bill. "Finally, the Truth about Disney's 'Hidden Sexual Messages' Revealed." *Huffington Post*, Jan. 14, 2015. https://perma.cc/R3N9-WA7Z.

Brandom, Robert B. "Insights and Blindspots of Reliabilism." *The Monist* 1, no. 3 (June 1998): 371–393.

Bricklin, Dan. "The Idea." Dan Bricklin's Web Site. Accessed Sept. 30, 2018. https://perma.cc/55SU-NBSM.

———. "Patenting VisiCalc." Dan Bricklin's Web Site. Accessed Sept. 30, 2018. https://perma.cc/3UF9-UPAW.

"A Brief History of Spreadsheets." *DataDeck Blog*, Jan. 31, 2018. https://perma .cc/U3DQ-CU4R.

Broderick, Damien, ed. *Year Million.* New York: Atlas, 2008.

Bulik, Mark. "Which Headlines Attract More Readers." *Times Insider*, June 13, 2016. https://www.nytimes.com/2016/06/13/insider/which-headlines-attract -most-readers.html.

Butler, Samuel. *Erewhon.* 2nd ed. N.p.: A. C. Fifield, 1910. https://perma.cc /L2JR-6YQQ.

Buytaert, Dries. "Driesnote." Slide deck, DrupalCon, Vienna, Sept. 2017. https://perma.cc/6SKS-4XWS.

Callioni, Gianpaolo, Xavier de Montgros, Regine Slagmulder, Luk N. Van Wassenhover, and Linda Wright. "Inventory-Driven Costs." *Harvard Business Review*, Mar. 2005.

Campbell-Dollaghan, Kelsey. "Here's How Much Better NASA's Weather Models Have Gotten since Katrina." Gizmodo, Aug. 24, 2015. https://perma.cc/A7QU-RWTK.

Canales, Jimena. *The Physicist and the Philosopher*. Princeton, NJ: Princeton University Press, 2015.

Carlson, Nicholas. "At Last—The Full Story of How Facebook Was Founded." *Business Insider*, Mar. 5, 2010. https://www.businessinsider.com/how-facebook-was-founded-2010-3.

Carr, Nicholas. *The Shallows*. New York: Atlantic Books, 2011.

Carson, Rachel. *Silent Spring*. New York: Houghton Mifflin, 1962.

Caruana, Rich, Yin Lou, Johannes Gehrke, Paul Koch, Marc Sturm, and Noémie Elhadad. "Intelligible Models for HealthCare: Predicting Pneumonia Risk and Hospital 30-Day Readmission." *KDD '15: Proceedings of the 21st ACM SIGKDD International Conference on Knowledge Discovery and Data Mining* (2015): 1721–1730.

Casas, Josefina. "5 Tricks for Writing Great Headlines on Twitter and Facebook as Awesome and Clickable as Buzzfeed's." Postcron. Accessed Nov. 2, 2018. https://perma.cc/ZW9Z-NQ74.

Cellan-Jones, Rory. "Google DeepMind: AI Becomes More Alien." BBC, Oct. 18, 2017. https://perma.cc/EEC4-N859.

Chan, Dawn. "The AI That Has Nothing to Learn from Humans." *Atlantic*, Oct. 20, 2017. https://perma.cc/4EQ8-Z73X.

Cheramie, Kristi Dykema. "The Scale of Nature: Modeling the Mississippi River." *Places Journal*, Mar. 2011. https://perma.cc/DR5X-3Y34.

Chopra, Aneesh. "From Silicon Valley to Main Street Virginia." *White House Blog*, Aug. 11, 2011. https://perma.cc/EE6Q-W94G.

Christian, Brian. "The A/B Test: Inside the Technology That's Changing the Rules of Business." *Wired*, Apr. 25, 2012. http://perma.cc/H35M-ENAA.

Churchill, R. C. *A Short History of the Future: Based on the Most Reliable Authorities with Maps, Etc.* London: Werner Laurie, 1955.

Cirasino, Massimo, Thomas Lammer, and Harish Natarajan. "Solving Payments Interoperability for Universal Financial Access." World Bank, Feb. 25, 2016. https://perma.cc/79D6-E9RQ.

Claudy, C. H. "A Great Brass Brain." *Scientific American*, Mar. 7, 2014, 197–198. https://perma.cc/7CQL-G5XG.

Clausewitz, Carl von. *On War*. 1832. Translated by J. J. Graham. Vol. 1. London, 1874. https://perma.cc/3GTU-XPGY.

Coldewey, Devin. "Uber in Fatal Crash Detected Pedestrian but Had Emergency Braking Disabled." TechCrunch, Apr. 24, 2018. https://perma.cc/W4L3-SVCM.

Condorcet, Marquis de. *Outlines of an Historical View of the Progress of the Human Mind, Being a Posthumous Work of the Late M. de Condorcet*. London: M. Carey, 1796. https://perma.cc/AD6J-T2MH.

Cornford, F. M. *From Religion to Philosophy*. London: Edward Arnold, 1912.

Crawford, Kate. "Artificial Intelligence's White Guy Problem." *New York Times*, June 25, 2016. https://www.nytimes.com/2016/06/26/opinion/sunday/artificial-intelligences-white-guy-problem.html.

Crusie, Jenny. "Rules for Golden Age Mystery Writing: Thank God It's Not 1928 Anymore." *Argh Ink* (blog), Jan. 8, 2016. https://perma.cc/G4CA-PSKQ.

Dennett, Daniel C. *Darwin's Dangerous Idea: Evolution and the Meaning of Life.* New York: Simon and Schuster, 2014.

Doshi-Velez, Finale, and Been Kim. "Towards a Rigorous Science of Interpretable Machine Learning." Preprint, submitted Feb. 28, 2017. https://perma.cc /2PSA-NZR4.

Doshi-Velez, Finale, and Mason Kortz. "Accountability of AI under the Law: The Role of Explanation." Paper presented at the Privacy Law Scholars Conference, George Washington University, Washington, DC, 2018. https:// perma.cc/L275-MH4N.

Duncan, John. *Any Colour—So Long as It's Black.* Titirangi, New Zealand: Ex-isle, 2008. Kindle edition.

Dunley, Richard. "Machines Reading the Archive: Handwritten Text Recognition Software." *National Archives Blog*, Mar. 19, 2018. https://perma.cc /NQ9R-NCZR.

Dylan. "The Mississippi River Basin Model." Atlas Obscura. Accessed Sept. 30, 2018. https://perma.cc/WL52-R2MG.

Edwards, Paul N. *A Vast Machine.* Cambridge, MA: MIT Press, 2013.

Eliot, Charles William. *Prefaces and Prologues to Famous Books.* New York: P.F. Collier and Son, 1910. http://www.gutenberg.org/ebooks/13182.

Elliot, Larry. "The Computer Model that Once Explained the British Economy." *The Guardian*, May 8, 2008, https://perma.cc/T88G-RQDB.

Ernst, Breisach. *On the Future of History: The Postmodernist Challenge and Its Aftermath.* Chicago: University of Chicago Press, 2003.

Esposito, Elena. "A Time of Divination and a Time of Risk: Social Preconditions for Prophecy and Prediction." *Fate,* Aug. 2011, issue 5. https://perma .cc/UNH6-US2Q.

Evans, David S. *Platform Economics: Essays on Multi-sided Businesses.* Conception Policy International, 2011. https://perma.cc/WY8W-XFCW.

"The Evolution of Scenario Planning." Jisc, Feb. 20, 2008. https://perma.cc /KAB9-HG3S.

Faith, Nicholas. *Black Box.* Minneapolis: Motorbooks International, 1997.

Falk, Dan. *In Search of Time.* New York: Thomas Dunne, 2008.

Ferris, Kerby. "Duck Typing the Gender Gap." Media Temple, Feb. 17, 2016. https://perma.cc/394U-XVQY.

Figuier, Louis. *Les grandes inventions anciennes et modernes dans les sciences, l'industrie et les arts.* Paris: Hachette, 1870.

———. *The Tomorrow of Death.* Translated by S. R. Crocker. Boston: Roberts Brothers, 1872.

"The First 'Official' Castle Smurfenstein Home Page." Accessed Aug. 21, 2018. https://perma.cc/9AL3-T7S4.

Foot, Philippa. "The Problem of Abortion and the Doctrine of the Double Effect." *Oxford Review*, no. 5 (1967): 1–7. https://perma.cc/GT2D-GVFN.

Foster, J. E. *History and Description of the Mississippi Basin Model.* Mississippi Basin Model Report 1-6. Vicksburg, MS: US Army Engineer Waterways Experiment Station, 1971.

Foster, Rusty. "Don't Go Chasing Waterfalls: A More Agile Healthcare.gov." *New Yorker*, Oct. 28, 2013. https://perma.cc/M4SG-JS7S.

Foucault, Michel. *The Order of Things.* New York: Pantheon, 1971.

Frankfort, Henri. *Before Philosophy.* Harmondsworth, UK: Penguin, 1971.

Freedman, Lawrence. *Strategy: A History*. Oxford: Oxford University Press, 2013.

Frischmann, Brett, and Evan Selinger. *Re-engineering Humanity*. Cambridge: Cambridge Unversity Press, 2018.

"From 0 to $1B—Slack's Founder Shares Their Epic Launch Strategy." First Round Review. Accessed Aug. 21, 2018. https://perma.cc/73XZ-C3B7.

Frost, Natasha. "Was the First Eclipse Prediction an Act of Genius, a Brilliant Mistake, or Dumb Luck?" Atlas Obscura, Aug. 8, 2017. https://perma.cc /26AF-72DL.

Fuller, Matthew. "The Forbidden Pleasures of Media Determining." In *Media after Kittler*, edited by Eleni Ikoniadou and Scott Wilson, 95–110. London: Rowman & Littlefield, 2015.

Gardner, Martin. "The Fantastic Combinations of John Conway's New Solitaire Game 'Life.'" *Scientific American*, Oct. 1970, 120–123. https://perma.cc /ER58-TGV3.

Geitgey, Adam. "Machine Learning Is Fun!" Medium, May 5, 2014. https:// perma.cc/FQ8X-K2KQ.

Gershgorn, Dave. "By Sparring with AlphaGo, Researchers Are Learning How an Algorithm Thinks." Quartz, Feb. 16, 2017. https://perma.cc/V9YY-RTWQ.

———. "Google Is Using 46 Billion Data Points to Predict the Medical Outcomes of Hospital Patients." Quartz, Jan. 27, 2018. https://perma.cc/NHS2-HU2G.

Gibbs, Alexandra. "Chick Sexer: The $60K a Year Job Nobody Wants." NBC News, Mar. 4, 2015. https://perma.cc/7FYE-6KZR.

Gibney, Elizabeth. "The Scant Science behind Cambridge Analytica's Controversial Marketing Techniques." *Nature*, Mar. 29, 2018. https://perma.cc /8LR5-LCLG.

Giratikanon, Tom, Erin Kissane, and Jeremy Singer-Vine. "When the News Calls for Raw Data." Source, Aug. 21, 2014. https://perma.cc/D9MR-HJQE.

Gitlin, Jonathan M. "Krakatoa's Chilling Effect." Ars Technica, Jan. 9, 2006. https://perma.cc/XET2-GY9K.

Gleeman, A. G. "The Phillips Curve: A Rushed Job?" *Journal of Economic Perspectives* 25, no. 1 (Winter 2011): 223–238.

Gleeson-White, Jane. "Mathematics, Art and God: The Divine Proportion of Luca Pacioli with Drawings by Leonardo da Vinci." *Bookish Girl* (blog), Feb. 15, 2012. https://perma.cc/KW8M-YANT.

Gleick, James. *Chaos: Making a New Science*. New York: Penguin, 1987.

———. *Isaac Newton*. New York: Pantheon Books, 2003.

———. *Time Travel*. New York: Pantheon, 2016.

GlobalData Healthcare. "Six Tech Giants Sign Health Data Interoperability Pledge." Verdict Medical Devices, Aug. 20, 2018. https://perma.cc/B5L7 -QRZW.

Gordon, David, ed. *The Turgot Collection*. Auburn, AL: Ludwig von Mises Institute, 2011. https://perma.cc/858Q-2WV7.

Green, Ben. *Smart Enough Cities*. Cambridge, MA: MIT Press, 2019.

Gray, Mary L. "Your Job Is About to Get 'Taskified.'" *Los Angeles Times*, Jan. 8, 2016. https://perma.cc/DM9X-C9F6.

Grier, David Alan. *When Computers Were People*. Princeton, NJ: Princeton University Press, 2005.

Gruning, Herb. "Divine Elbow Room." In *Polyphonic Thinking and the Divine*, edited by Jim Kanaris, 43–54. Amsterdam: Rodopi, 2013.

Gunders, Dana. "Wasted: How America Is Losing up to 40 Percent of Its Food from Farm to Fork to Landfill." NRDC Issue Paper 12-06-B, National Resources Defense Council, Aug. 2012. https://perma.cc/DF6M-FECX.

Gunn, James E., ed. *Man and the Future.* Lawrence: University Press of Kansas, 1968.

Hache, Emilie, and Bruno Latour. "Morality or Moralism?" *Common Knowledge* 16, no. 2 (2010): 311–330.

Hagel, John. "The Untapped Potential of Corporate Narratives." *Edge Perspectives with John Hagel* (blog), Oct. 7, 2013. https://perma.cc/E7SC-XCGD.

Hagel, John, III, John Seely Brown, and Lang Davison. *The Power of Pull.* New York: Basic Books, 2010.

Haines, Catherine M. C. *International Women in Science: A Biographical Dictionary to 1950.* Santa Barbara: ABC-CLIO, 2001.

Hamamuro, Akimitsu. "Gravity Points." Accessed Aug. 27, 2018. https://perma .cc/MFT6-8UN7.

Hammer, Michael, and James Champy. *Reengineering the Corporation.* New York: HarperCollins, 1993.

Hardt, Moritz. "Equality of Opportunity in Machine Learning." *Google AI Blog*, Oct. 7, 2016. https://perma.cc/6L8P-USQZ.

"Harvard Library Annual Report FY 2013." Harvard Library. Accessed Aug. 21, 2018. https://perma.cc/JZM2-YQYZ.

Hashmi, Khurram. "Introduction and Implementation of Total Quality Management (TQM)." iSixSigma. Accessed Aug. 21, 2018. https://perma.cc /W2HT-8CWX.

Heidegger, Martin. "The Question Concerning Technology." In *The Question Concerning Technology and Other Essays*, translated by William Levitt, 3–35. New York: Harper, 1977.

Hey, Tony, Stewart Tansley, and Kristin Tolle, eds. *The Fourth Paradigm: Data-Intensive Scientific Discovery.* Redmond, WA: Microsoft Research, 2009.

Hildalgo, Cesar. *Why Information Grows.* New York: Basic Books, 2015.

Hillis, W. Daniel. "2014: What Scientific Idea Is Ready for Retirement?" The Edge. Accessed Aug. 27, 2018. https://perma.cc/X9JT-SE55.

Hindle, Tim. "Scenario Planning." *Economist*, Sept. 1, 2008. https://perma.cc /TFF7-VAYT.

"History of Modding." *From Pacman to Pool* (blog). Accessed Oct. 7, 2018. https://perma.cc/R94H-FEMS.

"History of Tidal Analysis and Prediction." NOAA Tides & Currents. Last revised Aug. 8, 2018. https://perma.cc/XMZ2-6KD2.

Hollister, Sean. "After Two Weeks of Anarchy, 100,000 Simultaneous 'Pokémon' Players May Actually Beat the Game." The Verge, Feb. 26, 2014. https://perma.cc/6EWB-2QCG.

———. "Here's Why Samsung Note 7 Phones Are Catching Fire." CNET, Oct. 10, 2016. https://perma.cc/HKM2-VQBB.

Horsey, Richard. "The Art of Chicken Sexing." *UCL Working Papers in Linguistics* 14 (2002): 107–117. https://perma.cc/4M6Z-LGNX.

"H2O." Berkman Klein Center for Internet & Society. Last updated June 21, 2018. https://perma.cc/FBR6-KAUM.

Ihde, Don. *Postphenomenology and Technoscience.* Albany: State University of New York Press, 2009.

"Is Earth as Smooth as a Billiard Ball?" Stack Exchange. Question posed on Sept. 6, 2012. https://perma.cc/PN3X-SUFH.

Jarvis, Adrian. *Samuel Smiles and the Construction of Victorian Values*. London: Sutton, 1997.

Jeffries, Adrianne. "Why Obama's Healthcare.gov Launch Was Doomed to Fail." The Verge, Oct. 8, 2013. https://perma.cc/LJ7Z-Z9BN.

Johnson, Steven. *Emergence*. New York: Simon and Schuster, 2001.

———. *Everything Bad Is Good for You*. New York: Riverhead Books, 2005.

———. *Future Perfect*. New York: Riverhead Books, 2012.

Kearns, Michael, Seth Neel, Aaron Roth, and Zhiwei Steven Wu. "Preventing Fairness Gerrymandering: Auditing and Learning for Subgroup Fairness." Preprint, submitted Nov. 14, 2017. https://perma.cc/9EC5-QJ9T.

Kelly, Kevin. *The Inevitable*. New York: Viking, 2016.

Kemp, Martin. "Moving in Elevated Circles." *Nature*, July 2010, 33. https://perma.cc/GW3N-VY6Y.

Kennedy, Sidney. "How AI Is Helping to Predict and Prevent Suicide." The Conversation, Mar. 27, 2018. https://perma.cc/D8K4-ERZV.

Kesby, Rebecca. "How the World's First Webcam Made a Coffee Pot Famous." BBC News, Nov. 22, 2012. https://perma.cc/DNF7-PTA6.

Kevic, Katja, Brendan Murphy, Laurie Williams, and Jennifer Beckmann. "Characterizing Experimentation in Continuous Deployment: A Case Study on Bing." *ICSE-SEIP '17: Proceedings of the 39th International Conference on Software Engineering: Software Engineering in Practice Track* (2017): 123–132. https://doi.org/10.1109/ICSE-SEIP.2017.19.

Kinni, Theodore. "Rita Gunther McGrath on the End of Competitive Advantage." *Strategy+Business*, Feb. 17, 2014. https://perma.cc/D78W-YH37.

Kirkpatrick, David. *The Facebook Effect*. New York: Simon and Schuster, 2010.

Knox, Bernard. *Backing into the Future*. New York: W. W. Norton, 1994.

Knutti, Reto, Gabriel Abramowitz, Matthew Collins, Veronika Eyring, Peter J. Gleckler, Bruce Hewitson, and Linda Mearns. "Good Practice Guidance Paper on Assessing and Combining Multi Model Climate Projections." Paper presented at the IPCC Expert Meeting on Assessing and Combining Multi Model Climate Projections, Boulder, CO, Jan. 25–27, 2010. https://perma.cc/3NC2-7V6K.

Koselleck, Reinhart. *Futures Past*. Cambridge, MA: MIT Press, 1985.

Kubrin, David. "Newton and the Cyclical Cosmos: Providence and the Mechanical Philosophy." *Journal of the History of Ideas* 28, no. 3 (July–Sept. 1967): 325–346. https://perma.cc/G9UW-NT8J.

Kuhn, Thomas. *The Road since Structure: Philosophical Essays, 1970–1993, with an Autobiographical Interview*. Edited by James and John Haugeland. Chicago: University of Chicago Press, 2002.

Kurzweil, Raymond. *The Singularity Is Near*. New York: Penguin Books, 2006.

Kushner, David. *Masters of Doom*. New York: Penguin, 2003.

Lalande, Monique Gros. "Lepaute, Nicole-Reine." In *Biographical Encyclopedia of Astronomers*, edited by Thomas Hockey, Virginia Trimble, Thomas R. Williams, Katherine Bracher, Richard A. Jarrell, Jordan D. Marché II, F. Jamil Ragep, JoAnn Palmeri, and Marvin Bolt, 690–691. New York: Springer Science and Business Media, 2007.

Lambert, Fred. "A Number of Companies Are Now Using Tesla's Open-Source Patents and It Has Some Interesting Implications." Electrek, Nov. 10, 2015. https://perma.cc/49GJ-SZCF.

Landay, Elizabeth. "From a Tree, a 'Miracle' Called Aspirin." CNN, Dec. 22, 2010. http://perma.cc/HTT2-FR5C.

Landes, David. *Revolution in Time: Clocks and the Making of the Modern World.* Cambridge, MA: Belknap Press of Harvard University Press, 1983.

Lanzani, Giovanni. "A Brief History about the Pendulum." *EP Magazine,* Aug. 1, 2006. https://perma.cc/3K2L-YD5Q.

Laplace, Pierre-Simon. *A Philosophical Essay on Probabilities.* Translated by Frederick Wilson Truscott and Frederick Lincoln Emory. New York: John Wiley and Sons, 1902. https://archive.org/details/philosophicaless00laplaiala /page/n5.

"Laplace's Demon." Information Philosopher. Accessed Aug. 6, 2018. https:// perma.cc/S89N-P4BB.

Latour, Bruno. *We Have Never Been Modern.* Cambridge, MA: Harvard University Press, 1993.

Lessig, Lawrence. *The Future of Ideas.* New York: Random House, 2001. http:// www.the-future-of-ideas.com.

Levin, Sam, and Julia Carrie Wong. "Self-driving Uber Kills Arizona Woman in First Fatal Crash Involving Pedestrian." *The Guardian,* Mar. 19, 2019. https://perma.cc/VB4P-27HG.

Levy, Steven. "How Google Is Remaking Itself as a 'Machine Learning First' Company." *Backchannel,* June 22, 2016. https://perma.cc/N6T7-DDT2.

———. "A Spreadsheet Way of Knowledge." *Wired,* Oct. 24, 2014. https://perma .cc/YQ8H-CCRK.

Locke, Christopher, Rick Levine, Doc Searls, and David Weinberger. *The Cluetrain Manifesto.* Boston: Basic Books, 2000.

Lorenz, Edward. "Predictability: Does the Flap of a Butterfly's Wing in Brazil Set Off a Tornado in Texas?" Address at the American Association for the Advancement of Science, Dec. 29, 1972. https://perma.cc/L5J3-BSF7.

MacFarquhar, Larissa. "The Mind-Expanding Ideas of Andy Clark." *New Yorker,* Apr. 2, 2018. https://perma.cc/MW93-6HUN.

Mainzer, Klaus. *The Little Book of Time.* Göttingen, Germany: Copernicus Books, 2005.

Malafouris, Lambros. *How Things Shape the Mind.* Cambridge, MA: MIT Press, 2013.

Malik, Momin M., and Hemank Lamba. "When 'False' Models Predict Better Than 'True' Ones: Paradoxes of the Bias-Variance Tradeoff." Unpublished manuscript, version 1.6, Dec. 2017. https://www.mominmalik.com/false _models_in_progress.pdf.

Markley, O. Q., and Willis W. Harman, eds. *Changing Images of Man.* Oxford: Pergamon, 1982.

Mathis, Miles. "On Laplace and the 3-Body Problem." Miles Mathis's website, Aug. 6, 2009. https://perma.cc/F32C-9CD8.

Matloff, Maurice. *US Army in WW2: War Department, Strategic Planning for Coalition Warfare.* Washington, DC: Government Printing Office, 1959. http://history.army.mil/html/books/001/1-4/CMH_Pub_1-4.pdf.

Mbiti, John S. *African Religions and Philosophy*. Oxford: Heinemann Educational, 1969.

McCrum, Robert. "The 100 Best Nonfiction Books: No 99—The History of the World by Walter Raleigh (1614)." *Guardian*, Dec. 25, 2017. https://perma.cc/49YC-MMGZ.

McGrath, Rita Gunther. *The End of Competitive Advantage: How to Keep Your Strategy Moving as Fast as Your Business*. Boston: Harvard Business Review Press, 2013.

McGraw, Judith A., ed. *Early American Technology*. Chapel Hill: University of North Carolina Press, 1994.

McHale, John. *The Future of the Future*. New York: George Brazillier, 1969.

Meißner, Burkhard. "Strategy, Strategic Leadership and Strategic Control in Ancient Greece." *Journal of Military and Strategic Studies* 13, no. 1 (Fall 2010): 3–27.

Metz, Cade. "The Sadness and Beauty of Watching Google's AI Play Go." *Wired*, Mar. 11, 2016. https://perma.cc/UPD4-KVUR.

Meyer, Robinson. "The Secret Startup That Saved the Worst Website in America." *Atlantic*, July 9, 2015. https://perma.cc/3X7S-5A8Q.

Microsoft. "Cortana and Structured Data Markup." Cortana Dev Center, Feb. 8, 2017. https://perma.cc/Z76L-CFJ6.

Miotto, Riccardo, Li Li, Brian A. Kidd, and Joel T. Dudley. "Deep Patient: An Unsupervised Representation to Predict the Future of Patients from the Electronic Health Records." *Scientific Reports* 6 (2016): article 26094. https://perma.cc/R2GY-YBQQ.

Mitchell, Julian. "This A.I. Search Engine Delivers Tailored Data to Companies in Real-Time." *Forbes*, May 11, 2017. https://perma.cc/L3JP-8D38.

Mix. "Google Is Teaming Up Its AlphaGo AI with Humans So They Can Learn from It." TNW, Apr. 10, 2017. https://perma.cc/5MMZ-5FXL.

Mlodinow, Leonard. *The Drunkard's Walk: How Randomness Rules Our Lives*. New York: Pantheon Books, 2008.

Monk, James Henry. *The Life of Richard Bentley*. Vol. 1. London: C. J. G. & F. Rivington, 1830. https://perma.cc/N5MN-JMZ6.

Monteleoni, Claire, Gavin A. Schmidt, Shailesh Saroha, and Eva Asplund. "Tracking Climate Models." In "Best of CIDU 2010," special issue, *Statistical Analysis and Data Mining* 4, no. 4. Published ahead of print, July 8, 2011. https://doi.org/10.1002/sam.10126.

Mordvintsev, Alexander, Christopher Olah, and Mike Tyka. "Inceptionism: Going Deeper into Neural Networks." *Google Research Blog*, June 17, 2015. https://perma.cc/RU2C-58DH.

Moseley-Williams, Sorrel. "Adopt a Siren, Avert Disaster." Atlas of the Future, Oct. 10, 2015. https://perma.cc/SFZ9-JUB9.

Multhauf, Robert P. "Some Observations on the State of the History of Technology." *Technology and Culture*, Jan. 1974, 1–12.

Mumford, Lewis. "From Erewhon to Nowhere." *New Yorker*, Oct. 8, 1960, 180–197.

———. *Technics and Civilization*. San Diego: Harcourt Brace, 1934.

———. "Tools and the Man." Review of *A History of Technology*, by Charles Singer, E. J. Holmyard, A. R. Hall, and Trevor I. Williams. *Technology and Culture* 1, no. 4 (Autumn 1960): 320–334.

Murray, Cara E. "Self-Help and the Helpless Subject: Samuel Smiles and Biography." *Nineteenth-Century Literature* 69, no. 4 (Mar. 2015): 481–508.

Musk, Elon. "All Our Patent Are Belong to You." *Tesla Blog*, June 12, 2014. https://perma.cc/CYS7-V5ZP.

Narayanan, Arvind. "FAT* 2018 Translation Tutorial: 21 Definitions of Fairness and Their Politics." Paper presented at the Conference on Fairness, Accountability, and Transparency (FAT*), New York University, New York, Feb. 23–24, 2018. https://perma.cc/8NLE-XKVU.

Newsome, Rosetta, Chris G. Balestrini, Mitzi D. Baum, Joseph Corby, William Fisher, Kaarin Goodburn, Theodore P. Labuza, Gale Prince, Hilary S. Thesmar, and Frank Yiannas. "Applications and Perceptions of Date Labeling of Food." *Comprehensive Reviews in Food Science and Food Safety* 13 (2014): 745–769. https://perma.cc/Q3JR-PPJE.

Newton, Isaac. *Newton's Principia*. Translated by Andrew Motte. New York: Daniel Adee, 1846. https://archive.org/details/100878576/page/n7.

Nigin, Alexy. "New Spaceship Speed in Conway's Game of Life." *Nigin's Blog*, Mar. 7, 2016. https://perma.cc/WY2D-5KRF.

Nisbet, Robert A. *Social Change and History: Aspects of the Western Theory of Development*. New York: Oxford University Press, 1969.

Nisbett, Richard E. "What Your Team Can Learn from Team Obama about A/B Testing." *Fortune*, Aug. 18, 2015. https://perma.cc/922Z-5PMA.

"Now You Can Dial. Western Electric. 1954 or 1955." YouTube video, 9:51. Posted June 9, 2011. https://perma.cc/W5TX-J23A.

"Number of Possible Go Games." Sensei's Library. Last modified June 25, 2018. https://perma.cc/2JPY-KMVF.

Nussbaum, Martha C. *The Fragility of Goodness: Luck and Ethics in Greek Tragedy and Philosophy*. 2nd ed. Cambridge: Cambridge University Press, 2001.

Oestreicher, Christian. "A History of Chaos Theory." *Dialogues in Clinical Neuroscience* 9, no. 3 (Sept. 2007): 279–289. https://perma.cc/6U5L-QKXH.

O'Neil, Cathy. *Weapons of Math Destruction*. New York: Crown, 2016.

O'Reilly, Tim. "Gov. 2.9: It's All about the Platform." TechCrunch, Sept. 4, 2009. https://perma.cc/N39K-CDTQ.

"Organization of Schemas." Schema.org. Accessed Aug. 27, 2018. https://perma.cc/Y9RU-N8GW.

O'Toole, Garson. "Phrase: More Wood behind, All the Wood behind One Arrow." LinguistList listserv, Sept. 4, 2011. https://perma.cc/8W8H-A7PQ.

Ovans, Andrea. "What Is a Business Model?" *Harvard Business Review*, Jan. 23, 2015. https://perma.cc/W2HW-B8BN.

Oxford Museum of the History of Science. "Armillary Sphere." Epact: Scientific Instruments of Medieval and Renaissance Europe. Accessed Sept. 30, 2018. https://perma.cc/6ZPN-LPK6.

Packard, Vance. *The Hidden Persuaders*. Philadelphia: David McKay, 1957.

Palfrey, John, and Urs Gasser. *Interop*. New York: Basic Books, 2012.

Pasquale, Frank. *The Black Box Society*. Cambridge, MA: Harvard University Press, 2015.

Patel, Kasha. "Since Katrina: NASA Advances Storm Models, Science." NASA, Aug. 21, 2015. http://perma.cc/RFN4-94NZ.

Patey, Douglas Lane. "Ancients and Moderns." In *The Cambridge History of Literary Criticism*. Vol. 4, *The Eighteenth Century*, edited by H. B. Nisbet and Claude Rawson, 32–73. Cambridge: Cambridge University Press, 2005.

Payne, Emily. "Do You Speak 'Pilot'? The 300-Word Language That Senior Air Crew Must Speak—WHATEVER Their Nationality." *Sun*, Oct. 16, 2017. https://perma.cc/X3SM-2HGW.

PC Magazine. "Searching the Web." Dec. 5, 1995, 55.

Pearce, J. M. S. "The Controversial Story of Aspirin." *World Neurology*, Dec. 2, 2014. http://perma.cc/2TAJ-RC2T.

Pearl, Judea. *The Book of Why*. New York: Basic Books, 2018.

Perrault, M. *Le siècle de Louis le Grand*. Paris: chez Jean-Baptiste Coignard, 1687. https://perma.cc/V8RJ-2KLB.

Peters, Tom. "Leadership for the 'I-Cubed Economy.'" *Tom Peters's Blog*, Oct. 11, 2006. https://perma.cc/M3UQ-8EK.

Pigliucci, Massimo. "The End of Theory in Science?" *EMBO Reports* 10, no. 6 (June 2009): 534. https://perma.cc/7BQE-TT79.

Pilkey, Orrin H. *Useless Arithmetic: Why Environmental Scientists Can't Predict the Future*. New York: Columbia University Press, 2007.

Pink, Daniel. *Free Agent Nation*. New York: Warner Business Books, 2001.

"A Pioneering Economic Computer." Reserve Bank Museum. https://perma.cc/W7MH-5HLK.

Plato. *The Theaetetus*. Translated by Benjamin Jowett. https://perma.cc/U55R-3ZUE.

Pollard, Sidney. *The Idea of Progress: History and Society*. New York: Basic Books, 1968.

Prigogine, Ilya, and Isabelle Stengers. *Order out of Chaos*. Toronto: Bantam Books, 1984.

Ramsey, Richard N. "Swift's Strategy in *The Battle of the Books*." *Papers on Language and Literature* 20, no. 4 (Fall 1984): 382–389.

Raphals, Lisa. "Fate, Fortune, Chance, and Luck in Chinese and Greek: A Comparative Semantic History." *Philosophy East and West* 53, no. 4 (Oct. 2003): 537–574. https://perma.cc/6WGB-7H5T.

Ries, Eric. *The Lean Startup*. New York: Crown Business, 2011.

Roberts, Siobhan. "John Horton Conway: The World's Most Charismatic Mathematician." *Guardian*, July 23, 2015. https://perma.cc/64WC-9JRG.

Rouet-Leduc, Bertrand, Claudia Hulbert, Nicholas Lubbers, Kipton Barros, Colin J. Humphreys, and Paul A. Johnson. "Machine Learning Predicts Laboratory Earthquakes." *Geophysical Research Letters* 44, no. 18 (Sept. 28, 2017): 9276–9282. https://perma.cc/566D-JAB4.

Rudin, Cynthia. "Please Stop Doing Explainable ML." Webcast, Oct. 2, 2018. https://perma.cc/CWG3-4HUK.

Rushkoff, Douglas. *Present Shock*. New York: Current, 2013.

Rusli, Evelyn. "Behind Healthcare.gov: How Washington Is Drawing Inspiration from Silicon Valley, Twitter." TechCrunch, Aug. 6, 2010. https://perma.cc/L6QY-3RL9.

"Sales of Grand Theft Auto Products Have Generated $2.3 Billion for Take Two since GTA5 Launch." *ZhugeEx Blog*, Jan. 3, 2016. https://perma.cc/7EKK-PBHA.

Saltzer, Jerome H., David Reed, and David Clark. "End-to-End Arguments in System Design." *ACM Transactions on Computer Systems* 2, no. 4 (Nov. 1984): 277–284. https://perma.cc/77H4-WRES.

Samuelson, Kate. "A Brief History of Samsung's Troubled Galaxy Note 7 Smartphone." *Time*, Oct. 11, 2016. https://perma.cc/NQ7F-9ZCT.

Schiffman, David (@WhySharksMatter). "Our hotel room has a rotary phone . . . and there's a QR code on the wall to download a video that explains how to use it." Twitter, May 19, 2018. http://perma.cc/W7Y2-U3TP.

Schlender, Brenton R. "Who's Ahead in the Computer Wars?" *Fortune*, Feb. 12, 1990. https://perma.cc/J9SA-JQKH.

Schlenoff, Daniel C. "The Future: A History of Prediction from the Archives of *Scientific American*." *Scientific American*, Jan. 1, 2013. https://perma.cc /UHD4-EVPG.

Schliesser, Eric. "Without God: Gravity as a Relational Property of Matter in Newton." PhilSci Archive, Oct. 2008. https://perma.cc/4Y2X-4E78.

Schwartz, Peter. *The Art of the Long View: Planning for the Future in an Uncertain World.* New York: Doubleday, 1995.

Selinger, Evan, and Kyle Powys Whyte. "Nudging Cannot Solve Complex Policy Problems." *European Journal of Risk Regulation*, Jan. 2012. https:// perma.cc/6STS-X2ZG.

Seward, Zachary M. "The Steve Jobs Email That Outlined Apple's Strategy a Year before His Death." Quartz, Apr. 5, 2014. https://perma.cc/A5CV -SVL5.

"Showing Pebblers Love with Longer Device Support." Fitbit Developer, Jan. 24, 2018. https://perma.cc/SLE8-NV8F.

Silver, Nate. *The Signal and the Noise.* New York: Penguin Books, 2012.

Singer, Charles, E. J. Holmyard, A. R. Hall, and Trevor Williams, eds. *A History of Technology.* London: Oxford University Press, 1958.

Siroker, Dan. "How Obama Raised $60 Million by Running a Simple Experiment." *Optimizely Blog*, Nov. 29, 2010. https://perma.cc/TW5M-PHJ5.

"The Slack Platform Launch." *Slack Blog*, Dec. 15, 2014. https://perma.cc/4AC2 -W5ZT.

Smiles, Samuel. *The Lives of the Engineers.* Vol. 4. London: Murray, 1865.

Smith, Bryant Walker. "Human Error as a Cause of Vehicle Crashes." Stanford Center for Internet and Society, Dec. 18, 2013. https://perma.cc/9DR3 -6EVC.

Smith, Merritt Roe. "Technological Determinism in American Culture." In *Does Technology Drive History? The Dilemma of Technological Determinism*, edited by Merritt Roe Smith and Leo Marx, 1–35. Cambridge, MA: MIT Press, 1994.

Smith, Merritt Roe, and Leo Marx, eds. *Does Technology Drive History? The Dilemma of Technological Determinism.* Cambridge, MA: MIT Press, 1994.

Smolin, Lee. *Time Reborn.* Boston: Houghton Mifflin Harcourt, 2013.

Snobelen, Stephen D. "Cosmos and Apocalypse." *New Atlantis* 44 (Winter 2015): 76–94. https://perma.cc/X3UC-CJBK.

Standage, Tom. *The Victorian Internet.* London: Bloomsbury, 1998.

Staum, Martin S. Review of *Pierre Simon Laplace, 1749–1827: A Determined Scientist*, by Roger Hahn. *American Historical Review* 111, no. 4 (Oct. 1, 2006): 1254. https://perma.cc/2RYA-9AFP.

Stayer, Marcia Sweet, ed. *Newton's Dream*. Montreal: published for *Queen's Quarterly* by McGill-Queen's University Press, 1988.

Stiegler, Bernard. *Technics and Time*. Vol. 2, *Disorientation*. Stanford, CA: Stanford University Press, 2009.

Stone, Zak. "Celebrating Google TensorFlow's First Year." *Google AI Blog*, Nov. 9, 2016. https://perma.cc/NYU6-HDY8.

Struck, Peter T. "A Cognitive History of Divination in Ancient Greece." University of Pennsylvania Scholarly Commons, Jan. 2016. https://perma.cc/FG36-2YYP.

Sudbery, Anthony. "The Future's Not Ours to See." Preprint, submitted May 2, 2016. https://perma.cc/P3J6-CYRM.

Sutcliffe, David. "Could Counterfactuals Explain Algorithmic Decisions without Opening the Black Box?" Oxford Internet Institute, Jan. 15, 2018. https://perma.cc/HT5X-CV4L.

Swift, Jonathan. "A Full and True Account of the Battel Fought Last Friday, between the Antient and the Modern Books in St. James's Library." In *A Tale of a Tub, to Which Is Added "The Battle of the Books" and "The Mechanical Operation of the Spirit,"* edited by A. C. Guthkelch and D. Nichol Smith. Oxford: Clarendon, 1920. https://perma.cc/4TCC-SNPS.

Taleb, Nassim Nicholas. *Antifragile: Things That Gain from Disorder*. New York: Random House, 2012.

———. *The Black Swan: The Impact of the Highly Improbable*. New York: Random House, 2007.

"The Technical Side of the Bay Model." US Army Corps of Engineers. Accessed Sept. 30, 2018. https://perma.cc/WXZ3-3DSQ.

Teggart, Frederick J., ed. *The Idea of Progress: A Collection of Readings*. Los Angeles: University of California Press, 1949.

Tesla Team. "An Update on Last Week's Accident." *Tesla Blog*, Mar. 20, 2018. https://perma.cc/Q8CH-7HLP.

Thaler, Richard, and Cass Sunstein. *Nudge*. New Haven, CT: Yale University Press, 2008.

Thorp, Frank. "Only 6 Able to Sign Up on Healthcare.gov's First Day, Documents Show." NBC News, Oct. 31, 2013. https://perma.cc/574A-VLNV.

Toomey, David. "A Brief History of Time Machines." *Forbes*, Feb. 29, 2008. https://perma.cc/V5AC-MHVG.

Triulzi, Ananda. "Ancient Greek Color Vision." Serendip Studio, Nov. 27, 2006. https://perma.cc/XDU7-LDFJ.

Turkle, Sherry. *Alone Together*. New York: Basic Books, 2011.

Twain, Mark. *A Connecticut Yankee in King Arthur's Court*. New York: Charles L. Webster, 1889.

Vallor, Shannon. *Technology and the Virtues: A Philosophical Guide to a Future Worth Wanting*. Oxford: Oxford University Press, 2016.

Van Doren, Charles. *The Idea of Progress*. New York: Frederick A. Praeger, 1967.

Varhol, Peter. "To Agility and Beyond: The History—and Legacy—of Agile Development." TechBeacon. Accessed Aug. 21, 2018. https://perma.cc/3U6A-2J2D.

Vernon, Jamie L. "On the Shoulders of Giants." *American Scientist*, July–Aug. 2017, 194. https://perma.cc/DE9Q-PPYJ.

VersionOne. *10th Annual State of Agile Report.* VersionOne, 2016. https://perma
.cc/BP34-54YK.

Vincent, James. "Google and Harvard Team Up to Use Deep Learning to Predict Earthquake Aftershocks." The Verge, Aug. 20, 2018. https://perma.cc
/RJX5-DUCX.

Wack, Pierre. "Scenarios: Uncharted Waters Ahead." *Harvard Business Review*, Sept. 1985. https://perma.cc/3E3S-QC2Z.

Wakefield, Julie. *Halley's Quest.* Washington, DC: Joseph Henry, 2005.

Weinberger, David. "Austin's Flying Arrow: A Missing Metaphysics of Language and World." *Man and World* 17, no. 2 (1984): 175–195.

———. "Does the Moral Universe Arc?" Medium, June 18, 2015. https://perma
.cc/7TMJ-HGUE.

———. "Don't Make AI Artificially Stupid in the Name of Transparency."
Wired, Jan. 28, 2018. https://perma.cc/X9N4-8RBT. Longer version published as "Optimization over Explanation: Maximizing the Benefits of
Machine Learning without Sacrificing Its Intelligence." Medium, Jan. 28,
2018. https://perma.cc/H538-3Q2G.

———. *Everything Is Miscellaneous.* New York: Times Books, 2007.

———. "[liveblog][PAIR] Antonio Torralba on Machine Vision, Human Vision." *Joho the Blog*, Sept. 26, 2017. https://perma.cc/E9HB-DQQH.

———. "On the Merits of Obscurity." Rhapsody, Summer 2016.

———. "Our Machines Now Have Knowledge We'll Never Understand." (Also
known under the title "Alien Knowledge.") *Wired*, Apr. 18, 2017. https://
perma.cc/SP4T-AKZP.

———. "Present Shock: When Everything Happens Now—Douglas Rushkoff,
author of *Present Shock*, in Conversation with David Weinberger." Harvard
Law School, June 18, 2013. https://perma.cc/9N8Y-TD2Y.

———. "The Rise, Fall, and Possible Rise of Open News Platforms." Shorenstein Center on Media, Politics and Public Policy, July 10, 2015. https://
perma.cc/34CU-F7KD.

———. "Shift Happens." *Chronicle of Higher Education: Chronicle Review*,
Apr. 22, 2012. https://perma.cc/8XPS-84WN.

———. *Too Big to Know.* New York: Times Books, 2011.

Weiner, Eric. "What Made Ancient Athens a City of Genius?" *Atlantic*, Feb. 10,
2016. https://perma.cc/QE9X-TSZV.

Welchman, Lisa. "Keynote: The Paradox of Open Growth." Slide deck, DrupalCon, Prague, Sept. 25, 2013. https://perma.cc/7WNS-VAN6.

Wells, H. G. *The Discovery of the Future.* New York: B. W. Huebsch, 1913.
https://perma.cc/G9EP-3QFK.

———. *The Time Machine.* London: Heinemann, 1895. https://perma.cc/L55F
-PE7V.

"What Does a Chicken Sexer Do?" Sokanu. Accessed Sept. 30, 2018. https://
perma.cc/XYP5-FZVN.

White, Jonathan. *Tides: The Science and Spirit of the Ocean.* San Antonio, TX:
Trinity University Press, 2017.

White, Lynn, Jr. *Medieval Technology and Social Change.* Oxford: Oxford University Press, 1962.

Whitrow, G. J. *Time in History.* New York: Barnes and Noble, 1988.

"Why Isn't the Sky Blue?" *RadioLab*, May 20, 2012. Podcast, 22:23. https://
perma.cc/239Y-L2C6.

Wilkinson, Angela, and Roland Kupers. "Living in the Futures." *Harvard Business Review*, May 2013. https://perma.cc/L96E-5M9H.

Willis, A. J. "Forum." *Functional Ecology* 11 (1997): 268–271.

Wilson, Mark. "AI Is Inventing Languages Humans Can't Understand. Should We Stop It?" *Fast Company*, July 14, 2017. https://perma.cc/LS5L-85Q7.

Wolfram, Stephen. *A New Kind of Science*. Champaign, IL: Wolfram Media, 2002.

Wong, Kate. "Human Ancestors Made Deadly Stone-Tipped Spears 500,000 Years Ago." *Scientific American*, Nov. 15, 2012. https://perma.cc/ET3R-3KRJ.

———. "Oldest Arrowheads Hint at How Modern Humans Overtook Neandertals." *Scientific American*, Nov. 7, 2012. https://perma.cc/7H9E-V8G2.

Yala, Hesbon Ondiek, Harry Ododa, and Chelang'a James. "The Impact of Total Quality Management (TQM) Policy on Customer Satisfaction at Kenya Power and Lighting Company (KPLC) in Uasin Gishu County, Kenya (2010–2012)." *International Journal of Academic Research and Development* 3, no. 2 (Mar. 2018): 187–193. https://perma.cc/ZC5L-BG5L.

Yeen, Jecelyn. "AI Translate: Bias? Sexist? Or This Is the Way It Should Be?" Hackernoon, Oct. 6, 2017. https://perma.cc/2A7N-KKSX.

Young, Lauren. "The Battle over Net Neutrality Started with the 1920s-Era 'Hush-a-Phone.'" Atlas Obscura, Aug. 16, 2016. https://perma.cc/YY8K-VV5X.

Young, Paul. "VisiCalc and the Growth of Spreadsheets." RBV Web Solutions. Last updated May 7, 2000. https://perma.cc/2HRF-73RZ.

Zittrain, Jonathan. *The Future of the Internet, and How to Stop It*. New Haven, CT: Yale University Press, 2008.

INDEX

ACKNOWLEDGMENTS

As I have gotten older, I have become more and more grateful for the privilege—in both its senses—of living in communities where I'm surrounded by people who are simultaneously intelligent, curious, patient, and kind. The thoughts in this book have been formed by the endless tanglings of these networks.

First among these is, of course, my family, newly sweet with grandchildren, but not untouched by sorrow. Our children have sharp eyes for where the rails lead and when I would happily veer off of them. I owe an endless thanks to my wife, Ann Geller, who has seen me through the many years it has taken to write this book, always bringing her clear and sympathetic mind to my prose, and joy to my life. Everyone who knows us agrees that I am the luckiest person in the world.

I have benefited incalculably from being allowed to be part of Harvard's Berkman Klein Center for Internet & Society for the past fifteen years. It is a model of a community of scholars and researchers who care passionately about their work, the world, and one another—remarkable not only in its level of scholarship but also in its compassion.

Within that community, the members of the "Book Club"—people working on books—have been especially supportive.

Because I'm an old-school internet user, I also rely on mailing lists, some of which go back decades. Since they're private lists—there's that privilege again!—I'll designate them in ways their members will recognize: Thank you, IRR, BH, and Gordon!

In the final couple of months of this project, when I was cleaning up drafts and the like, I began a six-month tenure as a part-time writer-in-residence—an outsider embedded on the inside—at Google

PAIR (People + AI Research). While the book was fully drafted at that point, working literally next to machine learning developers and having the opportunity to pester them with endless and endlessly foolish questions has helped deepen my understanding and appreciation of the world we've entered.

Thanks to the Harvard Library Innovation Lab, from which I learned so much about the delicate and intricate connections among computer representations of ideas. Also thanks to the Lab for developing—under Jonathan Zittrain's direction—the Perma.cc service this book uses to provide stable referents for web links.

David Miller and Lisa Adams have been my literary agents and dear friends for almost twenty years. With extraordinary patience and clearheadedness, they helped me locate ideas worth talking about and shape them into the form of a book.

Then I had the incredible good fortune to work with Ania Wieckowski, an executive editor at Harvard Business Review Press. Ania worked through my drafts with an unparalleled commitment to challenging and clarifying the ideas and my expression of them. Her fierce patience, perfect pitch, and intellect were crucial, as were her enthusiasm and kindness. I could not have dreamed of a better editor.

Many other people and many conversations helped me, not least those who let me interview them for the book. Of course, I cannot capture all the other conversations that provided insights, steered me away from errors, and opened up entirely new lines of thought. So here are just a few of the people to whom I owe warm thanks— although more than a few of them will disagree with the broad themes or details of this book: Hal Abelson, Yannick Assogba, Dan Brickley, Greg Cavanagh, Judith Donath, Finale Doshi-Velez, Elena Esposito, John Frank, Brett Frischmann, Urs Gasser, Elyse Graham, Mary L. Gray, Jenn Halen, Timo Hannay, Eszter Hargittai, Tim Hwang, David Isenberg, Joi Ito, Reena Jana, Ansgar Koene, Jeannie Logozzo, Hilary Mason, Elliot Noss, Angelica Quicksey, Emily Reif, Angela Ridgely, Daniel Russell, Bruce Schneier, Evan Selinger, Zak Stone, Tim Sullivan, John Sundman, Peter Sweeney, Fernanda Viegas, Martin Wattenberg, Joel Weinberger, James Wexler, and Ethan Zuckerman.

I miss both of my wife's parents who passed away during the course of writing this book. Virginia and Marvin Geller were constant sources of support for me as an individual but more importantly as a member of a large, lively, and loving family.

I also miss my teacher Professor Joseph P. Fell who opened worlds when he taught, and was a model of scholarship, thoughtfulness, teaching, decency, and friendship.

This book's errors, mistakes, omissions, redundancies, misunderstandings, exaggerations, misrepresentations, inaccuracies, misspellings, biases, lacunae, typos, blind spots, missteps, lapses, redundancies, fallacies, misjudgments, flaws, slights, and redundancies are all that I can claim as fully mine.

ABOUT THE AUTHOR

From the earliest days of the web, **DAVID WEINBERGER** has been a pioneering thought leader about the internet's effect on our lives, on our businesses, and most of all, on our ideas. He has contributed in a range of fields, from marketing to libraries to politics to journalism and more. And he has contributed in a remarkably wide range of ways: as the author of books that explore the meaning of our new technology; a writer for publications from *Wired* and *Scientific American* to *Harvard Business Review* and even *TV Guide*; an acclaimed keynote speaker around the world; a strategic marketing vice president and consultant; a teacher; an internet adviser to presidential campaigns; an early social-networking entrepreneur; the codirector of Harvard's groundbreaking Library Innovation Lab; a writer-in-residence at Google; a senior researcher at Harvard's Berkman Klein Center for Internet & Society; a fellow at Harvard's Shorenstein Center on Media, Politics and Public Policy; a Franklin Fellow at the US State Department; and always a passionate advocate for an open internet. Dr. Weinberger received his doctorate in philosophy from the University of Toronto.